12 ⁵ᶜ

facts D/J

Modern Russian Historiography

V. O. KLYUCHEVSKY

В. Ключевскій

1905 г.

Modern Russian Historiography

a revised edition

Anatole G. Mazour

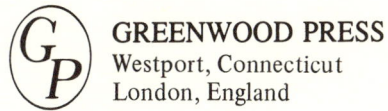

GREENWOOD PRESS
Westport, Connecticut
London, England

Library of Congress Cataloging in Publication Data

Mazour, Anatole Gregory, 1900-
    Modern Russian historiography.

        First ed. published in 1939 under title: An outline
    of modern Russian historiography.
        Bibliography: p.
        Includes index.
        1.   Russia—Historiography.   I.   Title.
    DK38.M3   1975   947'.007'2   75-16962
    ISBN 0-8371-8285-9

Library of Congress Catalog Card Number: 75-16962
ISBN: 0-8371-8285-9

First published in 1975

Greenwood Press, a division of Williamhouse-Regency Inc.
51 Riverside Avenue, Westport, Connecticut 06880

Printed in the United States of America

To Alex and Wayne

whose warm solicitude is
gratefully appreciated

Contents

[vii]

Illustrations

Preface to the First Edition

This study was undertaken at the suggestion of a number of professional colleagues. Upon commencing it, I found at once so great a number of writers to discuss or at least to mention—lest I be accused of ignorance of them—that for awhile I wondered if I should not abandon the project, and the difficulty of presenting many of the problems to readers who lack acquaintance with Russia only made me hesitate the more. However, I decided to keep on; and to facilitate the task, I determined to deal with Russian historians of Russian history only, leaving out the contributions that a legion of scholars of that country have made to ancient, Byzantine, and modern history. From the first sentence to the last, I have borne in mind that this work is designed merely as a guide for students who wish to acquaint themselves with Russian historiography. The degree of success attained in this endeavor is to be judged by others than the author.

I take pleasure in expressing gratitude to Professors Robert J. Kerner of the University of California, George Vernadsky of Yale, and Michael Karpovich of Harvard for their readiness not only to accept the laborious task of reading the manuscript in its original form, but particularly for sparing neither time nor effort in gathering bibliographical data and correcting errors. I also wish to express my thanks to the University of Chicago Press and the editors of the *Journal of Modern History* for allowing me to reprint parts of the outline that appeared as an article in the *Journal* for June 1937.

A.G.M.

Berkeley, California
April 1938

Preface to the Second Edition

Twenty years have passed since the appearance of the first edition of *Modern Russian Historiography*. The book has long been out of print. During these two decades an increased interest has made a new and revised edition more compelling and long overdue. The student of Russian history today finds it more rewarding to seek information that pertains to the recent period; the farther back he looks, the less material he is likely to find on Russian historiography. This is a regrettable situation, even if understandable, for any country produced a richer historical literature prior to 1917 than Russia. The general disregard of the prerevolutionary period and the disproportionate bulk of writings devoted to the "Stalinist Era" give one a distorted picture of Russian historiography. Furthermore, laboring within a limited scope of time seriously curbs a writer's field of historical vision and thereby deprives him of proper historical perspective. Writing in a tense atmosphere of what came to be known euphemistically as the "cold war," a writer exposes himself to further perils of seriously testing his nonpartisanship. Yet this generation cannot rest on its oars and wait for "historical perspective"; it must seek to chart the stormy sea into which it has been tossed, lest it surrender to aimless drifting and be carried away to unknown shores.

In undertaking the present work I have tried conscientiously to present in fair proportion the historiographic development in Russia prior to 1917 and not after. The subject of historiography after 1917 is treated specially in a study published in 1971 by the Hoover Institute.* I still adhere to the determination of some twenty years ago, for reasons cited in my first preface, "to deal with Russian historians of Russian history only."

*Anatole G. Mazour, *The Writing of History in the Soviet Union* (Stanford, Cal.: Hoover Institute Press, 1971).

[xii]

Furthermore, I continue to adhere to the original decision of supplying English-speaking students with only basic writings of Russian history in Russia.

Many reviews, personal letters, and much advice from colleagues of my profession motivated my revision, and to them I acknowledge my gratitude. Twenty years of teaching experience must not be discounted either. All together, these have led me in the present edition to make revisions, additions, and several retreats from former views, which I recognize in all humility. Whether these changes enhance the value of this study I shall leave to the fair judgment of the reader.

Once again, as in the earlier edition, I must express my thanks to the University of Chicago Press and the editors of the *Journal of Modern History* for allowing me to incorporate with minor changes an article that appeared under the joint authorship of Professor Herman E. Bateman, University of Arizona, and myself in the *Journal* for March 1952. It is my genuine pleasure to acknowledge my profound indebtedness to my colleagues and coauthor for graciously consenting to let me utilize the published article in the present study.

A.G.M.

Stanford, California
June 1958

A Brief Note to the Present Edition

This preface must begin with an expression of gratitude to several of my colleagues and students who urged me to bring up to date a study that initially goes back almost forty years. For various reasons, by correspondence or orally, these persons kept urging me to undertake the up-to-date revision that bygone years have imposed.

Having decided in favor of revision, I began by rereading the old reviews in various publications, some of which offered constructive suggestions for future editions. Aside from this source of aid, I sought and was given assistance by personal consultations. Among the latter I am particularly obliged to Professor Mark M. Szeftel of the University of Washington (Seattle) for his kind cooperation, for reading the chapter on annalistic literature and offering helpful advice. To many other colleagues I am equally indebted for their counsel and for giving generously of their time. It goes without saying that despite this generous assistance, they are all absolved from any responsibility for errors that critics may find in this study. The author alone bears the responsibility for the entire work.

A.G.M.

Stanford University
January 1975

Modern Russian Historiography

СЛЫШАТИ ДАСЛЫ
ШИТЬ :⁓

ЦА · МАРТА · СТРЛ
СТЫХЪ МКЪ · М⁚·
ЕВА · ОТЪ МАТ · ГЛА · С ·⁓

РЕЧЕ ГЪ ПРИТЪ
ЧЖ СИЖ ПОДО
БЬНО ЮСТЬ ЦРЬ
СТВИИ НБСЬНОЮ
ЧЛКОУ ДОМОВИ
ТОУ ИЖЕ ИZИДЕ
КОУПЬНО ZАОУТРА

[1]

Early Period

Annalistic Literature

The pageantry of historical writing can be traced mainly to the Kievan and Novgorodian periods. Most historians rightly consider annalistic literature as the earliest and most significant source of historical information. The chronicles available today can be considered as the earliest historiographic records of Russia. One of these, the so-called *Laurentian* (*Lavrentyevskya letopis"*), dating from 1377, is the oldest among all the Russian primary chronicles and includes the *Narrative of Bygone Years*, followed by the chronicle of Vladimir-Suzdal'. Some time between the fourteenth and early fifteenth centuries appeared the *Ipatiev Chronicle*, which also incorporated the *Narrative of Bygone Years* and other accounts. Thus, it may be noted, the chronicles, during a long period of time, kept expanding, altering, and incorporating what seemed to the scribes of vital importance in Russian historiography.[1]

In numerous Russian monasteries and in virtually all principality courts, scribes kept recording events "of bygone years" or about the origins of "the land of Rus' "; they rendered accounts of the first Kievan princes and listed the sources of the past and "earliest times." For this reason, if no other, cultural developments during the Middle Ages centered mainly in the various monasteries or courts of local principalities such as Kiev, Vladimir,

Rostov, Novgorod, Pskov, Tver, Pereyaslavl', Volhyn, Ryazan', Suzdal', or Moscow.[2]

The chroniclers usually recorded what they considered as events that were "newsworthy." Some of them included valuable information relevant to negotiations and concluded treaties between the Kievan prince and the Greeks during the tenth century; others incorporated material concerning Russian linguistics and early Russian writing. To these they would usually add their own version, often reiterating themselves or altering the narrative to favor local authorities. Experts have shown how these additional "layers" or versions usually cast light on environmental conditions, commented on cultural developments, or interpreted political peculiarities of the times or places they were familiar with best. Though many of the records were either repetitious or questionable in accuracy, they have usually rendered much material that students of history were able to utilize profitably after cautious scrutiny and comparative study.

Ordinarily the chronicles contain a variety of historical information, political references, or sources of literary content. This is best demonstrated by such records as the *Testament of Vladimir Monomakh* (*Poucheniye Vladimira Monomakha*), *A Narrative About the Mamay Battle* (*Skazaniye o Mamaevom poboishche*), or the *Travels Beyond the Three Seas of Afanasii Nikitin* (*Khozhdeniye za Tri Morya Afanasiya Nikitina*), and many others. Of all the chronicles, probably the most significant one is the *Narrative of Bygone Years* (*Povest' vremennykh liet*) that dates to 1113. The author of the chronicle is generally considered to have been Nestor, prior of the Crypt Monastery at Kiev. Modern historians have seriously questioned this. By comparative study they have shown that this *Primary Chronicle* is not the product of a single author, but is rather a compilation, some parts of which are traced to other texts.

The Kievan chronicles were usually recorded at the Crypt Monastery, while other recordings were kept up at the court of the Kievan prince. Southern chronicles are best represented by the so-called *Ipatiev Chronicle*, which includes the *Narrative of Bygone Years* or the *Primary Chronicle*. Compiled approximately about the year 1110, some believe perhaps earlier, it was revised by the abbot of Saint Michael's Monastery in Kiev.[3] It was completed about the year 1200. The Galician-Volhyn' record ends with the years 1289-1292. Other locations of chronicle writings were at the princely courts of Vladimir, Suzdal', and Pereyaslavl', site of the well-known *Laurentian Chronicle*.[4] This record starts with the traditional *Narrative of*

Bygone Years, continues with local events, and leads up to 1116. Finally, mention should be made of the chronicles of Novgorod, compiled mostly in monasteries, churches, or the court of the archbishop.

The Mongolian invasion delivered a fatal blow, particularly to the southern and Kievan chronicle-writing, which was not revived until the early fifteenth century. The writing of chronicles was revived in other principalities such as Pskov, Tver, Rostov, and Moscow. These usually recorded the lives and deaths of princes and the election of high local officials in Novgorod and Pskov; they recorded frequent outbreaks of war, periodic epidemics, crop failures followed by famine.

During the fifteenth century we begin to find references to such developments as the ascendancy of Moscow with its campaign for national leadership. This time the *Troitsky Chronicle* assumed a leading part in the annalistic movement. The original copy of this early fifteenth-century record perished during the Moscow fire of 1812.[5] The annual accounts show that some periods were noted for being colorless, marked by events of only local interest, while others reveal more dramatic developments. The style and contents vary; while some are devoid of literary grace, others show noticeable talent and occasionally even demonstrate true poetic gift. For this reason some of the annalistic records are not only of historical value, but constitute a literary treasure. The spirit with which the records are imbued often indicates the prevailing political atmosphere of the time at which the document was compiled. As the influence of Kiev declined, particularism became more pronounced. Yet three factors—common memories, common faith, and a common language—bound them together. For these reasons most of the chronicles would begin with the same "Primary Story," or with the *Narrative of Bygone Years*, then proceed to embellish the story with current events of local bias, the "first" Kievan princes, and the source "from which the land of Rus' had its beginning." The process was natural to the spirit of the time; there was no intention of plagiarism, as some seem to interpret the procedure; it was merely a *continuation* of a former story in a different local framework.

The various princes and princelings employed chroniclers not only to record the past or passing events, but to present their irredentist aspirations. Chroniclers were employed to settle genealogical disputes, proving or disproving priorities, as the occasion might require. The writing of chronicles was not always a flourishing occupation. Thus, during the reign of Ivan IV, of Boris Godunov, or of Peter I, the recording was done under outright intimidation and severe official censorship. As a result the accounts were pallid from a literary point of view, devoid of interpretive quality, and historically not always reliable. Much depended on the political climate, as these periods convincingly prove.

It was a common practice to change the location of described events to fit the narrative to one or another principality in order to please the local prince. One fact, however, always remained vital: by his dependence on the *Primary Chronicle* each writer had to begin with the oft-repeated version concerning the origin of the "land of Rus'." Traditionally this became the initial step, the standard interpretation of virtually every medieval chronicler. After the chronicler copied his predecessor's text, without, of course, reference to the source he used, he considered it his right to attach his own name. Moreover, the compiler handled the material liberally; he expanded, abridged, or altered the previous version to suit his own. It is for this reason that many of the chronicles in our possession call for caution, knowledge, or ingenuity in dissection to detect the real author or authors, precise date, or location of the newly added details.

If some chronicles emphasized the frequent wars in which the particular principality had been engaged, others stressed the bitter social strife or the protracted struggle against aggressive rulers. But the striking feature remained the same: the traditional desire or, at least, pretense to record faithfully, even though occasionally with a touch of fancy, all past and current events for posterity. In some cases the chroniclers proved themselves well-informed persons even concerning the outside world. Virtually all the earlier writers began with the year 860 A.D. (6368). A few would begin the narrative "With the flood, the sons of Noah, and the earth divided among them." Most chroniclers considered the year 862 as a logical date, the year when the Varangians were "invited" to the land "that was great" although there was no order in it; therefore they had "come to rule and reign over us."

The methodology employed by the early chroniclers was a subject of careful scrutiny by such eminent scholars as A. A. Shakhmatov, M. D. Priselkov, and others, who uncovered a few common methods. A local chronicler would begin to compile events he was most familiar with or had personally witnessed. To this he would "glue on" other accounts that appealed to him from the records of other principalities, embellish them with stylistic flare, dramatize some of the events to the best of his literary ability. At the end there would appear an account of "how and when the Russian land and people came from."

As an illustration, let us take the introduction of Christianity in Kievan Rus'. Thus the *Nestor Chronicle* presented the historical event as follows:

> It so fell out, by the will of God, that Vladimir was ailing with his eyes, and his vision failed him, and he was greatly troubled thereat. The Empress counseled him: "If thou wouldst be free of thy affliction, accept baptism without delay. If not thou will not be rid thereof."
> Thereupon Vladimir said: "If it be truly thus, then is your Christian God great indeed." And he issued orders for his baptism.[6]

It was only after the rise of Moscow and the elimination of many of the principalities that local history yielded to a broad "national" interpretation, and the narrative assumed the character of a more modern version. Here the Muscovite version came to dominate the presentation of the past while writers in most cases followed the "Great Russian" line and came closer to modern methodology.

For over two centuries a legion of Russian scholars studied the extensive annalistic literature. Earlier and later historians such as V. N. Tatishchev, N. M. Karamzin, M. D. Priselkov, A. N. Nasonov, A. I. Andreyev, L. V. Cherepnin, B. D. Grekov, S. V. Bakhrushin, or M. N. Tikhomirov, all searched these records minutely to find material for their own presentation. To the students of history the chronicles were of special interest since on many occasions the records cited a multitude of data and episodes that would fit into their broader historical syntheses. Furthermore, it is worth bearing in mind that the distinguishing characteristic of all medieval writings in Russian annalistic literature was the extraordinary quality that might be called historicalness placed before entertainment. This quality was of indispensable value to the historian.

Primary and Other Chronicles

We may now take a closer glance at the nature of the chronicles. In annalistic literature the *Primary Chronicle* occupies a special place. This chronicle has been commonly attributed to Abbot Nestor; hence it is often referred to as the *Nestor Chronicle*. Modern scholarship has conclusively shown that Nestor had only a part in the authorship. At the beginning the chronicle states that the purpose of presenting *The Narrative of Bygone*

Years was to explain the origin of the land of Rus' and of the principality of Kiev.[7]

A large part of the chronicle is of compilatory nature: it incorporates colorful folklore, local traditions, legendary tales, hearsay, and quotations from Arabic, Byzantine, and Bulgarian sources. All these were skillfully woven into the general pattern of a narrative that in the end presented a composite story of "bygone years." It called for a good deal of information, and archaeological, paleographical, and historical ingenuity, to dissect its components and trace each to its original source. In the end it demonstrated that the so-called *Nestor Chronicle* was not the work of a single man, but a composition of writings originating in earlier periods.

Still, despite some of its components of earlier date that had been incorporated later, it is a unique document. It is noted for its predominant general theme, for its political unity that describes the period of Kievan preeminence. The narrative explains "whence did the history of Russia begin, who ruled in Kiev first, and how did the land of Russia originate."

That Byzantine influence must have exerted a strong influence on chronicle writing is commonly accepted. With the decline of the Empire in the south, Byzantine influence was bound to cease and the quality of annalistic literature commenced to decline. In some principalities, such as Vladimir, Suzdal, Tver, Pereyaslavl, chronicle recording survived for a considerably longer period of time. But as the political breakdown continued and isolationism progressed, the contents of the chronicles became more impoverished, shallow, and increasingly preoccupied with local events.

Of the numerous chronicles, only one or two came down in their original form. Under careful scrutiny they have been identified as the *Laurentian* and *Ipatiev* chronicles, the most authoritative of them all. The first bears the name of the latest author, the monk Laurence (Lavrenty), who copied it in 1377 from an earlier manuscript for the prince of Suzdal. A single copy of this chronicle is known to be in existence, while the original has never been found. In 1792 the document came into possession of the eminent historian, archaeologist, and collector of antiquities, A. I. Musin-Pushkin (1744-1817). Eventually the document reached the Leningrad Public Library, where it remains to this day. The period covered by the *Laurentian Chronicle* is from 859 to 1305. The first complete text appeared in print in 1846. However, it was not until 1926-1928 that a scholarly, three-part edition with proper annotations by eminent scholars made its appearance. Rarely do we find along with local events reference to account of much broader nature.

The *Narrative of Bygone Years* (*Povest' vremennykh liet*) has its own history. It includes the version of Sylvester, the prior of Saint Michael's Monastery of Kiev, and the edition of Nestor dates to 1113 and is the nearest version of the *Primary Chronicle* that has reached the modern historian.

The *Ipatiev Chronicle* was so named because it was found in the Ipatievsk monastery near Kostroma. Copied from the original some time during the early part of the fourteenth century, the narrative was brought to the year 1292. It is a lengthy record of over six hundred sheets and consists of two parts: first, *The Narrative of Bygone Years*; the second, a copy of a Galich-Volhyn' chronicle of the thirteenth century. Published for the first time in 1843, it appeared in a second edition only some eighty years later, with more modern commentaries and scientific accuracy. Presently the original copy, beginning with the fifteenth century, is owned by the Soviet Academy of Sciences.

The *Laurentian* and *Ipatiev* chronicles are the earliest records of Russian history, dating back to the twelfth century. They are fairly identical and we may safely assume that they present us with the best general account of early Russian society. Later chronicles, aside from the local accounts, tried to incorporate interpretations based on events in the principality of the writer. The presentation of the *Laurentian Chronicle* might be considered as "Western" in orientation, though eventually it adopted the Muscovite version for its main thesis.

Other chronicles worthy of mention are the ones recorded in Novgorod, first uncovered and published by Tatishchev in his *Russian History from Earliest Times*. The Novgorod chronicles are considered particularly significant in the field of economic and political history of medieval Russia as well as giving testimony of literary development. One of the chronicles, known as the *Sophia Chronicle* (*Sofiisky vremennik*), can be regarded as a rare source of the period of the Novgorod Republic. It is also accepted by historians as a genuine source of Novgorodian church history until the third quarter of the seventeenth century. The *Sophia Chronicle* colorfully presents the strife between the general public and the domineering Boyar class, as well as the stubborn opposition of the Novgorodians to the idea of unification with Moscow.[8]

Most of the Novgorodian chronicles, as elsewhere, were compiled by monks or clergymen. In the nineteenth century S. M. Solovyev had observed that one of the main characteristics of Novgorodian chronicles was their succinct, businesslike style; it lacked the poetic flare, the drama,

the meditative quality that one finds, for instance, in the Kievan chronicles.

Also worthy of mention are the chronicles of Pskov of the thirteenth through the seventeenth centuries. These annals usually begin with the account of the rule of Prince Dovmon, leader against Germanic aggression. Some chronicles represent various orientations such as the chronicles of Kornily, champion of the Boyar cause and others who were opponents to unification with Moscow. Those who favored unification were represented by Abbot Filofei of the Eleazarov monastery, the strong advocate of cooperation with Moscow.

The Pskov chronicle also sheds light on the *veche* or popular assembly as well as on the medieval struggle with the Livonian order.[9] The general tone of the Pskov chronicles reflects the frontier community with all its vicissitudes and hazards, the periodic sieges and raids accompanied by destruction of property and crops, followed either by victories or defeats. It is an endless tale of rulers and usurpers, of Swedish and Livonian aggression until the election of the Romanovs and the termination of the independence of Pskov.[10]

Many chronicles reveal what might be generally considered as a Western orientation. This is usually detected in the annalistic literature from the thirteenth century. This is noted in a general way throughout, but particularly after the Mongolian invasion; it is partly explained by the prolonged antagonism and struggle against Poland and Lithuania. The narratives often deal with the tragic lot of the refugees who desperately sought protection either against the invading Tartar hordes, forcing the native population to flee and seek security in the West, mainly in Lithuania and Galicia. The increased flow of refugees, mainly from the East, added manpower to Lithuania or Poland. But the tragic development carried with it a double edge, adding Russian minorities in the countries to which these fled. Discrimination against the eastern refugees increased particularly after the union of Poland and Lithuania. This in turn was bound to result in sharper antagonism for centuries to come between the latter two and Moscow.

The transitional period following the Mongolian invasion was largely marked by noticeable shifts toward centralization of national government. The centripetal force was witnessed in such principalities as Tver and Ryazan, and it eventually led to Muscovite ascendancy. The shaky political situation and gradual Muscovite consolidation were bound to result in profound political changes, well reflected in chronicle narration that recorded events. The ascendancy of Moscow to national leadership is best shown in such chronicles as the Nikon annals. Thus the chronicles can be grouped into three categories: the *Primary* and early annals (*Povest' vremennykh liet*), the local annals, and finally, the Muscovite chronicles.

In the Moscow chronicles the predominant theme was national unification motivated by common resistance to Mongolian domination or, secondly, by resistance against obstreperous local princelings. Amid the lengthy and frequently recurring discussions of local events lurks Muscovite bias or argumentation. The chronicles were often used as a political weapon by Muscovite grand princes and rendered political assistance of inestimable value. In most instances the chroniclers were not merely pious hermits consciously dedicated to Clio, but were down-to-earth men motivated by political ideologies as well as by mundane interests.

For nearly seven centuries annalistic writings prevailed in Russia, lasting almost until the eighteenth century. In the end the chroniclers left the nation with a heritage of several hundred chronicles, constituting a depository of documentary evidence of inestimable historical value. The frequent territorial disputes of the Muscovite princes were often based on evidence extracted from the chronicles. Claims to various areas by the various principalities were often based on references to chronicles. The texts must have been known by some contestants by heart, judging by the frequent references to them. Endless discussions and similarly asserted rights, whether in peace or wartime, in diplomatic pronouncements or state correspondence, frequently referred to "formerly owned lands for which we have absolute proof in the chronicles." Some territorial disputes, especially between Moscow and Poland or Moscow and Lithuania, lasted for centuries. These invariably involved lengthy citations from the chronicles, and were often quoted and as often misquoted. Small wonder that local princes competed for men of learning who would be able to copy or compile data to be utilized by the prince in the future.

The annalistic literature therefore proved useful not only as an arsenal of historical information, but served as an instrument in diplomacy and in political aspirations. The text also served to crystallize the national philosophy or was exploited on occasion as a diplomatic tool. For this reason the early period of Russian history seems inconceivable without reference to annalistic literature.

With the exception of a few local principalities, the seventeenth century marked a decline in annalistic literature. Of the late chronicles we could mention the Siberian. Among these are the so-called *Stroganov* and *Yesipov* chronicles of the first half of the seventeenth century. Briefly the story of these is as follows. In 1621 participants of the well-known expedition led by Yermak composed a collective document on the conquest of Siberia. A year later the archbishop of Tobolsk, Kiprian, basing himself on the above-mentioned record, composed the *Synodik*, which included the most important events of Yermak's campaign. Then a scribe by the name Savva Yesipov recorded the narrative *About Siberia and Its Conquest*, which came to be known as the *Yesipov Chronicle*.

In the middle of the seventeenth century, at the request of the eminent Stroganov family, a scribe composed an essay *About the Conquest of the Siberian Land*. This record came to be known as the *Stroganov Chronicle*. The editor of this chronicle was a certain Spassky. The well-known nineteenth-century historian and ethnographer P. I. Nebolsin, firmly believed that the *Stroganov Chronicle* was based mainly on the work of Kiprian.

By the end of the seventeenth century, S. U. Remezov, a geographer and cartographer of Siberia, composed his own account, referred to as the *Remezov Chronicle*. In addition to the records cited in the previous *Yesipov* and *Stroganov* chronicles, Remezov added other accounts of the Siberian conquest as well as oral legends, folklore, and records of unknown writers. He covered a wide range of events in Siberia and dwelled on the period 1576-1598. The Remezov records were first discovered by G. F. Müller in the 1740s.[11]

Remezov also compiled an atlas of Siberia that can be rightly included in the annalistic literature of the time.[12] The atlas was discovered first by G. F. Müller and later utilized by Johann Fischer; both correctly estimated its historical value, although P. I. Nebolsin was less certain of its importance. Remezov's studies were not published until 1882 in an edition that included mainly the text and the maps. The narrative describes the life of the Siberian natives, leading up to 1649. Many scholars regard the atlas as an important piece of historical information.

Remezov's atlas of Siberia was not known until the eminent bibliophile and collector Count Rumyantsev acquired the text for his nationally known collection. In 1842 a bibliographical guide to Rumyantsev's collection appeared, but for some unknown reason at the time the atlas was not listed. The item, it was believed, was lost somewhere in Siberia. Then in 1857 the Russian Geographic Society was informed that a reproduction of the atlas

ПРЕДИСЛОВІЕ

had been found. Thus, of all the atlases ordered by the Czar, none of the original copies were to be found.

The preface to Remezov's atlas informs the reader that Siberian maps, which were usually made in Tobolsk in the 1660s, were for the most part inadequate. For historic reasons, however, the item became a bibliographic rarity and a valuable item. It included all kinds of local maps and one general one of Siberia. These were all based on the latest information Remezov gathered throughout the country. The total of twenty-three maps were made by Remezov with the assistance of his three sons.

The eminent Siberian ethnographer A. F. Middendorff, member of the Academy, valued the atlas highly. For its time the precision of the maps, particularly of Tobolsk and the Amur areas, or the ethnographic conditions described by Remezov, are in themselves a remarkable achievement. G. F. Müller had the identical view of the atlas.[13]

If Remezov's geographic data are at times less reliable, his ethnographic information remains valuable and historically important. Numerous details reveal the shifting population and the undermined ethnic unity in various parts of Siberia. Some settlements indicated on the maps are no more to be found in contemporary Siberia: migrations and severe economic conditions served to disperse the natives. In this connection the atlas offers data rarely found elsewhere. This is particularly applicable to northern and central Asia and to Russian colonization.

Until Remezov the world knew little of Russia, even less of Siberia, and almost nothing of Siberian cartography. Peter I, eager to have the Western world know more about Russian civilization, did not mind if native map makers passed their products to foreigners. Prior to Peter I, Russian cartography was not to be revealed to any foreigner for fear that it might be utilized by potential enemy states such as Poland or Sweden. Since the atlas of Remezov appeared during the reign of Peter I, secrecy was relaxed and the circulation of Russian maps became relatively free.

In the course of time the atlas prepared by Remezov assumed historical as well as ethnographic importance. It was completed in 1697. For years the Remezov atlas passed unnoticed in library depositories. During his travels in Siberia Müller discovered a copy of the atlas and donated it to the Foreign Ministry archives. Later a copy reached the private collection of Vorontsov-Dashkov, a fact proved by the stamp the copy bears. The same copy later passed into the hands of the Archeographic Commission. In 1914 it was lent to the committee for the settlement of migrants in Siberia. Shortly thereafter, the copy vanished during the war years and the turmoil of the revolution. By some mysterious route it reached a private dealer and then the Harvard Library. Though it was agreed that the copy be reprinted, it proved "impossible to finance such a scheme." It was only in 1958 that a facsimile edition was produced by Mouton and Company in Holland, with an introduction by Leo Bagrow, a former owner who sold the copy. Historic documents travel mysterious and devious ways before they become universally recognized.

One additional note concerning the "wandering years"—1697-1958. As in the case of belle-lettres, so in historical writing, Russia demonstrated an extraordinary outburst of vigorous talent and productive scholarship throughout the century and a half discussed. Yet it would be remiss to bypass this period, which left a legacy no student of history can possibly afford to overlook. The eighteenth century assured later historians of convenient access to formerly unknown archival material; it was a period of the *Geschichtssammler,* to use the apt term of A. L. Schlözer, which enabled the nineteenth-century *Geschichtserzähler* to exploit more effectively the work of their predecessors. It is only proper that Russian historiography pay tribute to one more pioneer historian whose historical sensitivity set in motion a synthesized narration of the past of enduring usefulness—Innokenty Giesel (c.1600-1683).

The Synopsis

In 1674 a history of Russia appeared under the title of *The Synopsis,* written by Giesel. For several reasons the work served as a landmark in Russian historiography. It represents an earnest effort at a constructive, unified narrative of "bygone years." Moreover, the author made a significant endeavor to present a pragmatic, unified narrative, even though it was overburdened with many irrelevant details and long lists of Russian, Polish, and Lithuanian rulers and Kievan Metropolitans.

Despite some excessive details, *The Synopsis* represents an attempt to present the past in a truly historical perspective. In this pioneer undertaking the author at times oversimplified matters; the line of continuity was at times excessively stretched, implications here and there softened to get around "delicate situations." For these reasons later scholars, beginning with Schlözer, came to accept *The Synopsis* with a degree of skepticism.

Nonetheless its value must not be minimized. In current terms the presentation may seem trifling; in terms of the seventeenth century it was a significant achievement.

It was also the intention of Giesel to introduce Kievan-Muscovite history in a fairly popular form, comprehensive to the literate person. It reflects its period's historical method, literary style, and an aspiration to utilize the available sources, scanty as these were. Evidence was drawn from a variety of sources, Polish, Lithuanian, Byzantine, and Latin, and the intention was to weave a narrative around a central theme and lead the entire story to a favorable interpretation, with, incidentally, a touch of patriotic pathos.

The author of *The Synopsis*, Innokenty Giesel, was born in Prussia and as a youth came to Kiev, where he embraced Greek Orthodoxy. In due course he was sent abroad to avail himself of additional education. While abroad Giesel devoted his time mainly to the study of history and jurisprudence. Upon his return to Kiev in 1634, he assumed the responsibility of teaching history at the Kievan Academy, an institution later to be known as the Kievan Theological Seminary, of which Giesel was to become rector. It was in this capacity that he was able to attract some of the most eminent Orthodox theologians of his time to teach the seminary young people.

Giesel corresponded with many prominent personalities, particularly those who concerned themselves with problems related to monastic institutions. In 1654 he visited Moscow, where he represented the Ukrainian clergy and discussed the status of the Ukraine. Two years later he was named Archimandrit and teacher at the Kiev Crypt Monastery, a post he held until the end of his life. Though Giesel favored unification with Moscow, he simultaneously championed the cause of Ukrainian autonomy. In this capacity, as well as for his work as a historian, he was considered as one of the most educated clergyman of the seventeenth century. He participated in the negotiations with representatives of the Roman Catholic church, delivered sermons, studied and taught theology in the light of Greek Orthodoxy. After his death the Patriarch of Moscow came to suspect Roman Catholic influence in his activities, but for all practical purposes Giesel served as the champion of the Orthodox church and even wrote an essay in which he severely criticized the Jesuit order. In 1674 Giesel published his *Synopsis*, which was adopted widely as a history textbook for several generations.[14]

Faithful churchman as Giesel was, he also demonstrated a keen interest in the politics of his time. As a strong Ukrainophile he favored close cooperation with Moscow, though he continually stressed the idea of preserving Ukrainian autonomy. By the terms of the Andrusovo Treaty of 1667, the area west of the Dnieper River was to be held by Poland, while the east bank of the river and all its territories were to be ceded to Moscow. Since Kiev was on the right bank of the Dnieper, the city was to be ceded to Moscow only for two years, after which it was to revert to Poland, a stipulation that, incidentally, was never carried out. The Treaty of Andrusovo left a number of vital issues either poorly defined or simply omitted entirely. Among these was the question of the status of the Ukrainian church, complicated by the fact that after 1667 the office of the Kievan Metropolitan found itself in Polish-controlled territory and vacant. This resulted in endless controversies, which Giesel skillfully maneuvered.

Giesel judiciously avoided all the conflicts inherent in the advocacy of Russo-Ukrainian unity. He dwelled on the common past and gingerly handled the issues resulting from the struggle between Kiev and the Galician principalities, particularly concerning the affairs of the Kievan church. He frequently reminded statesmen of the Mongolian invasion and all its tragic consequences that evolved from the absence of unity for which all of Slavdom paid dearly. The narrative dwelled mostly on the Ukrainian struggle against its two traditional rivals, Poland-Lithuania and Mongolia, and stressed the urgent need for Moscow and Kiev to realize their common interests.

Many writers regard *The Synopsis* as the first history textbook in Russia. Published in Kiev in 1674, the work passed through no less than thirty editions between 1674 and 1881 and became the springboard of Russian historiography during the eighteenth century. It was used even during the nineteenth century as a textbook, and many later eminent historians read it in their school days. Among these was no other than M. Lomonosov.[15] Beginning with the origins of the Russian state and the early life of the people, Giesel ended with the third quarter of the seventeenth century. He often indiscriminately incorporated factual and legendary data, and he paid attention predominantly to Kievan Russia, until the rule of Vladimir Monomakh, followed by the period of Mongolian invasions. The data are accompanied by long lists of military leaders, churchmen, and princes.

If the contents of *The Synopsis* were factual or elementary, it is mainly because its purpose was to serve the general reader. The book lacks stylistic elegance, most likely because the author was mainly preoccupied with more practical aspects—the preservation of harmony between Kiev and Moscow as the two national centers. At the time the book was written the theme was a touchy one, and the author successfully managed to balance the two issues, not permitting one to dominate the other. With utmost caution Giesel cited some of the conflicting issues involved in the rivalry for leadership and retention of political or clerical leadership. He delved into earlier history and described the sharp struggle Kiev had experienced while facing various opponents or outright enemies. He included an account of the Crypt Monastery and the common aspiration that cemented that institution with the Kievan principality.

The novelty in *The Synopsis* was the degree of unity the author attained throughout the text. A common aspiration accompanied by national self-assertion is detectable throughout the story. At times Giesel failed to maintain balanced distribution of related subjects, being carried away by his effort to prove the need of the common purpose between Moscow and Kiev. Some historians found this a serious negative feature of Giesel's thesis, while Schlözer called Giesel a "historical rascal." Still, if one considers the *Zeitgeist* of his lifetime, it is difficult not to be impressed by the author's genuine effort to attain historical unity and national purpose throughout the entire length of past events.[16]

Mankiyev's Kernel of Russian History

Another eminent name among the early synchronizers of Russian history is that of Aleksey Ilich Mankiyev (? -1723).[17] By an accident of history Mankiyev was projected into presenting a historical account: he served as secretary to the Russian envoy to Sweden, Prince A. Y. Khilkov. At the outbreak of the Northern War in 1700, both were unlawfully detained in Stockholm and released only in 1718. Forced leisure inspired Mankiyev to devote himself to the study of Russian history. The result of his labor was a seven-part study, beginning with the national origin of the Russian people and leading to the reign of Peter I. Death of the author in 1723 interrupted the final chapter, on the reign of Peter I. The work appeared in print only in 1770, and for many years its author was considered to be Prince Khilkov. The man who first discovered the manuscript was G. F. Müller.

The historical narrative produced a favorable impression, and was highly praised for the utilization of previously unknown sources as well as for its original interpretation. The author divided the entire work into seven parts that followed the old periodization, accompanied by a helpful summary that proved superior to the presentation by Giesel in his *Synopsis*. Furthermore, whereas Giesel's *Synopsis* was based mainly on annalistic sources, Mankiyev was able to incorporate records formerly unknown to writers. The title itself betrayed a degree of originality as well as modesty on the part of the author: *The Basis of the Russian Empire: Information That Might Satisfy the Curious*. The longevity of the work proved its popularity: it passed through several editions, in 1770, 1784, 1791, and 1799. Solovyev was the first to correct the originally mistaken authorship. Mankiyev's work became a popular guide to general Russian history for many years.

As stated above, Mankiyev divided Russian history into seven parts, beginning with the origin of the Russian people, the invitation of the Varangians as rulers, and ending with the retreat of the Polish army from Moscow and the eventual ascendancy of Peter I. Many parts followed orthodox patterns, and the author frankly admitted from the start that while handling the early part of Russian history he had to face a sparsity of documentary evidence. For this reason, he explained, the early period had to be brief. As the narrative kept unfolding and evidence became more abundant, the narrative lengthened. Even more significant was the fact that Mankiyev had endeavored to present Russian history within the framework of world events rather than confine the narrative to local or provincial happenings, thereby adding an original touch of universality to his interpretation. Thus Mankiyev incorporated such events, and their implications, as the discovery of America, the westward expansion of the Turkish Empire, or the fall of the Byzantine Empire. Occasionally Mankiyev cited Biblical versions, such as in tracing the origins of the Russian people to Noah. In most cases, however, the author handled the material with greater sensitivity and reliability than Giesel. Thus Mankiyev unfolded the reign of Ivan IV as a dramatic clash between autocracy and entrenched hierarchy.

During the eighteen years of forced leisure in Sweden, Mankiyev was enabled to examine numerous historical records and to consult many ancient writings either formerly ignored or totally unknown to preceding historians. He consulted Swedish and Italian historical sources and ably incorporated relevant material into the narrative. Only the last part is a bit garbled, most likely because he had to deal virtually with contemporary events; nor did he write this part with adequate poise. Still, the entire work came to enjoy popularity mainly because of lucidity in style or helpful brevity. In many respects Mankiyev's work reflected the Petrine age. The sources he utilized at home and abroad undoubtedly raised the standard of his study, despite the inevitable errors scattered throughout the text.

From all available evidence Mankiyev completed his account of Russian history about 1715 and shortly before his death submitted it for approval to Peter I. For reasons not very clear, the manuscript was lost, to be uncovered many years later by Tatishchev, who was immediately impressed by its contents. Tatishchev was particularly impressed by the fact that the author utilized new and entirely unknown chronicles such as the Voskresensky chronicle, the *Book of Ranks* (*Stepennaya kniga*), or some of the Polish records, to mention a few.

The popularity of Mankiyev's study can also be ascribed to the time of its appearance. The country witnessed a rising interest in national history, best illustrated by such government acts as the order issued by Peter I on November 20, 1720. This order requested that "in all monasteries, dioceses and cathedrals formerly granted charters, all letters, historical manuscripts and books be examined, copied and sent to the Senate." It was by the same order that the so-called Radzivil chronicle, located at Königsberg, was copied and utilized. Regrettably the author died in 1723, and two years later he was followed by the sovereign himself, Peter I, whom he had so deeply admired. Undoubtedly the unexpected deaths explained the loss of the manuscript for several decades to come.

We hope the reader has noticed that the writing of history in Russia began not with the universities or learned societies, but either by way of government orders or with amateurs. It was not until the nineteenth century that history became an organized field of study, approached in a systematized fashion, transferred from privated studies to university lecture halls and seminars, where the teaching and writing of history became the profession of men who devoted themselves exclusively to a thorough investigation of the past. However, those amateurs who had begun to write history in the preceding century must not be scoffed at. Confronting them was a problem of enormous complexity—to sift through all legendary, unauthenticated material and place the study on an entirely new and scientific basis, turning back for this purpose to the original documents in order to reconstruct the true story. Formerly, Biblical legends had been the chief source for a national interpretation of the earlier time; it was with frank patriotic bias that the historian traced the origins of the national state. Eighteenth-century

Russian historians slowly began to liberate themselves from medieval influence, utilize dependable annalistic records, trace duplication, search the original authors. Henceforth no historian would begin his narrative with the flood and its aftermath, when "the sons of Noah divided the earth among them."[18]

The historian of the later half of the eighteenth century came face to face with complex problems—the examination of voluminous materials gathered by a legion of pioneering students. Newly discovered chronicles required not only a reevaluation of former writings, but also knowledge to read the texts correctly. The old canvas on which writers kept freely embellishing their narratives with fanciful brush strokes had to be cast overboard and the story of the past entirely rewritten. One can imagine the nature of the struggle in which the modern historian found himself engaged during the eighteenth century.

In summary, over two centuries of careful research was carried on in the field of annalistic literature. These appeared in print in the first half of the nineteenth century; three-quarters of a century later Russian scholars initiated a complete collection of all chronicles, which by 1968 reached thirty-one volumes. Among the pioneer historians who began to utilize the chronicle, two men stand out prominently: V. N. Tatishchev and Prince M. M. Shcherbatov. A. L. Schlözer spent his lifetime studying, examining, and editing the text of the *Primary Chronicle*. Later, men like P. M. Stroyev, M. P. Pogodin, or I. I. Sreznevsky expanded the wealth of information, basing it mostly on annalistic literature. Even more profound changes were introduced by scholars like A. A. Shakhmatov, who initiated minute comparative scrutiny, and collected and interpreted factual and genealogical data, of the fourteenth- and fifteenth-century chronicles. Annalistic studies became a field of special study in which numerous scholars have gained interpretation and sound judgment, along with profound erudition and impressive achievement.

Notes

1. D. S. Likhachev, *Russkaya letopis' i ikh kul'turnoye znacheniye* (Moscow, 1947); V. S. Ikonnikov, *Opyt russkoy istiograffi* (Kiev, 1908), Vol. 2, Book 1.
2. *Polnoye sobraniye russkikh letopisey* [Complete Collection of Russian

Chronicles], 31 vols. (St. Petersburg, Moscow, Leningrad, 1841-1968). Among the numerous studies of Russian annalistic literature the following may be suggested: M. O. Koyalovich, *Istoriya russkogo samosoznaniya* [A History of Russian Self-Realization] (St. Petersburg, 1884), particularly Chapter 2, pp. 10-42; V. S. Ikonnikov, *Opyt russkoy istoriografii* [A Study of Russian Historiography] (Kiev, 1908), particularly Vol. 2, Part 1; A. E. Presnyakov, *Lektsii po russkoy istorii* [Lectures on Russian History] (Moscow, 1938); A. E. Gruzinsky, ed., *Istoriya russkoy literatury* [A History of Russian Literature] (Moscow, 1916), particularly the part contributed by A. E. Presnyakov; A. A. Shakhmatov, *Obozreniye russkikh letopisnykh svodov XIV-XVI vv.* [A Survey of Russian Chronicle-Writing of the XIV-XVI Centuries] (Leningrad, 1940); D. S. Likhachev, *Russkie letopisi i ikh kulturno-istoricheskoye znachenie* [Russian Chronicles and Their Cultural-Historical Importance] (Moscow, 1947); M. D. Priselkov, *Istoriya russkogo letopisaniya XI-XV vv.* [A History of Chronicle-Writing of the Eleventh to the Fifteenth Centuries] (Leningrad, 1940); M. N. Tikhonov, "Razvitiye istoricheskikh znanii v Kiyevskoy Rusi, feodal'no-razdroblennoy Rusi, i Rossiiskom tsentralizovannom gosudarstve (X-XIII vv.)" [The Development of Historical Knowledge in Kievan Rus', in the Feudally Decentralized Rus, and the Russian Centralized State (Tenth to Thirteenth Centuries], *Ocherki istoricheskoy nauki v SSSR* (Moscow, 1955), 1: 48-105; A. N. Nasonov, *Istoriya russkogo letopisaniya XI-nachala XVIII vv.* [A History of Chronicle-Writing from the Eleventh to the Early Eighteenth Century] (Moscow, 1969).

3. *The Russian Primary Chronicle: Laurentian Text*, trans. and ed. Samuel Cross and Olgred P. Shervowiyz-Wetzor (Cambridge, Mass., 1953).

4. The latest publication of this chronicle was issued under the editorship of V. P. Adrianova-Perets and D. S. Likhachev. See *Povest' vremennykh liet*, 2 vols. (Moscow, 1950).

5. See M. D. Priselkov, *Troitskaya letopis'. Rekonstruktsiya teksta* (Moscow, 1950).

6. Bernard Guilbert Guerney, ed., *A Treasury of Russian Literature* (New York, 1943), p. 2.

7. See *The Russian Primary Chronicle: Laurentian Text.*

8. See *Polnoye sobranie russkikh letopisei* [Complete Collection of Russian Chronicles], Vols. 3-4. Also *Novgorodskaya pervaya letopis' starshego i mladshego izvodov* (Moscow, 1950); D. S. Likhachev, *Russkie letopisi i ikh kul'turnoye znacheniye* [The Russian Chronicles and Their Cultural Significance] (Moscow, 1947).

9. *Polnoye sobranie russkikh letopisei* [Complete Collection of Russian Chronicles], Vol. 5, *Pskovskie i Sofiiskie letopisi* [Pskovian and Sophia chronicles] (St. Petersburg, 1851); *Pskovskie letopisi* [Pskovian Chronicles], Issue 1

(Moscow-Leningrad, 1941); see also A. N. Nasonov, "Iz istorii pskovskogo letopisaniya" [History of Pskovian Chronicle Writing], *Istoricheskiye zapiski* 18 (1946): 255-94; M. N. Tikhomirov, *Istochnikovedeniye istorii SSSR s drevneyshikh vremyon do kontsa XVIII v.* [Source Study Concerning the History of the USSR from Earliest Times to the End of the Eighteenth Century] (Moscow, 1940), Vol. 1.

10. See L. Marasinova, *Noviye Pskovskiye gramoty 14-15 vv.* [New Pskov Charters of the Fourteenth and Fifteenth Centuries] (Moscow, 1966).

11. V. S. Ikonnikov, *Opyt russkoy istoriografii*, Vol. 2, Book 2; S. V. Bakhrushin, "Tuzemniye legendy v Sibirskoy istorii Remezova" [Native Legends in Remezov's Siberian History], *Istoricheskye izvestiya*, Vols. 3-4, 1916; S. V. Bakhrushin, *Ocherki po istorii kolonizatsii Sibiri XVI-XVII vv.* [Sketches of the History of Siberian Colonization of the Sixteenth to the Eighteenth Centuries] (Moscow, 1928); A. M. Stavrovich, "Sergei Kubasov i Stroganovskaya letopis' " [Sergei Kubasov and the Stroganov Chronicle], in *Sbornik statei po russkoy istorii, posvyashchennykh Platonovu* (Petrograd, 1922).

12. See review of S. U. Remezov's "Chertezhnaya kniga, sostavlennaya synom boyarskim Remezovym v 1701 godu" [The Atlas Compiled by the Boyar Son Remezov in 1701], in *Zhurnal ministerstva narodnogo prosveshcheniya* 6 (1882): 311-19. Also A. I. Andreyev, *Ocherki po istochnikovedeniyu Sibiri* [Studies of Resources on Siberia] (Moscow, 1960), pp. 207-23; S. V. Bakhrushin, *Trudy* [Works] (Moscow, 1955), 3: 17-32.

13. See G. F. Müller, *Unter Tungusen und Jakuten* (Leipzig, 1882), p. 133.

14. N. F. Sumtsov, "Innokenty Giesel," *Kievskaya starina*, Vol. 10, 1884; V. S. Ikonnikov, *Opyt russkoy istoriografii* (Kiev, 1908), 2: 1554-1559; M. O. Koyalovich, *Istoriya russkogo samosoznaniya* [A History of Russian Self-Realization] (St. Petersburg, 1893), pp. 86-88; M. I. Marchenko, *Ukrain'ska istoriografiya* [Ukrainian Historiography] (Kiev, 1959), pp. 59-63; Innokenty Giesel, *Synopsis, ili kratkoye opisaniye ot letopistsev o nachale slavyano-russkogo naroda* [A Synopsis or Brief Description from the Chronicles about the Origins of the Slavic-Russian People] (St. Petersburg, 1810).

15. "K istorii izdaniya Kievskogo 'Synopsisa' " [About the History of Publication of the Kievan 'Synopsis'], in Sbornik, *Izvestiya otdeleniya yazyka i slovesnosti Akademii Nauk* (Leningrad, 1928), Part 3; A. S. Lappo-Danilevsky, "Ocherk razvitiya russkoy istoriografii" [An Outline of the Development of Russian Historiography], *Russky istorichesky zhurnal* 101 (1920): 23-26.

16. See A. S. Lappo-Danilevsky, "Ocherk razvitiya russkoy istoriografii." [An Outline of the Development of Russian Historiography], *Russky istorichesky zhurnal* 101(1920): 23-26.

17. A. I. Mankiyev, *Yadro rossiiskoy imperii ko ugozhdeniyu proiskatelnykh* (Moscow, 1770). On Mankiyev see M. Obolensky, "Svedeniya ob avtore 'Yadro rossiiskoy imperii'," *Bibliograficheskiye zapiski*, No. 2, 1858; M. O, Koyalovich, *Istoriya russkogo samosoznaniya po istoricheskim pamyatnikam i nauchnym sochineniyam* (St. Petersburg, 1893); A. V. Starchevsky, *Ocherk literatury russkoy istorii do Karamzina* (St. Petersburg, 1845); N. L. Rubinstein, *Russkaya istoriografiya* (Moscow, 1941); S. P. Peshtich, *Russkaya istoriografiya XVIII veka* (Leningrad, 1961), Part I.
18. *The Russian Primary Chronicle: Laurentian Text*, p. 51.

[2]

The Eighteenth Century

The Bibliophile Collectors: Rumyantsev and Musin-Pushkin

During the eighteenth and part of the nineteenth century a number of persons became earnestly engaged in the writing of history while others, motivated by a similar spirit, turned to the collection of historical resources. Among the latter, two eminent figures stand out. One of them is Count N. P. Rumyantsev, the other Count A. I. Musin-Pushkin. These two enthusiasts spent a lifetime gathering historical records most of which contributed a good deal to historical research.

Count Nikolay Petrovich Rumyantsev (1754-1826) lived for several years abroad, where he studied history and related subjects. Upon his return he served in the Ministry of Foreign Affairs and simultaneously kept a watchful eye on every possible object that might be instrumental in the promotion of the study of history. It was under his inspiring leadership that the Commission for the Publication of State Charters and Treaties was founded. It was also at his initiative and, incidentally, at his personal expense that Rumyantsev started the collection of items of various kinds that might have any historical value. The collection eventually assumed national importance and proved of incalculable value to many students of history; it covered a period of several hundred years, beginning at about the thirteenth century and including sixteenth-century charters, official acts dated to the Time of Troubles. Rumyantsev was equally responsible for the publication of the Code of Laws of Ivan III and of Ivan IV (edited by P. M. Stroyev). It was under Rumyantsev's stimulating sponsorship that the *Sophia Chronicle* appeared in printed form. He took an active part in the expedition that sought to uncover all conceivable historical and archaeological data scattered throughout the national depositories as well as in the archives of the Foreign Office. As a result of his life-long labor and accumulated resources consisting of manuscripts, numismatic collections, and ethnographic records, Rumyantsev laid the foundation for the well-known Rumyantsev Museum.

Count Rumyantsev also formed a group of enthusiastic collaborators, among whom we find such leading archivists and explorers as Stroyev, A. K. Vostokov, E. Bolkhovitinov, K. F. Kalaydovich, and others. Rumyantsev's museum and library was used extensively by many history students, among whom were such historians as Karamzin, Boltin, and others.

The other nationally known collector and bibliophile was Count Aleksey Ivanovich Musin-Pushkin. During the last quarter of the eighteenth century he managed to gather a large number of chronicles, government acts, and unpublished parts of manuscripts of various writers, historians, and poets. It was Musin-Pushkin who uncovered the *Laurentian Chronicle*, the original text of the medieval Code of Laws (*Russkaya pravda*), the *Testament* of Vladimir Monomakh (*Poucheniye Vladimira Monomakha*), and numerous other equally important records related to history, ethnography, genealogy, and geography. It was also under his encouragement that the well-known eighteenth-century publisher N. Novikov published the *Russian Library* (*Drevnyaya Rossiiskaya Vivliofika*), reproduced recently by Mouton in the Hague (twenty volumes). As in the case of other bibliophiles and collectors, the material was gathered largely as the result of a dilettantish hobby. Nonetheless, though lacking systematic concept or historical vision, much of the gathered material proved of considerable value to future historians.

The collected records included the rarest items such as the original text of the *Russkaya pravda* and the Monomakh *Testament*, already mentioned, and also the well-known thirteenth-century poem *The Lay of Igor's Raid* (*Slovo of Polku Igoreve*), which describes the lament of Igor's wife who vainly awaited her slain husband on the battlefield against the Polovetsky hordes in the south. The poem has been well translated and cited by Leo

Wiener in his anthology of Russian literature. Musin-Pushkin located it in 1792 and published it eight years later, as his monumental discovery.

The fate of Musin-Pushkin's collection is a sorrowful story. Shortly after the French reached Moscow, the fires devoured a good part of that city, including the house of Musin-Pushkin, which burned to the ground. With the house perished the entire collection he had gathered during his lifetime. By a stroke of good fortune, Musin-Pushkin had presented the *Laurentian Chronicle* as a gift to Alexander I before the catastrophe, and Alexander in turn presented the document to the Imperial Public Library, where it was saved from the devouring fires of Moscow.[1]

We must now turn our attention to the historians of the same century. Among them stands out prominently the name of Vasily Nikitich Tatishchev (1686-1758), the man who conceived modern historical writing as well as the utilization of more promising resources now available to the student of history.

Tatishchev

With Tatishchev, it can be said, historical science in Russia begins to move forward from the simple annalistic accounts to a more modern form of historical narrative. From this point of view we can therefore consider Tatishchev as one of the pioneering modern Russian historians. He envisioned Russian history on a scale hardly imagined by previous writers; he was among the first to endeavor the writing of history as a pragmatic narrative of "bygone years."[2]

Vasily Nikitich Tatishchev was of noble birth, a graduate of an engineering school, trained in artillery in the army, and a true son of the age of Peter the Great. An ardent admirer of the Petrine reforms, he gazed westward, not to forsake the past, but to comprehend it more rationally. Under direct encouragement from Peter I himself, Tatishchev set out to demonstrate to the Western world that Russia, too, had a history of which her people might well be proud.

Tatishchev began his career in the army like most of his contemporaries and took part in the most decisive conflict of his time, the battle of Narva and Poltava. Later, as a product of his time, he became a mining engineer and in this capacity was commissioned on several occasions to assume administrative responsibilities. In 1724 he was sent to Sweden to meet mining engineers and entice them to come to Russia to lend their skill and talent. Here for the first time he came in contact with the West and was able to observe closely Western political and economic life. Still later, he held a number of responsible government positions in the Ural districts and served for four years (1741-1745) as governor of Astrakhan province.[3]

For Tatishchev history came as a by-product; his main interest was the economic development of national resources. However, in pursuing his studies, he came to realize the utilitarian advantages of historical knowledge in general.[4] While he studied the economic resources of the nation, Tatishchev was also impressed by the abundance of documentary historical sources scattered throughout the country. Tatishchev soon began to collect these from various parts of the vast empire and later extended his search throughout foreign countries, where he employed special copyists. His final aim was not merely to compile but also to master thoroughly and exhaustively the sources and to write an interpretive history; he sensed intuitively the presence of some pattern in the past, instead of a chain of unrelated episodes. His great ambition was to free Russian history from the current Germanic interpretation, particularly the theory concerning the origin of the Slavs. It was for this reason that he emphasized the early history of the Republic of Novgorod. While on his mission to Sweden he had met many scholars of that country, authorities on the early relations between Sweden and Novgorod.[5] Unfortunately his work was handicapped by his preoccupation with politics, while his utter lack of literary style and an inability to read Greek and Latin prevented him from personally familiarizing himself with important sources at home and abroad.

In 1738 Tatishchev submitted to the Russian Academy of Sciences two documents he came upon in his work: the texts of the medieval Code of Laws (*Russkaya pravda*) and the Code of 1550 *(Sudebnik)* accompanied by extensive commentary notes. In this manner two of the most valuable sources of earlier Russian history came to light for the first time. Despite the errors that Tatishchev committed in interpretation, basically his approach and commentary notes proved surprisingly sound. While endeavoring to interpret the earlier period of history, he determined to push aside the so-called Norman theory, the thesis concerning the origins of the Russian state. Tatishchev came to view the current Norman thesis as a product of the German members of the Academy of Sciences, who professed neither respect for nor an understanding of Russia's past and were therefore prone to distort the entire subject.

A year later, in 1739, Tatishchev presented his *magnum opus* to the august body of the academy, his *Russian History from the Earliest Times*, consisting of five parts.[6] These included a history of the Scythian and early Slavic tribes to 860, followed by developments leading to 1557; the period after that date is covered in fragmentary form. This bulky undertaking was motivated by strong patriotic sentiments, and the author, with candid pride, stated that he did it in order to acquaint Western Europe with Russian history. His work, he hoped, would dispel the calumnies and misunderstanding caused by German, Polish, and other unfriendly writers and prove that Russia had a great past of her own. Tatishchev ignored Biblical legends, basing his interpretations on ''man's achievements only.'' Three factors, according to Tatishchev, played a most important part in the development of Russia as well as other countries: the art of writing, the Christian faith, and the art of printing. In this pronouncement it is not difficult to detect the dawn of the Age of Enlightenment.

Throughout his volumes Tatishchev not only demonstrated an unusual mastery of documentary sources of the sixteenth and seventeenth centuries, but revealed an advanced grasp of the forthcoming historical consciousness. The chief link between the eighteenth and nineteenth centuries was the common awareness of the need to gather all historical records and to publish them. Both generations ardently sought means to enable the future *Geschichtsmaler* to recreate the past and the *Geschichtschreiber* to compose a historical synthesis of the entire course of history. At the same time the historian began to free himself from extreme patriotic fervor and to follow, at times unconsciously, the wise counsel of Schlözer—to pursue historical truth without patriotic, national, religious, or political bias. The sole allegiance of the historian, said Schlözer, must be to truth.

By slow degrees Russian historical writing began to dissociate itself from Biblical chronology, from annalistic methods, preconceived patterns and legends; it commenced to cast off the crude utilitarianism of some writers and the panegyrical pomposity of others. Already eighteenth-century writers began to insist on more scholarly methods in recording the past. Tatishchev refused to incorporate miracles and Biblical legends in his writings; Boltin denounced LeClerc and Shcherbatov for failure to substantiate their interpretations with authentic documentary evidence; Müller insisted on handling genuine source material, while Schlözer spoke in terms of universal history. Together they left an impressive legacy that helped to crystallize nineteenth-century thought. Ironically, although both Müller and Schlözer came to be associated with the Norman school, they also demonstrated the need for rational evaluation of past events as well as those of their time. To all this must be added the prevailing spirit of the age of Peter I and its significant historical departure from the past.

All this Tatishchev absorbed and utilized as he undertook to write the history of his land. According to Tatishchev, the monarchical form of government came about as a result of a contract, a theory he evidently borrowed from Locke. Of the three forms of government—oligarchy, monarchy, and democracy—Tatishchev considered the second as the most appropriate for Russia. Oligarchy, he argued, prevailed in countries well protected by natural boundaries such as mountains or seas, such as Sweden or England. Democracy arose only in small countries and where cities played a predominant part in national life. In Russia, a country of vast and poorly protected territories where the masses were inadequately enlightened, monarchy was the only effective government. Tatishchev did not believe in a national destiny, but rather in social order best suited to the country and in the highest caliber of leadership the state could produce. Tatishchev also demonstrated a keen interest in subordinate disciplines such as ethnography or national geography, fields of human knowledge that he considered vitally important for history. This is best proved by his effort to compile an encyclopedia, which he never managed to complete in his lifetime, ending with letter "K."

The amazing thing about Tatishchev's work is the enormous body of sources that he utilized for the first time. He consulted all the writings then available: the chronicles, diplomatic correspondence, letters exchanged between Prince Kurbsky and Ivan IV, and widely scattered archival material found in Moscow, Perm, Astrakhan, Kazan, and other localities throughout Russia; he also sought and on many occasions obtained copies of documents related to Russian history that were to be found in foreign archives. In 1725 he wrote to the University of Uppsala, Sweden, ordering all "useful books" and sources. Tatishchev was unable to organize properly or to evaluate critically the bulk of his gathered sources. Yet, taking into consideration the general cultural atmosphere in which the author labored and his lack of training as a student of history, it is surprising how much he did manage to accomplish.

When at last the manuscript was submitted to the Academy of Sciences, the dignitaries looked at it askance and severely censured it because of its forbidding size, dubious conclusions, and stylistic defects.[7] The author was compelled to undertake a revision of his thesis in order to suit the views of the German members of the academy. Tatishchev died while in the midst of revising his manuscript. Later other complications occurred when a fire destroyed a good portion of his writings. The entire work had to be reproduced from copies in the possession of Tatishchev's colleagues. Thanks particularly to G. F. Müller, the work of Tatishchev was saved from complete loss.[8]

Notwithstanding well-deserved criticism, Tatishchev was one of the first historians in Russia with a vision broad enough to realize the relationship among the various factors that collectively account for national life. It is only by embracing all phenomena that one was able to comprehend and reconstruct a nation's past as well as to arrive at a philosophy of history. Tatishchev keenly appreciated the relationship to history of such sciences as economics, geography, or ethnography.[9] If his attempts were not entirely successful, at least he gave impetus to others and served to presage a more enlightened method in the art of historical writing.

Bayer

Although feelings against the German members of the academic family in Russia were not always cordial, the antagonism derived from an emotional rather than a rational source. For this reason the clashes often produced more heat than light. With few exceptions the Germans, invited to membership in the Academy of Sciences initiated in 1725, proved of inestimable cultural value to Russia, serving as links between Russian and Western Europe. Prominent among these was Gottlieb Siegfried Bayer (1694-1738), who was invited in 1725 and arrived in St. Petersburg on February 6, 1726. Hardly thirty-two years of age, Bayer had already proved himself a noted scholar in the fields of philology and history. A linguist and research student, Bayer was among the pioneer academicians to bring to Russia the traditional ideas of Western scholarship. One of Bayer's main principles of research was his insistence on the historian's meticulous examination of sources to establish authenticity before determining conclusions.

Even before arriving at the Russian capital, Bayer had an impressive list of publications, which he lengthened further while at the academy. Of these, some monographic studies were devoted to various aspects of ancient Scythia, others to such subjects as Kievan geography (*Geographia Russica ex Constantino Porphyrogenito*), or to the Varangians (*De Varagis*), or to the origins of Rus' *(Origines Russicae)*, or to the earlier Russian campaign against the Byzantine Empire *(De Russorum prima expeditione Constantinopolitana)*.[10] Bayer has been justly considered the founder of the so-called Norman school, which expounded the theory that the Russian state was of Scandinavian origin. The decade 1730-1740 in Russian history is well known for the ascendancy of the German party at the court of St. Petersburg. In the light of what took place during that decade, it seems understandable that some observers might have deduced the Norman theory. But the thesis was destined to touch off a fierce debate, which continues to recur in historical literature to this very day.

As a linguist, Bayer arrived at his deductions largely by means of comparative philology, collating names and terms in the Russian and Scandinavian languages, associations that were at times neither sound nor convincing. Though of speculative nature and vulnerable to much criticism, as any hypothesis is apt to be, the Norman theory led in some cases to curious allegations, such as the statement that anything constructive to be found in the formative process of the Russian state was due entirely to the invited Normans. This armed some with convenient political weapons and instilled others with patriotic indignation. In the end the debates recurred with increasing heat and diminishing light on a subject stubbornly cloaked in the midst of the past. What seemed a purely historical issue was quickly to be converted into a battleground on which a questionable hypothesis and an injured national pride were to clash and scar many participants. One wonders if Bayer himself had not experienced melancholy thoughts over the subsequent disputes.

The Norman theory came to regard the Varangians (Normans) as true founders of the Russian state. The founding of this Norman school dates back to the first half of the eighteenth century, traced largely to a group of German scholars, members of the Russian Academy of Sciences who were invited to collaborate within the recently founded institution. Among these stood out such men as Bayer, Müller, Schlözer, and others. The Norman theory was based on the account presented in the *Narrative of Bygone Years*. The chronicle narrates the story of the invitation of the three Scandinavian brothers in 862 from abroad to come and govern the land of the Kievan Slavs, "the land which was extensive, but unable to maintain order."

The awakened nationalists argued that the version was included much later in an effort to counteract Byzantine political aspirations. Among the early opponents of Normanism was M. V. Lomonosov, who began to gather material for a history of Russia in which he might present his own view of the Russian state. Lomonosov as well as others, particularly the later Slavophiles, even tried to prove that the Varangians were themselves Slavs. The struggle between the Normanists and the nationalists flared up recurrently. Normanism was resented particularly for its tendency to consider the Slavs not only as backward people, but as incapable of governing themselves; hence the "invitation" they extended to the Varangians to govern them. The political implications during the twentieth century need not be stressed here, except to point out that even at this period in history the issue was by no means a mere historic episode.

Perhaps the latest case, and best illustration, of the conflict was in the late 1940s, with the condemnation of N. L. Rubinstein's study of Russian historiography.[11] Reviewing the work of Rubinstein several years later, when the postwar period had allowed other issues to move to the foreground, M. N. Tikhomirov wrote:

> It is known that Bayer did not know Russian, though, according to N. L. Rubinstein, he was an "eminent linguist," a master of ancient and oriental languages, who knew Greek, Latin, Sanskrit, Chinese. The question then is, why did such a great philologist not have any desire to study only one language, the language of the country that invited him to enlighten it? In a word, Why did he not study the Russian language? Answer: Because he was a giftless, little cultivated, militant German, without genuine interest in science and its problems outside of that narrow, smelly "academic" cubicle, where science ruled not as a proud goddess, but as an ordinary all-around cook.[12]

Bayer's eight-year sojourn in Russia had a strong effect; it not only initiated a debatable hypothesis, but also stimulated an opposition that was forced to study the past and thereby encourage historical research. During his last four years, Bayer assumed the editorship of the historical journal of the Academy of Sciences.[13] Constant friction among the members often distressed him to such a degree that he would seriously scheme of severing his relations with the Academy of Sciences and returning to his native city of Königsberg. He failed to carry out his decision, for he suddenly died in the prime of his career at hardly forty-four years of age. Behind him he left a profound influence on standards of scholarship, for which the academy became universally noted, and an interpretive philosophy concerning the origin of the Russian state that still divides the ranks of historians into two inimical groups, the Normanists and the anti-Normanists.

Müller

Despite the academic tension that prevailed between the native and German members, most constructive work was accomplished by the Academy of Sciences, as subsequent development shows. We must begin with the name of another member of that group, Gerhard Friedrich Müller (1705-1783), the phenomenally prodigious and versatile worker who was instrumental in opening up to students of Russian history forgotten or unsuspected archival wealth.[14] A successor of Bayer and one of the first German historians to settle permanently in Russia, Müller emulated Bayer's diligence, though not his erudition. "I do not demand," Müller wrote on one occasion, "that the historian must narrate everything he knows, not even everything that is genuine, for there are things that could not be told or that are not interesting enough to be narrated to the public; but whatever the historian does state must be strictly true and never should he give any cause for suspicion to be directed toward himself."[15]

Müller was only twenty years of age when he arrived in the Russian capital from Leipzig in 1725. As one German observer wrote:

In those days there was a popular movement from Germany to Russia, particularly among the students. These fools thought that nowhere was one likely to strike fortune more easily than in Russia. Everyone had in mind the student of theology expelled from the University of Jena, the son of a Westphalian priest [Baron, later Count, Johann Friedrich Ostermann] who subsequently became Russian State Chancellor.

Müller might have been one of those "foolish" young men whose high hopes for rapid advancement soon proved to be illusory. For a while he served in the capacity of instructor at a *gymnasium*, where he was compelled to teach whatever was assigned to him. Among the subjects he taught, besides history, were geography, Latin, elocution, and even the "art of letter writing."

After eight years of residence in the Russian capital with no definite assurance of a position, Müller decided to join Behring's second expedition to Siberia. The trip, for Müller a mere escape from insecurity, proved of such consequence as to place him eventually among the notable pioneers in the field of historical research in his adopted country. The purpose of the expedition was further exploration of Siberia and the coast of Kamchatka, and it also called for a study of "the various subjects related to science." Müller courageously assumed the responsibility of exploring "the geography of the earth, antiquities, customs, usages of the various natives." Above all, the government expected more pragmatic results: it wished to know about the potential natural wealth of Siberia, about possible exploration, commercial opportunities in the East, and to learn whether Asia and America were separate continents. All data that were collected, the government instructed, were to be kept secret so as to avoid the attention of foreign nations.

Though a historian by training and remote from the sciences that he was expected to know for his assignment, Müller extended his research to widely separated fields of knowledge. He gathered data about the location of mineral deposits and possible areas for exploitation, incorporated his findings in his *Notes on Siberian Commerce*, and mailed them to the capital where they stirred interest among numerous officials. In the field of history Müller's travels in the East resulted in a two-volume study that represents no small achievement. The work not only devotes many pages to the history of that hardly known eastern domain, but includes accounts of Russian relations with Asian countries. It is based mostly on documents he uncovered throughout Siberia and, in many instances, in various local dialects. These contained also ethnographic, geographic, and diplomatic data, as well as local folklore revealed for the first time in historical literature.

It is difficult to imagine the obstacles that Müller had to overcome while collecting his source material. He examined some twenty archives in widely scattered localities of Siberia. Many records, as he described them, were found in chaotic piles and in a deplorable state, often stained by dampness or chewed away by mice. The sorting out of these huge piles required the patience of a dedicated man. Müller interviewed many people, especially the oldest survivors among the natives, to confirm local legends. Together with his compatriot, Johann Georg Gmelin (1709-1755), he made some archaeological explorations, visited caves where he found and copied carved figures and inscriptions, investigated legendary burial places, and on one occasion came into possession of a Tartar chronicle.

Even the severe critics of the "German elements" in the Academy of Sciences in the eighteenth century, such as the late M. Tikhomirov, had to admit that "Bayer and Müller did not belong to the same German group that regarded Russia merely as a "feeding trough" (*kormushka*). The name of Müller, Tikhomirov stated, became clearly associated with Russian historical science thanks to the decade he spent in Siberia in search of sources. It was in Siberia that Müller nearly lost his eyesight, reading gathered material during long Siberian winter nights in dwellings poorly heated and supplied with inadequate light. In all fairness, Tikhomirov stressed, Müller was first an archaeographer and only second a historian, and therefore he cannot be compared with men like Tatishchev or Lomonosov, who sought to paint on a wide canvas an all-embracing picture of Russian history.[16]

The first volume of Müller's *History of Siberia* appeared in 1750. The publication proved to be an even greater strain than the Siberian expedition, for numerous difficulties had to be overcome before the author could see his laborious manuscript in print. A special commission appointed by the academy to subject the manuscript to minute scrutiny resulted in endless disputes with Müller. The work had to be translated from German into Russian, and to this project a certain Golubtsov was assigned. He proved to be a drunkard and became involved in frequent bouts with Müller, who bitterly complained to the authorities not only about Golubtsov's drinking habits, but about his stealing of valuable papers as well as quills that were entrusted to him. The translated text was another source of friction. In desperation Müller wrote to the academy authorities that his translator would lead him prematurely to his grave.

As one examines the materials amassed by Müller, one must conclude that he was in the true sense primarily a compiler, a *Geschichtssammler*, and never a *Geschichtsmaler*, for had he been the latter he would never have been able to perform such valuable spadework. With typical German diligence and persistence, he set out to copy voluminous collections of government records in the distant towns of Siberia. He combed all the settlements of western and eastern Siberia, visited its natives, sailed its rivers. During his journeys he located the Siberian chronicle of Remezov; he copied or examined voluminous records, took many with him, and shipped others to St. Petersburg. During the same time he also discovered many records that pertain to the Time of Troubles, charters issued by Boris Godunov, Prince Shuisky, and others. Altogether Müller invested ten years of arduous labor (1733-1743), as a result of which he was able to hand over to the Archaeographical Commission a mass of material that the commission continued to publish for the next century and a half. Though begun incidentally, the collection of manuscripts gathered from Siberian archives and known as the "Müller's Portfolios" (thirty-eight in all and for the most part still unpublished) opened a mine of sources from which students of Russian history, particularly of Russian eastward expansion, draw material to this day.[17] The originals of many of these documents are no longer available, so that the "Portfolios" remain the only valuable records of Siberian history at present.

Until the work of Müller appeared, almost all the historians had based their studies entirely or chiefly on the only chronicles known to them. Müller's material, which makes up the larger part of the later supplements to documents published by the Archaeographical Commission,[18] revealed new and more authentic sources, including numerous government decrees, orders, charters, and official correspondence. His papers contained extracts from the chronicles of the early seventeenth century, various statistical data, sources pertaining to Siberian ethnography, and descriptions of the more important expeditions and personal adventures in eastern Siberia.[19] Besides offering these new documents, Müller was the first to direct attention to totally unknown Tartar and Mongolian sources; he interrogated natives and recorded their versions of bygone events, explored Siberian tumuli, and collected archaeological, linguistic, and genealogical data. His discoveries led to an increasing interest in further search for archival material as well as in historical writing, particularly concerning later periods of Russian history. Moreover, they gave an insight into Moscow's eastward and Siberian colonization, a subject barely touched at that time and one still awaiting due appreciation in Western historical literature. Müller's publication in German of the *Sammlung russischer Geschichte* further attracted the attention of Western scholars—among them Schlözer—to Russian sources; and Müller's *History of Siberia*, though a lifeless account, remains to this day a source to which students make frequent reference.[20]

The investigation of Siberian archives was followed by similar study of documentary evidence located in western Siberia, especially in the archives of Moscow, which the government was long unwilling to open to curious scholars. In 1748 Müller was so carried away by enthusiasm for his work (and to a degree by the animosity within certain academic circles) that he consented to abandon his Prussian allegiance (after twenty-three years of residence in Russia!) and become a Russian subject. Eventually he decided even to change his name to Feodor Ivanovich Meeller. There is good reason to believe that his frequent quarrels in the academy were, in part at least, responsible for his decision to abandon his former citizenship. Anti-German feeling was rising, and frequent attacks by Lomonosov and other Russian members of the academy who suspected Müller as "politically unreliable" motivated him to prove his loyalty. Personal experience, the fate of some of his compatriots in Russia, and particularly the conduct of Gmelin, who, while on leave for a year, decided never to return to Russia, made Müller's position even more vulnerable to criticism. In 1752 Gmelin published his *Travels in Siberia* abroad without obtaining permission from the Russian government. As years passed, Müller mellowed, became more sensitive and cautious, and finally surrendered to his fate. In 1764 he settled down permanently in Moscow, where two years later Catherine II appointed him to the superintendency of the Russian archives, a post Müller had long craved and which he held for the rest of his life. His departure from St. Petersburg ended the publication of the journal *Sammlung russischer Geschichte* and the monthly Russian publication, *Yezhemesyachniye sochineniya*. The two journals contain much valuable historical material in both German and Russian.

Russian historiography is considerably indebted to Müller for having had Tatishchev's *History* edited before its publication. Müller regarded this work as one of the outstanding achievements in Russian historical writing. Müller also edited the Code of Laws of 1550 (*Sudebnik*), including the commentaries of Tatishchev, and several other sources of value to later scholars. In 1748 Müller requested that the academy acquire the entire collection of materials painstakingly gathered by Tatishchev; he urged similar requests concerning other private libraries and collections of sources. He published the letters of Peter I to Sheremetev and was instrumental in the publication of a second edition of Krasheninnkov's *History of Kamchatka* (referred to below), not to mention numerous other documentary collections and historical accounts. Finally, Müller was the pioneering figure in the field of Russian archaeology and Siberian ethnography. Simultaneously he continued the compilation of all the sources, state and privately owned, on which he could possibly lay his hands. His toil was compensated by the fruitful research of later scholars, who began to exploit the material he had so meticulously gathered. He had not expected more. Realizing that his age did not permit him to undertake ambitious projects and that archival work demanded unremitting attention, he sought younger men to continue his work, at first among his compatriots—like Schlözer—and later among the rising Russian generation represented by men like N. N. Bantysh-Kamensky, who succeeded Müller as director of the Moscow archives, or A. F. Malinovsky, who was later followed by two of the most eminent archivists, K. F. Kalaydovich and P. M. Stroyev.

One more name must be added to the story in connection with Müller, that of S. P. Krasheninnkov (1711-1755). This man went east with the second expedition of Behring and under the direction of Müller and Gmelin explored the Kamchatka peninsula. The result of this ten-year investigation and guidance of his senior scholars, Krasheninnkov produced a monumental study of Kamchatka.[21] The two-volume study constitutes an excellent companion to Müller's two-volume *History of Siberia*. Historically speaking, Krasheninnkov's achievement is also significant in marking the beginning of the rise of a new generation of native intellect and talent that was soon effectively to challenge the cultural preponderance of the German elements among the members of the Russian Academy of Sciences during the eighteenth century.

Schlözer

According to August Ludwig von Schlözer (1735-1809), there are four kinds of historians: the collector (*Geschichtssammler*), the analyst (*Geschichtsforscher*), the writer (*Geschichtsschreiber*), and, finally, the historian-artist (*Geschichtsmaler*). If Müller can be classified as the outstanding collector, Schlözer was undoubtedly one of the most distinguished analytical historians.[22] The two other kinds of historians were yet to appear on the scene of Russian historiography.

A former student of Oriental languages and theology and later of medicine, Schlözer eventually decided to devote himself to history. Already, while temporarily residing in Sweden (1755-1758), he had written an *Essay on the General History of Trade and of Seafaring in the most Ancient Times.* He soon came to extend his interest beyond the subject of trade, realizing that there was a need for widening the field of history.

Müller had already visualized the historian as a man "without a fatherland, without religion, without a sovereign." Schlözer went farther: he maintained that history must be universal, embracing more than mere political development; the historian must therefore abandon his academic isolation and seek a closer acquaintance with the wide world of reality.[23] He was among the first to urge a scientific systematization of *all* sources on which critical historical writing might be based. Whatever source material the historian finds, Schlözer insisted, must be analyzed objectively. Historical writing must be founded on sources that are without doubt authentic, but the narrative based on these sources must be absolutely unbiased, regardless of racial or national affiliation of the author. "The first law of history," declared Schlözer in a famous utterance, "is to state nothing false; it is better to remain ignorant than to be deceived." The arts of writing history and of writing novels must never be confused; in the former there is no place for fancy, dreams, or invention. This new enunciation was delivered at a time when discord between the German and Russian members of the Academy of Sciences was at its boiling point. The debates between Lomonosov and Müller over the Norman theory in history led to the question of what was the first and foremost purpose of the historian.

Schlözer found himself in Russia at the invitation of Müller in 1761. Here he hoped to find employment that would enable him to proceed with his studies and to travel in the Near East; while in Russia he found his interest aroused by the abundance of medieval sources of his patron, Müller. The reason the latter extended his hospitality to the young scholar was that he hoped to gain his cooperation in examining the gathered sources.[24] With Schlözer's assistance Müller hoped to make use of the documents he brought from Siberia and to write an extensive history.[25] The cherished scheme was not, as some writers seemed to assume, based merely on seniority. Schlözer came to Russia as an intellectually mature person, carrying with him an air of erudition that Müller realized he himself sadly lacked. Schlözer, on the other hand, resentfully sensed his patron's scheme. With a degree of ill-concealed disdain he observed how poorly trained Müller was, largely because of his prolonged absence from Western Europe. He thought even less of Russian historians, with the exception of Tatishchev, and to some degree of Shcherbatov and Boltin. Therefore a sharp disagreement between the two men was a foregone conclusion. Relations were further strained by the fact that Müller jealously guarded all the sources that Schlözer was eager to examine. After several years of hopes and disillusionments, Schlözer accepted an invitation from the University of Göttingen and left his scheming host empty-handed.

The impression Schlözer carried away about the state of scholarship in

Russia was a very negative one. The most serious handicap, he felt, was the lack of proper training and familiarity with Byzantine and northern European history. Another reason for the academic backwardness was poor linguistic preparation among Russian historians. Schlözer regarded even Bayer as an unsuitable scholar since he never managed to learn the Slavic languages adequately. As to his opinion of Müller, Schlözer considered him a superb day-to-day workman.

Realizing quickly the importance of linguistic equipment to the historian, Schlözer came to master Russian as few foreign scholars ever did. With the aid of the native tongue he soon extended his study from history into other fields, economics and ethnography particularly, both of which Schlözer came to regard as indispensable to history. It is to be regretted that Schlözer left Russia without ever familiarizing himself with the nature of the documentary material in Müller's possession. Though arrangements were made for a wide exchange of sources between the Academy of Sciences and the University of Göttingen, still much remained beyond Schlözer's reach. Without the knowledge of the content or general nature of many of the sources, he was bound to follow the outmoded method, relying almost entirely on the chronicles rather than on the records more recently uncovered in the East. Still it must be said that Schlözer felt intuitively that other documentary materials must be sought before a well-rounded history could be written.

The periodization of Russian history Schlözer outlined in his *Probe russischer Annalen*, while in the *Tableaux de l'histoire de Russie* he revealed a surprising lack of originality. The first period, according to Schlözer, began with the orthodox story of the invitation extended to the Varangians and ended with the death of Vladimir, 862-1015; he labeled it *Russia nascens*. The second period, 1015-1216, Schlözer named *Russia divisa*. Here he dealt with the process of Kievan decline and the rise of the appanage system. The third, *Russia oppressa*, 1216-1462, dealt with the Mongolian ascendancy and ended with the death of Basil II. The fourth he named *Russia victrix*, 1462-1696. Finally, the climactic period, 1696-1762, begun with the ascendancy of Peter the Great, ends with the ascendancy of Catherine II, which Schlözer exultingly entitled *Neueverändertes Russland* (Resurrected Russia).

The writing of a complete Russian history, Schlözer believed, was a premature undertaking unless (1) all national sources (*studium nomumentorum domesticorum*) and (2) those to be found in foreign archives (*studium monumentorum extrariorum*) had first been gathered and properly edited. While at the University of Göttingen he began to prepare materials for such a forthcoming collection. In 1768 he published his *Probe russischer Annalen*, to be followed shortly by other works much as *Allgemeine nordische Geschichte* and *Neuverändertes Russland*. Finally, in 1802, Schlözer published the first volume of his monumental work, the study of that "old sage, Nestor." This work stands out as a unique accomplishment for its time, even in German historical literature. The first volume, his labor of love, Schlözer dedicated to Alexander I. In his preface the author expressed the hope that the work might inspire others to write a history of Russia with the *Gründlichkeit* of Markow, the *Geschmack* of Robertson, the *Unbefangenheit* of Giannone, and the *Anmut* of Voltaire.

Long before he published the *Nestor Chronicle*, Schlözer, with keen perception, outlined the preliminary work necessary to establish the authenticity of the *Primary Chronicle*. This called for a careful collection of all annalistic literature and an analytic study of each chronicle. It involved a minute comparative study in order to determine the influence of one chronicle on another, and to detect, through the influence of one chronicler upon another and the borrowed textual parts, the time each was recorded. The analysis would further necessitate a comparative study of Scandinavian, Byzantine, Arabic, and other Eastern sources from which, most likely, some Russian chronicles must have borrowed parts of the texts for their own accounts. When such a *Corpus historiae russicae* was accomplished, and only then, scholarship could hope to attain its goal. This was the pious hope of many Russian scholars for over a century and a half and is far from fulfillment to this day.

Schlözer's method of tracing the genuine *Primary Chronicle* and weeding out the spurious parts demonstrated an astounding erudition and originality. This method was to become the basis of subsequent research throughout most of the nineteenth century. Though Schlözer was inclined to accept the Norman theory, he did so with some qualification. Thus he pointed out that within two centuries after the arrival of the Normans there was hardly a trace left of Scandinavian linguistic influence on the Russian tongue, which led him to the conclusion that the Normans who descended upon the Slavs must have been numerically very few and therefore quickly absorbed. This interpretation was not challenged, and it even pleased some nationalists and Slavophile elements.

But Schlözer also maintained that prior to the arrival of the Normans the

Russians lived in a state of barbarism. This led to later accusations that Schlözer's Germanic loyalties were stronger than the historical methods he advocated, that in effect what he endeavored to show was that the Normans (later to be considered Germans) were instruments in civilizing the Slavs. The Slavophiles in particular were militantly opposed to such a contention, since they were most sensitive on this issue. They disregarded the fact that Schlözer also stressed the high literary standard that, prior to the arrival of the Normans, obviously prevailed among the Slavs and enabled them to create a rich annalistic literature. However, this consideration was brushed aside by the nationalists, but it was not lightly ignored by the Slavophiles, who never failed to respond to the least challenge.

Objective judgment did not entirely depart from the ranks of scholars, but even during his lifetime Schlözer was recognized for his contribution to Russian historiography. His analytical study of the *Nestor Chronicle* was soon acknowledged as an outstanding accomplishment, and a request was made that it be translated from German into Russian. In recognition of his scholarship he was elected honorary member of the Society of Russian History and Antiquities. Schlözer's research convinced Russian scholars of the necessity to publish all available chronicles and other documentary sources (a subject discussed in detail elsewhere). A more recent evaluation by Herbert Butterfield characterized Schlözer thus: "There are defects in his critical practice. . . . It is not even true to say of him that he was a mind of the first rank; though he is certainly the most interesting figure in the Göttingen story, and the range of his activities is astonishing."[26]

Though Schlözer left Russia to escape the enervating squabbles within the academy family, he did not find the peace he sought in his native country either. At Göttingen he was annoyed by other experiences, mainly resulting from his utterances of personal views. He insisted, for example, that the historian must keep his faith apart from the institution of the church when dealing with the latter in history, that one must also dissociate from historical truth the superstitions accumulated over the centuries. Being an admirer of Voltaire, Mably, and other thinkers of the Age of Enlightenment, Schlözer came to be regarded by his colleagues as an atheist; for expressing approval of the execution of Charles I, Schlözer was labeled a dangerous radical who favored regicide and therefore should be watched with suspicion.[27] The path of Schlözer, like the path of historians of his caliber at any time, was not a smooth one, and it was only his devotion to historical truth that made the treading endurable.

Lomonosov

Mikhail Vasilevich Lomonosov (1711-1766) was not in a strict sense a historian; yet his name can hardly be dissociated from Russian historiography. Though a many-sided genius he was primarily a man of science; his learning embraced a wide range of knowledge. His intellectual and scientific versatility was remarkable. He was a poet, philologist, and historian; he was also the father of Russian science and scientific research, particularly in the field of physical chemistry. He conducted astronomical observations and proved proficient in physical science. Above all he was an enlightened patriot and champion in research both in the applied sciences and in the field of arts.

Lomonsov carried out pioneering experiments in modern quantitative analysis and sought solutions to problems related to expansion of gases and metals. He made a mosaic portrait of Peter I and wrote odes dedicated to his favored sovereign as well as to Empress Elizabeth, in which he extolled their virtues. He improved the rhythm of Russian verse and modernized the literary language as distinct from Old Church Slavonic, thereby helping it to become a vehicle of much more eloquent expression. He was the author of a new Russian grammar that remained for many years the standard textbook. Lomonosov held the post of professor of chemistry, later was named rector of the University of St. Petersburg, and ranked high among his academic colleagues.[28]

It was as a member of the academy that Lomonosov became embroiled in the sharp debates and assumed the leadership of the opposition against his German colleagues. Some of the Germans were pure careerists who had gained membership in the academy through special favors and whose presence caused much feuding. Another source of even more militant opposition was the notorious Norman interpretation of history, which Lomonosov came to consider as a purely German invention. In the heated debates the entire affair was bound to lead to indiscriminate attack against any German influence whatsoever. Though chiefly a scientist, he laid aside his laboratory research, plunged headlong into battle with historians, and took up the literary cudgels to defend his own thesis—that the Russian state had developed long before the Normans arrived on the scene of history. His knowledge of history or of available sources was scant, and yet the influence Lomonosov exerted proved lasting in a historiographic sense.

The Norman incident was provoked by a paper delivered at the academy by Müller in 1749 on the subject of the origin of the Russian state and the derivation of the name *Rus'*. A self-made man with a profound sense of national pride, Lomonosov instantly attacked Müller and soon expanded the offensive along a wider front, against Fischer, Bayer, and Schlözer, criticizing their entire philosophy and method of approach; he stressed the fact that they had not learned the Russian language sufficiently and did not even have any intention to learn it; he pointed out that they failed to consult native sources and depended exclusively on documentary evidence in foreign languages abroad, and, therefore, they falsified the entire course of Russian history.

In defense of his own national philosophy of history Lomonosov argued that the historian was obliged not merely to compile factual data, but to synthesize these and to show the interdependence of all past events in the long process of history. This, continued Lomonosov, required lucid vision, consistent thinking, integrity of character, and the ability to discern historical unity. When such a narrative of the past is successfully composed, he concluded, it must serve to awaken in the reader an understandable pride, admiration, and respect for his native history. The verdict was thus simple: Müller had dismally failed to accomplish his task, for he vilified and falsified history.

Lomonosov's violent attack against Müller led to an official request that Lomonosov be assigned to write the history he so ardently advocated. This he readily accepted; with the pattern already designed, to show that the past of Russia "equals that of ancient Greece and Rome, except for the absence of historians to prove it," he immediately commenced preparing himself to play the part of a Russian Herodotus. He began to examine the *Nestor Chronicle*, the earliest Slavic codes of laws, the first part of Tatishchev's manuscript; he read Greek and Byzantine historians, consulted Helmold's *Annales Slavorum* and Martin Cromer's *De origine et rebus gestis Polonorum*; he gathered copious notes and citations to support his thesis and to prove that his opponents were entirely wrong. Lomonosov contemplated an extensive four-volume study, which he was not destined to complete or even to see partially in print: it was a year after his death, in 1766, that his first and only volume came off the press. It was entitled *Earliest Russian History from the Beginning of the Russian People Until the End of the Grand Prince Yaroslav I or to the Year 1054.*

Lomonosov started to gather his material in 1751, began to write three years later, and sent his manuscript to the press in 1758. According to his annual report to the academy, the three years were spent compiling citations from a wide range of documentary and secondary sources; he collected data on toponymy and comparative philology as part of the ammunition for his battle with the Normanists. He quoted Slavic names of settlements of the fourth century and sought proof of earlier civilization preceding the "coming of the Varangians." He contemplated accompanying the published text with lengthy commentaries similar to those of Tatishchev, but his death prevented completion of the plan. From the lengthy lists of original sources that Lomonosov incorporated in the text he argued that Müller's sources were selective and deliberate and that Müller had discarded any evidence that might conflict with his preconceived theories.

Lomonosov's general thesis can be summarized thus: History represents an endless process of the rise and decline of nations. Lomonosov came to regard the fifth century as the dividing period between ancient and medieval history. The latter began with the invasions of the Roman Empire by the Germanic and Slavic tribes and the ensuing internal disorders within the empire. To prove his thesis Lomonosov cited copiously from many writers, Pliny, Tacitus, Strabo, Procopius, Livy, Nepos, and Ptolemy among them. To Lomonosov history was a universal drama in which the Slavs played a part no less glorious than that of any other people. The Varangians or "invited Normans" had long been considered a homogeneous people of Baltic origin. On the contrary, Lomonosov contended, they included a most heterogeneous group of tribes and tongues, united by a common cause— plunder. He used philology as evidence, arguing that the origin of the name Rus' was Prus, or "Prussians," a contention that later scholars have convincingly disproved but which to Lomonosov was good enough for driving a point home.

Lomonosov's *History* cannot be considered as a contribution of enduring value to history; it serves rather as one sign of an awakened national consciousness that clamored for an end to foreign intrusion in its intellectual life and was destined to blossom a century later. Furthermore, it demonstrated with increasing evidence that in the absence of a complete publication of sources, as shown by Schlözer, history would provide a wide field for emotional discussion and writing, but never a truly integrated, scientifically reliable synthesis of Russia's past. This task was largely left to the succeeding century to accomplish.

Shcherbatov

Historical study and the publication of source material became, in the second half of the eighteenth century, the occupation of many many members of the Russian elite. The reign of Peter I and the following years of confusion, the struggle against domination in intellectual life, and the endeavor to create in Russia a genuine national culture, all conspired to bring the developments we are familiar with. In short, on the one hand there was an ardent effort to write a pragmatic history of Russia; on the other, a desire to explore all archival material in order to justify by documentary evidence every claim to intellectual independence, if not superiority. This was not precisely in agreement with the more scholarly concepts of Schlözer, but so far at least as students began to search for sources, it coincided with his ideas. Among these students two preeminent names claim our attention, Prince Mikhail M. Shcherbatov (1733-1790) and Major General Ivan N. Boltin.[29]

A descendant of an illustrious old family, Prince Shcherbatov was one of the most cultured Russians of his time. He had received an excellent education, spoke French, German, and Italian, was thoroughly familiar with world literature, and during his lifetime had built up a fifteen-thousand-volume private library. Prince Shcherbatov was a true product of his time: a rationalist, a political critic, an economist, a champion of a morally responsible aristocracy, and a moralist. He was seriously disturbed by the decline or, as he described it, "corruption of morals" since the death of Peter I, and particularly during the reign of Catherine II. Prince Shcherbatov strongly believed in progress, but any advance, he believed, had to depend on leadership and the latter could only be provided by a moral aristocratic class. Absolutism, he feared, could easily deteriorate into despotism, which could only be blocked by a genuine nobility that professed high moral principles and was motivated by a sense of duty to serve the country.

Our concern, however, is mainly Prince M. M. Shcherbatov as a historian. Shcherbatov was interested in history as an environmental product, as were some of his contemporaries, such as N. I. Novikov or I. N. Boltin. Shcherbatov's interest in the past was largely awakened by his aspiration to defend his aristocratic caste. For this purpose, he fully realized, he had to have a command of historical information and the ability to cite as well as interpret factual records. What he sought, it may be said, was "historical testimony," accompanied by moral integrity. Such was the main impulse that led Shcherbatov to study and write a history of Russia.

As a matter of the Legislative Assembly of 1766, Shcherbatov demonstrated an amazing acquaintance with the teachings of Beccaria and Montesquieu. In his observations on the relations between church and state he showed an equal familiarity with the literature of the Encyclopedists and most of all with Voltaire. He was familiar with the theories of the physiocrats, particularly concerning the role of agriculture in national economic life. He agreed with Schlözer on the importance of statistics and even attempted to write a "statistical survey" of Russia. Among his many political and social occupations, Shcherbatov became intensely interested in Russian history.[30] This was fortunate, for not only was his own library of great assistance, but he also had sufficient leisure and the access to some of the Papal archival materials and state archives as well, largely through the assistance of Catherine II. This enabled him to advance historical writing much farther than any of his predecessors had done.[31] The Emancipation Act of 1762, freeing the nobility from compulsory service to the state, allowed Shcherbatov the leisure to devote himself entirely to the writing of history.

Shcherbatov was familiar with many of the Russian sources of which Schlözer was hardly aware. For this reason his history encompasses a far wider scope and is not of the nature of chronicle writing. Yet Shcherbatov still shows the signs of the eighteenth-century dilettante historian rather than the *Geschichtsforscher* of the Schlözer caliber. It is to be regretted that Schlözer's erudition and the advantages derived from Shcherbatov's social position could not somehow have been amalgamated; for in spite of his prodigious industry and excellent opportunities, Shcherbatov sadly lacked training in handling historical sources, with the result that he committed more errors than a careful scholar would have made without any sources at all. In his work Shcherbatov displayed little originality either in approach or in organization of material and often followed the chronicles uncritically. Nor must we overlook the fact that Shcherbatov's compelling reason for writing history was the deep lament over the "corruption of morals in Russia."

Economic or social factors were alien to his concept, or at least not stirring issues; it was in politics that he was mainly interested, and the status of the nobility in society was of particular concern to him. An aristocrat to the core, he pursued a single theme: only in honest cooperation with the nobility could the monarchy remain strong and enduring. He referred at great length to the reign of Ivan IV, with its senseless persecution of the nobility, and quoted copiously from Prince Kurbsky's correspondence with the Czar; he interpreted Ivan's military defeats as proof of the dangers of divorcing the interests of the nobility from the state. The numerous peasant uprisings were cited as further proof of his thesis.

Let us now turn to his main work. Shcherbatov began his history in the 1760s and toiled over it for the rest of his life. At the time of his death he was working on the third part of the seventh volume, which was interrupted in the middle of a paragraph in 1790. The seven volumes that he produced (the last one incomplete) consisted of fifteen parts, beginning with Ryurik and ending in 1610. His introductory chapter goes back to an earlier period, to the Scythians. His entire narrative is dominated by factual presentation, rarely by interpretation. Only here and there does an interpretive effort manifest itself. One example is the oft-narrated story about the "invitation" of the Varangians, who, Shcherbatov significantly added, were never granted sovereign power except the duty to defend the land from the ravages of inimical people, along the borders.[32]

Prince Shcherbatov was particularly interested in Peter I and often demonstrated profound admiration of his reforms. According to Shcherbatov, prior to Peter I there was no enlightenment, no factories, no adequate defense forces or extensive trade. And if Peter I acted arbitrarily on frequent occasions, it was only because circumstances compelled him to conduct himself in this manner. In short, within the short distance of time since the turbulent age of Peter I, some men already began to sense the historic role of that Czar and the implications of his reforms. Shcherbatov does not fail, however, to remind us at intervals of the negative aspects of the Petrine age, the moral damage it was bound to cause, or the fallacies of haste. But he added, to counterbalance this negative aspect with positive accomplishments and a net result, that the constructive effects outweighed the moral damages inflicted during the Petrine reign. The true moral decline, Shcherbatov believed, came after Peter I, particularly during the reign of Catherine II.

Shcherbatov's thesis made a deep impression on some of his contemporaries such as the historians I. N. Boltin and N. M. Karamzin. The profound impact that Prince M. M.Shcherbatov had on other writers has been slowly recognized. But during his lifetime and for years after, few people noted either his constructive criticism or the beneficial influence he had on later historians in Russia.

For decades Prince Shcherbatov toiled over the bulky volumes of his *Russian History from the Earliest Times*, which he never managed to complete. The seventh and last volume ends with the year 1610; the author's original intention was to lead up to the reign of Peter the Great. At the end Shcherbatov himself acknowledged that he had not been entirely successful in his original endeavor to present a historical synthesis. He recognized his failure, but justified his labor by the hope that some future historian would utilize his writings and find in them the necessary material for a superior work. Besides his seven-volume history, Shcherbatov also published source material—*A Chronicle of Many Revolts: A History of the War with Sweden*—and various essays. His work is written in the ponderous style typical of his time, which makes tedious going for a modern reader. Being a rehash of the chronicles he had read indiscriminately, it therefore represents rather a guide than a study, as the author himself justly sensed at times. The chief merit of Shcherbatov's labor lies in the fact that he was the first to utilize some of the church and diplomatic documents, particularly the correspondence between the Muscovite sovereigns and the Crimean khans. During the following century Karamzin made good use of the materials Shcherbatov presented and of his bibliographical references in general.[33]

Shcherbatov lived during a period when the demarcation between the old and the new Russia was becoming more and more distinct. As a typical aristocrat of the old Russia, in spite of his flirtation with Voltairian philosophy and Freemasonry, he could see nothing good in the new ideas and could only lament over the moral decline that had come over his fatherland. For him the old Russian customs and institutions held a peculiar virtue that had deteriorated under the ruthless onslaught of Western ideas, forced through since Peter I, and led to the loose morals of Catherine II. He deplored the prominence that various court favorites came to assume during the ''Times of Catherine'' and often expressed his feelings with a rare and mordant frankness. Shcherbatov's last work, *On the Corruption of Morals in Russia*, is an obituary for old Russia and an appeal for the preservation of neglected virtues. Acknowledging the progress toward Western civilization that these sovereigns had assured in Russia, he was unable to overlook the price the country had paid for it in the disesteem that had befallen the virtues of the national character. His solution was not entirely encouraging, only hopeful that Russia must "beg God that this evil may be eradicated by a better reign. But this cannot be until we have a monarch who is sincerely attached to God's Law." Reform would also require an abhorrence of vice, willingness to take advice from wise men, the banishment of licentiousness, and the ability to delegate authority. The counsel of Shcherbatov, we may add, is sound at any age, but was hardly audible in the nation.

Boltin

Like Prince M. M. Shcherbatov, General Ivan Nikitich Boltin (1735-1792) was a true son of his age and a representative of the "amateur school" of historians. He was a familiar figure in the literary circles of St. Petersburg, knew Lomonosov, belonged to a group led by A. I. Musin-Pushkin, and actively participated in the publication of historical documents. He prepared the text of the medieval Russian Code of Laws (*Russkaya pravda*) for publication, based on several versions found by the late eighteenth century. Boltin was imbued with the spirit of the Age of Enlightenment. At one time he flirted with the ideas of the French *philosophes*, advocated religious tolerance, frequently quoted Voltaire, gently criticized the church and monastic orders for their accumulated wealth, cautiously favored legislation that would curtail the rights of serf owners or at least define their rights more precisely, and on occasions expressed faint hope of emancipation at some unforeseeable future. If Shcherbatov is labeled an "old-fashioned" historian, Boltin may be rightly regarded as "historian-philosopher." One literally lived in the past, the other sought meaning in the past; one endeavored to create an idyllic picture, the other was in search of meaningful courses of development; one championed conservation as a guiding light to the future, the other toyed with the past to improve the future.

Boltin spent a good deal of his spare time, which was none too plentiful, in gathering sources and familiarizing himself with archival materials and private collections. The work was greatly assisted by the well-known collector of Russian antiquities, Count A. I. Musin-Pushkin. The "antiquarian dilettantism" of Boltin proved to have a more serious aspect than the superficial observer might have detected. He was not interested, as was Shcherbatov, in a tedious, minutely detailed paraphrasing of the chronicles. "Trivialities mentioned in chronicles are irrelevant to history," Boltin wrote. It was the philosophy of history that fascinated him. This marks a step further in the progress of historical science in Russia.

Boltin was absorbed in a comparative study of Russian and Western European historical development: he showed keen interest in national origins of his country and in the institution of serfdom, a subject that was soon to become a national issue of major importance. In this respect, it may be added, Boltin was better qualified than his opponents, since few men of his time either fully grasped the essence of history so clearly or traveled so widely and knew conditions so intimately as Boltin did. Boltin was particularly familiar with the southern part of the country, where he spent many years as administrator in various official capacities. Catherine II sought his advice on many occasions and appreciated his wide knowledge in the fields of history, geography, and ethnography. Finally, it should be noted, Boltin devoted a great deal of his writing to an analytical study of other historians with whom he crossed swords. We must discuss one such duel.

In 1759 a French physician, N. G. LeClerc, visited Russia at the invitation of the royal court, and on the basis of this brief visit he wrote nothing less than a six-volume history of the country.[34] He boldly entitled his work *The Natural, Moral, and Political History of Early and Recent Russia.* This "brazen-faced slanderer" so deeply hurt Boltin's patriotic pride by numerous misrepresentations that the gallant general took up his literary weapons in defense of his country. LeClerc provoked Boltin, who regarded the writings of his opponent as a hodgepodge of small talk, or, as Klyuchevsky described it, as a small town store in which one is liable to find "velvet, facial cream, a microscope, and a copper ring—but no history" (V. O. Klyuchevsky, *Sochineniya*, VIII, 427). "Judging Russia by comparing her with other European states," Boltin declared, "is like fitting a dwarf's suit of clothes to a full-grown man." Since LeClerc had relied greatly on the first two volumes of Shcherbatov's history, Boltin unbridled his wrath against both writers. The criticism resulted in an impressive four-volume work, two volumes for each opponent. In these tomes the author displayed not only a considerable knowledge of the subject, as well as a good deal of historical acumen, but also a surprising capacity for original thought.[35] The criticism of LeClerc's work so impressed Catherine II that she ordered the two volumes to be published at state expense.

Boltin first challenged LeClerc's Norman theory that Russian political life dates to the coming of the Scandinavians. According to the chronicles, Boltin argued, Novgorod had been a self-governing state long before the

Scandinavians arrived on the national scene; the level of Slavic civilization, furthermore, was much the same as throughout medieval Europe. Agricultural development, growth of town life, trade in the Baltic area, and commerce were recorded by chroniclers long before the ninth century. Culturally the Scandinavians who descended on Kiev were no further advanced than the Slavic peoples with whom they came in contact. Similarly, Boltin denied the idea expounded by LeClerc that bondage was a typical Russian institution. He cited the institution of the *veche* (assembly) and similar democratic medieval institutions that allowed voting privileges, thus showing that LeClerc had neglected or was unaware of important aspects of Russian national life. There was feudalism in Russia, said Boltin, but that was an institution not unfamiliar in Western Europe. His theory, an original one, that Russian serfdom was similar to Western feudalism, was to be developed by other scholars more than a century later.

Boltin regarded Russian annalistic literature as one of the most valuable sources for historical study, far above any foreign accounts of his country. It was reliance on the latter that caused Prince Shcherbatov to commit some of the grave errors in his writings, Boltin stated. Yet he was entirely aware that one had to be cautious in relying on the chronicles, and he warned historians therefore that they must make comparative studies and carefully sift all evidence before their accounts could be accepted with any degree of finality. He correctly declared that the *Primary Chronicle* of Nestor must have been preceded by other chronicles. Finally, he cautioned, historians must not follow the pattern of events as cited in the chronicles—that was the error of Tatishchev and Shcherbatov—but must present an all-embracing picture of both the complex national life as well as of the nation itself. The historian, he advised, must see not only the achievements of individual leaders but the national accomplishments as well, and must explain the effects of historic causes on the course of events. Such a presentation must incorporate the interdependence of the general environmental conditions, the form of government, the prevailing judicial system, the peculiar geographic circumstances of the country, and the other factors that cumulatively were likely to contribute to the molding of Russian history.

Boltin was one of the earliest historians in Russia to attempt an analysis of historical processes; he held the view, as did Montesquieu and Bodin, that climate is one of the most important factors in determining social and political institutions. Criticizing LeClerc's thesis that Russia was a barbaric country governed by whimsical despotism, Boltin endeavored to show that, on the contrary, only through their cultural superiority and monarchical form of government had the Russian people succeeded in surviving and overcoming foreign domination. Like Shcherbatov, he was a typical aristocrat of eighteenth-century Russia, favoring the Muscovite period and skeptical of the reforms of Peter I and Catherine II;[36] unlike Shcherbatov, however, he demanded that the subject of westernization be presented critically. Boltin reminded Shcherbatov in no uncertain terms that if one lacks skill in handling historical sources, it is preferable to leave them alone altogether.[37] He also insisted, as did Schlözer some years later, that history could never be rightly recorded unless all the documents, within a country as well as without, were properly gathered and organized. This was not a task for one person or even for one generation; whoever undertakes by himself both to compile all the sources pertaining to national history and to write that history is bound to fail, as had Tatishchev or Müller. With rare insight Boltin wrote, while criticizing both Shcherbatov and LeClerc, that the labor that must precede the writing of history is as important and as difficult as the writing itself. To create history, particularly good history, is very difficult and is hardly possible for one man, no matter how long his life or how gifted he may be. Before such a history can be written, all the necessary sources must be collected, analyzed, clarified, and comprehended; this requires more time and labor than the writing itself.

Boltin's influence on many nineteenth-century Russian writers is much in evidence. He was particularly admired by the later Slavophile school, which held history to be a science of national self-realization. Utilitarian in his view, Boltin tried to link his own time with early periods and to derive practical lessons from them. Logical and level-headed, he maintained that historical interpretation should be based only on authentic sources. Schlözer, who held a very low opinion of Russian historians with the rare exception of two or three names, singled out Boltin as the only native historian worthy of special mention. Despite his original mind and intellectual foresight, Boltin, being a product of his time and intellectual climate, accepted erroneous theories. Some of his ethnographic theses and ideas concerning the origin of the Slavs, for example, are ludicrous.[38] He was incapable of grasping fully the implied historical importance of issues of his own time. Though searching for the origins of the institution of serfdom, he failed to appreciate the gravity of its national implications. He believed in solving the agonizing issue "step by step and slowly" and lived under mortal fear that precipitate action might be taken; in that case, he prophesied nothing but disaster for the peasants and economic ruin for the entire country.[39] The more, however, one studies Boltin's general approach to his philosophy of history, his views concerning methodology, purpose, and causation in history, the more one is prone to overlook his false views. Boltin is a symbolic figure in Russian historiography: he stood on the borderline of two distinct eras, halfway between the fading eighteenth century and the nineteenth century, a relentlessly advancing era with new developments in historical methodology. He keenly appreciated periodization in Russian history; correctly formulated the historical resources necessary to write history; and keenly stressed the importance of ethnographic, geographic, as well as economic resources. He insisted on laborious textual study of all resources and related fields. These alone move him into the front ranks of the early Russian historians.[40]

Golikov

Before we move on to the following century we must comment on one more "amateur historian," a man of the eighteenth century who diligently cultivated the field of historical science, Ivan Ivanovich Golikov (1735-1801). Golikov was a merchant from Kursk and a member of the Legislative Assembly summoned by Catherine II in 1766. Implicated in some illegal financial deal, he was convicted and pardoned in 1782.

From his early years he became interested in Russian history and for this reason came to represent the "amateur school" of historians. Though preoccupied during his entire lifetime, he managed to devote much attention to the gathering of sources, particularly those related to the reign of Peter I. Among these he succeeded in locating and purchasing many primary sources, memoirs of contemporaries, and folk tales about the colorful personality of Peter I. The net result was massive, a staggering thirty-volume publication: twelve volumes of *Acts of Peter the Great, Wise Reformer of Russia*, which appeared in 1788-1789, and an eighteen-volume *Addendum*, including extensive indices, which began to appear a year later.[41]

The imposing thirty-volume set includes a chronological narrative of the life of Peter I and numerous citations of rare documents painstakingly collected by Golikov. It includes also some two thousand letters of Peter I. All this was obtained at considerable labor and financial cost, gathered from many parts of the sprawling Russian Empire. The purpose of this voluminous collection in itself is revealing—to prove with almost reverential admiration the "acts of the wise reformer." Some historians came to look at the amassed material with skepticism and even unconcealed disdain; yet many writers relied heavily on its contents. Golikov himself never pretended to scholarship: he humbly confessed that he was not a man of learning and knew nothing about the rules of critical evaluation of sources; his sole aim was to gather documents that might cast more light on the time and the illustrious personality of Peter the Great.

To Golikov Peter I was the ideal "enlightened monarch." As a member of the merchant class he professed special interest in the economic policies of his hero-emperor and in Peter's aspiring drive to expand trade and commerce, to introduce industry, and to improve means of transportation. He praised Peter's policy of compulsory labor regardless of class origin, thereby expressing the views of the rising middle class. Contrary to the opinions of the aristocratic writers of history such as Shcherbatov, who expressed grave misgivings concerning the "demoralizing effects of westernization" and the decline of the indigenous virtues of the Russian people, Golikov took the opposite view; with the characteristic optimism of his class and the energetic drive for economic expansion, he detected in Peter's reforms only praiseworthy progress for the future. With Calvinistic admiration Golikov praised Peter for his personal diligence, his aversion to luxury, his economic aspiration, his simple way of life.[42] The very appearance of a man like Golikov in Russian historiography was symptomatic; it heralded some forthcoming changes during the following century.

A Summary of the Eighteenth Century

With Shcherbatov, Boltin, and Golikov we may bring to a close the story of Russian historical writing during the eighteenth century. In general it can be said that none of the eighteenth-century historians had accomplished any critical study. Schlözer, because of his departure from Russia, was unable to analyze the wealth of new material that Müller had gathered in the East. His only notable accomplishment by the turn of the century was the annotated publication of the *Nestor Chronicle*.[43] The vast bulk of documentation remained virtually unknown to students of history; such was the case with Müller collections. Golikov's represented a purely compilatory accomplishment from which later generations, especially the "Westerners," were to draw needed references during the nineteenth century. Its main purpose was the exaltation of Peter's reforms. The collection of sources remained, throughout the eighteenth century, largely an amateur hobby and was rarely a state-supported function. These private collectors nonetheless rendered an inestimable service to the field of history. It suffices to mention such faithful men as Müller, Tatishchev, and Boltin or such benefactors as Count Rumyantsev and Count Musin-Pushkin.

During the last quarter of the eighteenth century, a historian-economist, Mikhail Dmitriyevich Chulkov, succeeded in compiling an impressive seven-volume collection of statistical data on the history of Russian commerce.[44] This represents a rare labor of love and covers a wide range of information. It starts with the trade of pre-Mongolian Russia and the economic relations between the Republic of Novgorod and the Hanseatic League and continues with the development of trade in the Baltic, in Asia, in the North by way of Archangel, and in the West. As in the case of other writers, Chulkov's compilatory work proved to be of immense aid only to later students of history. The national archives were still *terra incognita* to almost all historians, partly because of the enormous difficulty of early investigations but chiefly because the government remained reluctant to open them to students of history.

It would be difficult to overestimate Müller's services to Russian historiography. His preoccupation with the gathering of source materials did not leave him time for the historical writing he had hoped to do; he remained basically a *Geschichtssammler* throughout his lifetime. His ambitious undertaking of the *Sammlung russischer Geschichte* (previously referred to); his *Monthly Publications*, which appeared in Russian from 1755 to 1764 (twenty volumes); and later his attempt to write a recent history of Russia— which incidentally, received the severe rebuke of Lomonosov—all these accomplished little except to provide the future *Geschichtsschreiber* with needed records.[45] Subsequently, with his appointment as archivist in Moscow, Müller had to abandon even his editorial work and devote his entire attention to the tedious yet vital labor of investigating hitherto unexplored archives. Again, it was only the generation to follow that reaped the benefits of his toil.

The second half of the eighteenth century stands out as a schooling period in the field of research and publication of available records. In this connection the year 1767 assumes special significance, for it was then that the first volume of the projected series of chronicle publications had been initiated. The planned series carried the characteristically long eighteenth-century title of *Russian Historical Library Containing Early Chronicles and Various Notations, as an Aid to the Understanding of the History of Geography of Early and Medieval Russia.* Eight volumes appeared between the years 1767 and 1792. During the very year that marked the appearance of the first volume of the chronicle, Tatishchev uncovered the rare historical document, the early Code of Laws (*Russkaya pravda*) of eleventh- and twelfth-century Russia. An enlarged edition of this valuable discovery was published twenty years later. It was, however, not until 1940 that the complete document was gathered from all later-found chronicles, edited, and annotated by the distinguished scholar of the period, B. D. Grekov. Another equally important discovery was the Code of Laws of 1550 (*Sudebnik*) during the reign of Ivan IV. This document was published in 1768 and accompanied by the commentary notes of Tatishchev. Various other source materials were gathered and published during the second half of the eighteenth century, including the decrees promulgated since 1550, and Golikov's voluminous collection covering the reign of Peter I. In summary, it can be safely said that the second half of the eighteenth century had laid the foundation for the enormous projects that unfolded during the following century.

Closely linked with the initial publications is the name that no historiographer can afford to overlook, that of N. I. Novikov (1744-1818). Novikov was not only one of the greatest publishers of his time but also one of the most eminent bibliophiles, with a special interest in history. In 1779 he rented the University of Moscow Press, and the ensuing years, according to one historian, could be called the "Novikov decade." Novikov successfully combed the country far and wide to try to locate church and state charters, which he published at a cost that at one time nearly ruined him financially. Already in 1773 he initiated a scheme that called for the publication of materials located in private, state, and church collections. The result was his *Early Russian Library* (*Drevnyaya rossiiskaya vivliofika*), which included a mass of historical though indiscriminately accumulated material.[46] It is to be regretted that the career of this pioneer publisher ended abruptly and sorrowfully: in 1792 Catherine, while in her last panicky years, detected "subversive Masonic tendencies" in Novikov's activities and ordered him imprisoned. Though released later by Paul I, Novikov never recovered from the experience: he retired broken in heart and in spirit and ruined financially for the remaining years of his life.

The chief link between the eighteenth and nineteenth centuries was the common awareness of the need to gather all historical records and publish them. Both generations ardently sought means to enable the future *Geschichtsschreiber* to create the historical synthesis of the entire course of history and the *Geschichtsmaler* to create in a true literary form the fascinating narrative of bygone years. At the same time the historian began to free himself from patriotic fervor and to follow, perhaps unconsciously, the wise counsel of Schlözer—to pursue historical truth without patriotic, national, religious, or political bias. The sole allegiance of the historian is to the truth.

By slow degrees Russian historical writing began to dissociate itself from Biblical chronology, from annalistic methods and patterns, and from folk legends; it commenced to cast off the crude utilitarianism of some writers and the panegyrical pomposity of others. Already eighteenth-century writers began to insist on more scholarly methods in recording the past. Tatishchev refused to incorporate miracles and Biblical legends in his writings. Boltin denounced LeClerc and Shcherbatov for failure to substantiate their interpretations with authentic documentary evidence. Müller insisted on the objective handling of source material, and Schlözer spoke in terms of universal history. Together they left an impressive legacy that helped to crystallize nineteenth-century thought. Ironically, both Müller and Schlözer came to be associated with the Norman school, whose views on the origin of the Russian state caused bitter feuds, endless and often totally futile controversies among historians. Nonetheless, the intellectual heritage that the eighteenth century passed on to Russian historiography is an impressive one and cannot be lightly dismissed in the analysis of subsequent progress in the field of historical writing. One more note on the subject. A comparative study of the period of annalistic writing was a relatively harmonious one when compared with the dynamically conflicting age of the forthcoming decades of the nineteenth century; retrospectively, the recent past assumes incredible dimensions of distance as well as the genesis of Russian historical science; simple information became increasingly manifold, evidence more demanding, synthesis more mandatory, and interpretation more critical.

Notes

1. *Ocherki istorii istoricheskoy nauki* [Studies of the History of Historical Science] (Moscow, 1955), Vol. 2; V. S. Ikonnikov, *Opyt russkoy istoriografii* [A Study of Russian Historiography] (Kiev, 1892), Vol. 1, Book 2; P. G. Sofinov, *Iz istorii russkoy dorevolyutsionnoy archeograffi* [History of Russian Prerevolutionary Archeography] (Moscow, 1957); V. O. Klyuchevsky, "A. I. Musin-Pushkin," in *Sobraniye sochineniy* [Collected Works] (Moscow, 1959), Vol. 8; "Zapiski dlya biografii gr. A. I. Musina-Pushkina" [Memoranda for a Biography of Count A. I. Musin-Pushkin], *Vestnik Evropy*, Part 72, Nos. 21-22, 1813; N. Popov, *Istoriya Imperatorskogo Moskovskogo Obshchestva Istorii i Drevnostey Rossiiskikh* (Moscow, 1884), Part 1; L. A. Dmitriyev, "Istoriya otkrytiya rukopisi 'Slovo o Polku Igoreve' " [A History of the Discovery of the Manuscript "The Lay of Igor's Raid"], in *Sbornik "Slovo o Polku Igoreve"—Pamyatnik XVII veka* (Moscow 1962).
2. V. N. Tatishchev, *Istoriya rossiyskaya* [Russian History], 7 vols. (Moscow, 1962-1968). This is the latest and fullest edition of Tatishchev's works. See also N. A. Popov, "Ucheniye i literaturniye trudy V. N. Tatishcheva" [Scientific and Literary Works of V. N. Tatishchev] *Zhurnal Ministerstva Narodnogo Prosveshcheniya*, June 1886; N. A. Popov, *Tatishchev i ego vremya* [Tatishchev and His Time] (Moscow, 1861); P. N. Milyukov, *Glavniye techeniya russkoy istoricheskoy mysli* [Main Currents of Russian Historical Thought] (Moscow, 1897), pp. 21-31; M. Tikhomirov, "Vasily Nikitich Tatishchev," *Istorik-Marksist* 6 (1940): 43-56. References to Tatishchev may also be found in P. P. Pekarsky, *Istoriya Imperatorskoy Akademii Nauk* [A History of the Imperial Academy of Sciences] 2 vols. (St. Petersburg, 1870).
3. A. M. Pypin, *Istoriya russkoy literatury* [A History of Russian Literature] (St. Petersburg, 1911), 3: 369-70.
4. *Russky biografichesky slovar* [Russian Biographical Dictionary], 20: 342-43.
5. P. P. Pekarsky, *Novye izvestiya o Tatishcheve* [New Information Concerning V. N. Tatishchev] (St. Petersburg, 1864).
6. V. N. Tatishchev, *Istoriya rossiiskaya s samykh drevneyshikh vremyen* [Russian History from Earliest Times] 5 vols. (Moscow, 1768-1848). The first edition of the five volumes was published posthumously at considerable intervals, as can be seen from the dates of publication.
7. Pypin, *Istoriya russkoy literatury*, 3: 372.
8. *Sbornik II otdeleniya russkogo yazyka i slovesnosti Imperatorskoy Akademii Nauk* 30 (1883): 51-53; Popov, *Tatishchev i ego vremya*, pp. 591-98 (see above, note 2).

9. K. N. Bestuzhev-Ryumin, *Biografii i kharakteristiki* [Biographical Essays] (St. Petersburg, 1882), pp. 141, 145-47.

10. E. Winter, *Halle als Ausgangpunkt der deutschen Russlankunde in 18. Jahrhundert* (Berlin, 1953); M. N. Tikhomirov, "Russkaya istoriografiya 18 stoletiya" [Russian Historiography of the Eighteenth Century], *Voprosy istorii*, No. 2, 1941; *Ocherki istorii istoricheskoy nauki SSSR* [Studies of the History of Historical Science of the USSR] (Moscow, 1955), Vol. 1. See G. S. Bayer, *Auszug der älteren Staatsgeschichte* (St. Petersburg, 1728).

11. N. L. Rubinstein, *Russkaya istoriografiya* [Russian Historiography] (Moscow, 1941). See A. G. Mazour, *The Writing of History in the Soviet Union* (Stanford, Cal., 1971).

12. *Voprosy istorii* 2 (1948): 94-99.

13. *Sammlung russischer Geschichte*, 9 vols. (St. Petersburg, 1732-1764). A posthumous volume, the tenth, was published in 1816, in Dorpat.

14. G. F. Müller, *Opisaniye Sibirskogo tsarstva* [A Description of the Siberian Kingdom], 2 vols. (St. Petersburg, 1750). There is also a later edition, Moscow, 1937-1941. *Sammlung Russischer Geschichte*, 9 vols.; a posthumous volume, the tenth, was published in 1816 in Dorpat. A. N. Pypin, *Istoriya russkoy etnografii* [A History of Russian Ethnography] (St. Petersburg, 1892); see particularly Vol. 4, the chapter on Siberia.

15. Pekarsky, *Istoriya Imperatorskoy Akademii Nauk*, 1: 381 (see above, note 2).

16. *Voprosy istorii* 2 (1948): 96.

17. N. N. Golitsyn, *Portfeli G. F. Millera* [The Portfolios of G. F. Müller] (Moscow, 1899). See particularly the more up-to-date account by N. Baklanova and A. Andreyev, "Obzor rukopisey G. F. Millera po istorii, geografii, etnografii, i yazykam narodov Sibiri, khranyashchikhsya v Moskovskikh i Leningradskikh arkhivakh i bibliotekakh" [A Survey of G. G. Müller's Manuscripts of History, Geography, Ethnography, and Languages of Siberian Peoples, Kept in the Moscow and Leningrad Libraries], in the 1937 edition of Müller, *History of Siberia*, 1: 543-69.

18. *Akty istoricheskiye, sobranniye i izdanniye arkheograficheskoyu kommissieyu* [Historical Documents, Collected and Published by the Archeographical Commission], 5 vols. (St. Petersburg, 1841-1842); *Dopolneniya* [Supplements], 12 vols., 1846-1872.

19. Pekarsky, *Istoriya Imperatorskoy Akademii Nauk*, 1: 418-24 (see above, note 2). See also *Goroda Sibiri, ekonomika, upravleniye i kultura v dosovetsky period 19 veka* (Novosibirsk, 1974).

20. The reader is referred to an excellent essay, "Müller as an Historian," by S. V. Bakhrushin, in the latest edition of Müller's *History of Siberia* (Moscow, 1937), 1: 5-55.

21. S. P. Krasheninnkov, *Opisaniye zemli Kamchatki* [A Description of

Kamchatka], 2 vols. (St. Petersburg, 1755); new edition, 1939. English ed., trans. James Grieve (London, 1764).

22. *Obshchestvennaya i chastnaya zhizn Augusta Shletsera, im samim opisannaya* [The Social and Private Life of August Schlözer Described by Himself], trans. V. Kenevich (St. Petersburg, 1809-1819). A. L. Schlözer, *Allgemeine nordische Geschichte* (Halle, 1771); *Histoire universelle* (Tübingen, 1781); *Neuverändertes Russland, oder Leben Catharina der Zweyten* (Riga, 1771-1772); *Probe russischer Annalen* (Bremen, 1768); *Nestor. Russische Annalen in ihrer slavonischen Grundsprache verglichen, übersetzt und erklärt von A. L. Schlözer*, 5 vols. (Göttingen, 1802-1809) (Vol. 1 dedicated to Alexander I); *Geschichte von Russland*, Vol. 1, 1768; *Tableaux de l'Histoire de Russie*, 1769. A Russian translation of *Nestor* appeared in St. Petersburg, 1809-1819.

On Schlözer see the following: V. S. Ikonnikov, *A. G. Schlözer. Istoriko-biografichesky ocherk* [A. G. Schlözer: A Historico-Biographical Sketch] (Kiev, 1911); Bestuzhev-Ryumin *Biografii*, pp. 177-203 (see above, note 9); Milyukov, *Glavniye techeniya*, pp. 63-73 (see above, note 2); S. M. Solovyev, *Sobraniye sochineniy* [Collected Works], pp. 1539-1616; N. L. Rubinstein, *Russkaya istoriografiya* [Russian Historiography] (Moscow, 1941), pp. 150-66; Herbert Butterfield, *Man on His Past* (Cambridge, England, 1955), pp. 52-59; "Schlözer i ego podkhod k 'universalnoy istorii' " [Schlözer and his approach to "universal history"], in B. G. Veber, *Istoriograficheskiye problemy* (Moscow, 1974), pp. 19-37.

23. It may be of interest to note also that Schlözer emphasized the significance of statistics, which he named *eine still-stehende Geschichte: Russky biografichesky slovar*, 23: 342.

24. *Sbornik II otd. russkogo yazyka i slovesnosti Imperatorskoy Akademii Nauk* 30 (1883): 1-3, 25, 30, 44.

25. Pekarsky, *Istoriya*, 1: 378 (see above, note 2).

26. Butterfield, *Man on His Past*, p. 60 (see above, note 22).

27. *Russky biografichesky slovar*, 23: 343-44.

28. M. V. Lomonosov, *Drevnyaya Rossiiskaya istoriya ot nachala rossiiskogo naroda do konchiny Velikogo Knyazya Yaroslava Pervogo ili do 1054 goda* [Earliest Russian History from the Beginning of the Russian People Until the End of the Grand Prince Yaroslav I or to the Year 1054] (St. Petersburg, 1766); Pekarsky, *Istoriya*, Vol. 2 (see above, note 2); Solovyev, *Sobraniye sochineny*, pp. 1317-88; Milyukov, *Glavniye techeniya*, pp. 31-33 (see above, note 2); M. N. Tikhomirov, ed., *Ocherki istorii istoricheskoy nauki v SSSR* [History of Historical Science in the USSR] (Moscow, 1955), 1: 193-204; Rubinstein, Russkaya istoriografiya, pp. 85-96 (see above, note 22); B. N. Menshutkin, *Chemist, Courtier, Physicist, and Poet—Lomonosov*

(Princeton, 1952); M. N. Tikhomirov, "Istoricheskiye trudy M. V. Lomonosova" [Historical Works of M. V. Lomonosov], *Voprosy istorii* 5, (1962); E. S. Kulyabko, *Lomonosov i uchebnaya deyatelnost Petersburgkoy Akademii Nauk* [Lomonosov and the Pedagogical Activity of the Petersburg Academy of Sciences] (Leningrad, 1962); M. I. Radovsky, *Lomonosov v Petersburgkoy Akademii Nauk* [Lomonosov in the Petersburg Academy of Sciences] (Moscow, 1961); V. P. Lystov, *M. V. Lomonosov—rodonachalnik russkogo prosvetitelstva* [M. V. Lomonosov: Ancestor of Russian Enlightenment] (Voronezh, 1961).

29. M. M. Shcherbatov, *On the Corruption of Morals in Russia*, ed. and trans. A. Lentin (Cambridge, England, 1969). See particularly the admirable essay "Shcherbatov the Historian," pp. 55-72.

30. V. A. Myakotin, *Iz istorii russkogo obshchestva* [Notes on the History of Russian Society] (St. Petersburg, 1902), pp. 112 ff.

31. M. M. Shcherbatov, *Neizdannye sochineniya* [Unpublished Works] (Moscow, 1935), pp. 112-13; *Russky biografichesky slovar*, 24: 115.

32. M. M. Shcherbatov, *Istoriya rossiiskaya* [Russian History], (St. Petersburg, 1901), 1: 271.

33. M. M. Shcherbatov, *Istoriya Rossiiskaya ot drevneyshikh vremyen* [A History of Russia from the Earliest Times], 7 vols. (St. Petersburg, 1770-1791); German translation, Danzig, 1779; *Neizdannye sochineniya* [Unpublished Works] (Moscow, 1935); Shcherbatov, *On the Corruption of Morals in Russia* (see above, note 29); N. Chechulin, "Khronologiya i spisok sochineniy kn. M. M. Shcherbatova" [A Chronology and List of Works of M. M. Shcherbatov], *Zhurnal Ministerstva Narodnogo Prosveshcheniya* 8 (1900): 337-64; Bestuzhev-Ryumin, *Biografii* (see above, note 9); Milyukov, *Glavniye* (see above, note 2); A. N. Pypin, "Russkaya nauka i natsionalniyi vopros v XVIII v." [Russian Science and the National Question in the Eighteenth Century], *Vestnik Evropy* 3 (1884) 212-56; Rubinstein, *Russkaya istoriografiya*, pp. 116-37 (see above, note 22); Tikhomirov, p. 286.

34. Nicolas Gabriel LeClerc, *Histoire physique, morale, et politique de la Russie ancienne et moderne*, 6 vols. (Paris, 1783-1794).

35. I. N. Boltin, *Primechaniya na istoriyu gospodina Leklerka* [Critical Notes on the History of Russia by Mr. LeClerc], 2 vols. (St. Petersburg, 1788); *Kriticheskiye primechaniya gen.-mayora Boltina na perviy-vtoroy tom istorii knyazya Shcherbatova* [Critical Notes of Major General Boltin to Volumes I and II of the History of Prince Shcherbatov], 2 vols. (St. Petersburg, 1793-1794); *Otvyet gen. mayora Boltina na Pismo Kn. Shcherbatova* [Reply of Major General Boltin to a Letter of Prince Shcherbatov] (St. Petersburg, 1793). On Boltin, see V. O. Klyuchevsky, *Ocherki i rechi* [Sketches and Speeches] (Moscow, 1913), pp. 163-98; P. N. Milyukov, *Glavniye*

techeniya, pp. 50 ff. (see above, note 2); Pypin, "Russkaya nauka i natsionalnyi vopros" (cited above, note 33); V. Ikonnikov, "Boltin," *Russky biografichesky slovar*, Vol. 3; Tatishchev, *Istoriya rossiyskaya*, 1: 210-214 (see note 2); Rubinstein, *Russkaya istoriografiya*, pp. 137-50 (see note 22).

36. *Russky biografichesky slovar*, 3: 199-200.
37. Ibid., 3: 193-94.
38. V. O. Klyuchevsky, *Ocherki i rechi*, p. 188 (note 35 above).
39. See Pypin, *Istoriya russkoy etnografii*, 1: 147 ff. (cited in note 14).
40. See M. I. Sukhomlinov, *Istoriya Rossiiskoy Akademii Nauk* [A History of the Russian Academy of Sciences] (St. Petersburg, 1880); V. S. Ikonnikov, *Istoricheskie trudy Boltina* [The Historical Works of Boltin] (St. Petersburg, 1902); Milyukov, *Glavniye techeniya* (cited above, note 2); Milyukov, ed., *Ocherki istorii*, Vol. 1 (note 28, above); Rubinstein. *Russkaya istoriografiya* (note 22, above).
41. Ivan I. Golikov, *Deyaniya Petra Velikogo, mudrogo preobrazovatelya Rossii: sobranniye is dostovernykh istochnikov i raspolozhenniye po godam* [Acts of Peter the Great, Wise Reformer of Russia; Collected from Authentic Sources and Arranged by Years], 12 vols. (Moscow, 1788-1789); *Dopolneniya* [Addendum], 18 vols. (Moscow, 1790-1797); 2nd ed., 15 vols. (Moscow, 1837-1843); *Ocherki istorii istoricheskoy nauki*, 1: 215-18 (note 28, above).
42. Soviet writers consider Golikov as the forerunner of "bourgeois historiography." See *Ocherki istorii istoricheskoy nauki,* 1: 215 (note 28, above).
43. *Nestor. Russische Annalen in ihrer Slavonischen Grundsprache verglichen, übersetzt und erklärt von August Ludwig Schlözer*, 4 vols. (Göttingen, 1802-1805); Russian translation by D. Yazykov, 3 parts (St. Petersburg, 1809-1819); *La Chronique de Nestor*, tr. en français d'après l'édition imperiale de Petersbourg, manuscrit de Königsberg, 2 vols. (Paris, 1834-1835); also translated by Leger (Paris, 1884). See also the edition of R. Trautmann, *Die altrussische Nestorchronik, Povest vremennykh lyet.* (Leipzig, 1931). The latest English edition: *The Russian Primary Chronicle: Laurentian Text*, trans. and ed. Samuel H. Cross and Olgred P. Sherbowitz-Wetzor (Cambridge, Mass., 1953).
44. M. D. Chulkov, *Istoricheskoye opisaniye rossiiskoy kommertsii pri vsekh portakh i granitsakh ot drevnikh vremyen to nynye nastoyashchego, i vsekh preimushchestvennykh uzakoneny po onoy Gosudarya Imperatora Petra Velikogo i Gosudaryni Imperatritsy Yekateriny Velikoy* [A History of Russian Commerce at All Ports and Boundaries from Earliest Times to the Present, and All Important Legislation of Peter the Great and Empress Catherine the Great], 7 vols. (St. Petersburg, 1788-1789).
45. Pypin, *Istoriya russkoy literatury*, 3: 510 (note 3, above); *Sbornik II otd.*

russkogo yazyka i slovesnosti Imperatorskoy Akademii Nauk [Collection of Works of the Division of the Russian Language and Philology of the Imperial Academy of Sciences] 30 (1883): 193-95.

46. In 1970 Mouton (The Hague, Holland) initiated a reproduction of Novikov's entire *vivliofika* under the editorship of C. H. Van Schooneveld as part of Slavistic Printings and Reprintings.

[3]

Russian Historiography Comes of Age: 1800 - 1850

Publication of Documents

Russian participation in the turbulent events of Western Europe during the early years of the nineteenth century must have left an indelible impact on the national self-consciousness of the country. The deep imprint was probably best expressed in the awakened interest of national history. The hit-or-miss historical work during the preceding century was not wasted. To students of the nineteenth century it proved of considerable aid either in planning the publication of recently discovered resources or in a further and more intensive search of still uncovered materials. Be that as it may, it became increasingly clear that Russian historiography entered a new stage of development when the increasing volume of studies was subjected to more severe analytical study and editorial preparation. The enormous assistance that the newly published historical records rendered to scholarship can hardly be overestimated.

The source material that had been or was soon to be uncovered was of various kinds. There was the ever-increasing volume of discovered chronicles, there were the government acts and legislation of the past centuries, there were a multitude of family, church, and monastic documents, there were accounts by foreign travelers in Russia and their observations. Collectively this constituted an invaluable boon to the historian.[1]

However, the publication of this impressive amount of historical material presented a number of problems. The first and seemingly insurmountable difficulty was that of coordinating the dispersed efforts while gathering the material; another was the evaluation and classification of gathered records, and the order in which these should be published to preclude a haphazard dumping into single and bulky volumes. Besides these fundamental questions there were also numerous problems concerning methods of publication, introductory remarks, form and extent of annotation that must accompany textual contents, elucidation of stylistic peculiarities of the various periods, a clear agreement on the meaning of obscure terms; there was the question, too, of whether to reproduce the text faithfully or change it to more recent spellings and modernized syntax. These were all pertinent issues that required serious study and called for urgent and specific answers. The quest for answers became more urgent as more and more source material was made available.

From the early part of the nineteenth century the search of historical records began with individuals; later the more effective efforts were undertaken more systematically by institutions. Thus Archbishop, later Metropolitan of Kiev, Y. A. Bolkhovitinov (Metropolitan Yevgeny), began to travel as early as 1804, examining all gathered materials either in various monasteries or churches.[2] Four years later a special commission was formed for the gathering of all historical sources in the northern Ukrainian cities. In 1811 the Commission for Publication of State Charters and Treaties emerged which would examine the archives of the Ministry of Foreign Affairs in Moscow. This commission, with the aid of the eminent Chancellor N. P. Rumyantsev, began to function a year later.[3]

One of the most difficult problems faced was the question of critical appraisal of recently discovered records. During the preceding century, students of history sadly lacked the knowledge that such editorial work inevitably involved. The new sciences vital in this field, paleography and archaeography, flowered much later, a fact that explains many of the errors committed during the initial stages. For the same reason, most of the eighteenth-century published materials called for a thorough editorial revision as well as more up-to-date textual annotations. The appearance in Göttingen of the *Nestor Chronicle*, edited by Schlözer in 1802, indicated the path scholarship must follow. This work produced such a favorable impression that after the third volume had appeared, Alexander I ordered the formation of a society for the advancement of historical science at one of the universities in the Russian Empire. The honor of sponsoring the society was bestowed upon the University of Moscow, and so in 1804 there was founded the first Russian historical organization, the Moscow Society of History and Russian Antiquities.[4] The society existed for 125 years, ending in 1929. Among its members were the most illustrious figures in the field of history: Count A. I. Musin-Pushkin, N. M. Karamzin, K. F. Kalaydovich, N. N. Bantysh-Kamensky, A. L. Schlözer, and others.

The fact that this was a government-sponsored organization carried with it a degree of restraint. By its charter the membership was limited and the presiding officer had to be approved by the Minister of Education. The activity of the society was limited to a critical analysis of Russian chronicles, for the prevailing political climate during the second half of the reign of Alexander I and throughout the reign of Nicholas I hardly favored the flourishing of free thought. When in 1848 the government was displeased with the choice of Giles Fletcher's *The Russe Commonwealth* for publication in Russian, it banned the society's annual *Studies* altogether. A year later this publication reappeared under a new name, and its contents, the administration was assured, were to be confined strictly to documentary materials. It was not until 1858 that the publication resumed its original nature and became a quarterly.

Despite the adversities the Moscow Society had to face, it managed to accomplish a surprising amount in the field of historical studies: aside from the stimulating effect it had on Russian historical scholarship, it kept pressing as well for a wider publication of national sources. Though fettered by official restrictions, the society nonetheless managed from time to time to publish materials, some of which proved later to be of considerable value to Karamzin and other historians in their writings. The Moscow Society managed to collect and edit not only chronicles but also charters, official and private records of historical interest, and accounts of travels by natives and foreigners; it searched out all available sources and published them in its quarterly or kept them for later study and eventual publication. The amassed materials led to the development of such other allied sciences as numismatics, paleography, diplomatics, and sphragistics. Under the influence of the Moscow Society various local archival institutions began to announce their inventories, carefully listing some of their most treasured accumulations. Furthermore, the Moscow Society eventually inspired other universities to organize similar groups, which were eventually destined to play an important part in the development of historical research. Within no more than a year after the founding of the Moscow Society, the University of Kazan initiated a similar organization; the University of Kharkov followed suit in 1817, as did in 1839 the University of Odessa, and gradually many other institutions. Each society became actively engaged in research and published its discoveries of materials pertinent to history in its own periodical *Studies.*

In St. Petersburg a different situation had developed. Here the Academy of Sciences took the initiative instead of the university. It was also the academy's good fortune to discover in the capital the presence of a veritable Maecenas, such as the distinguished diplomat, statesman, and benefactor, Count Nikolay Petrovich Rumyantsev (1754-1826). By a fortunate confluence of circumstances it came about that the collective efforts of the Moscow Society and the feverish activity of a dilettante drove a deep furrow in the field of historical research in Russia.

Russian historical science owes a profound debt to Count Rumyantsev for his enthusiasm and devotion to his cause. By his relentless drive in promoting research and the writing of history he left a monument that not even the revolution was able to delete from the records of the past. This effort led directly to the founding, in 1831, of the Rumyantsev Museum, to which the benefactor donated his immense private library. This library included valuable manuscripts, coins, maps, and a vast book collection among which were many bibliographic rarities. The museum was later transferred to Moscow and considerably expanded into what is now the Lenin Library.

When in 1809 Count Rumyantsev became State Chancellor and Minister of Foreign Affairs, the Moscow archives came under his jurisdiction. Rumyantsev was thus in a position to avail himself of every publishing opportunity, and he missed none. Since the Moscow Society had been entrusted with the publication of the chronicles, Rumyantsev determined to publish, at his own expense, the diplomatic sources that were kept in the Moscow archives. He spared neither money nor effort to make the edition a luxurious one. In 1813 he presented the academy with a sum of 25,000 rubles for the purpose of examining and eventually publishing the documentary sources to be found in the Moscow archives of the Foreign Office. The motivation, according to Rumyantsev, was that no adequate history could be written unless the historians were able to make use of all the available source material in the country.[5] For the publication of the State Charters and Treaties the historian owes most to Count Rumyantsev.[6]

The Collection of State Charters and Treaties of the Ministry of Foreign

Affairs included documents covering the period between 1229 and 1696. The editing involved many difficulties and conflicting opinions concerning annotations, spelling, preservation of the old orthography, punctuation, and correction of obvious errors. In this respect Rumyantsev had been fortunate in enjoying the advice of several of the most able experts in the field of archaeography and archival art, such as P. M. Stroyev, K. F. Kalaydovich, A. K. Vostokov, N. S. Artsybashev, and P. I. Koeppen. As the work advanced, both Rumyantsev and his assistants came to the conclusion that unless the complete collection of chronicles was added to the other sources at their disposal in the archives of Moscow, the entire undertaking would be a failure. Referring to the chronicles that were scattered hither and yon, Rumyantsev asked: "Is it believable that one of the greatest nations of the enlightened world and the single possessor of a treasure so significant not only for that nation, but also for all engaged in the writing of history—is it believable that this nation, which ought to be proud of its past, should not hasten to announce and display the treasure to the world?"[7] He therefore began to support lavishly the next plan, the completion of a complete collection of all available chronicles, and donated altogether forty thousand rubles for this purpose.[8] He urged that a commission be sent to explore such monastic repositories as those of Volokolamsk and New Jerusalem, where he hoped many treasures might be found.

The exploratory mission, as visualized in 1817, was to investigate all book and manuscript depositories scattered throughout the country. The head of this mission was the able young archivist P. M. Stroyev (1796-1876). Already in his early years Stroyev demonstrated a keen interest in history and in the preservation of historical records. At the age of seventeen he had written a *Short History of Russia for Beginners*, which became a popular textbook during the 1820s and 1830s. As editor of the *Contemporary Observer of Russian Literature* he contributed a number of articles to that periodical as well as to the national publication *Son of the Fatherland* (*Syn Otechestva*). In 1816, in recognition of his ability and interest, Count Rumyantsev invited Stroyev to serve as archivist of the Ministry of Foreign Affairs. A year later he was invited to head a projected archaeological mission. With the assistance of another able archivist, K. F. Kalaydovich, Stroyev set out with the assigned mission for some three years to search throughout the country for historical records.

Stroyev visited some of the oldest monasteries, with most gratifying results. Among the treasures found were such items as the records of

Svyatoslav, Prince of Chernigov (1027-1076), the Code of Laws of Ivan III, the documents concerning the Moscow Assembly of 1503, to mention only a few.[9] Stroyev managed during the same time to compile and publish, with Kalaydovich's assistance, *A Detailed Account of Slavo-Russian Manuscripts of the Moscow Library of Count F. A. Tolstoy.* Four years later appeared the *Detailed Account of Old Slavic and Russian Books of the Library of Count F. A. Tolstoy.* There appeared also in print for the first time a description of the archaeographic wealth of the monasteries, such as the inventories of four of the oldest of them, among these the monastery of Volokolamsk, located not far from Moscow. These became in due course bibliographical rarities.[10] This work on the monasteries also included a series of comments presented by Stroyev, with his interpretation of the uncovered chronicles, namely, that their textual contents represented in reality not the result of a single record, but of compilatory narratives, gathered through years by various authors, each adding his own available material, interpretation, and taste for embellishment—a theory elaborated much more conclusively a century later.[11]

In 1817 the archaeographic expedition only served to inspire Stroyev to press his campaign further; he insisted on the need for further research throughout the country to locate scattered historical material. Shortly after his return in 1823 he began advocating another expedition and offered a specific program for the search of the expected sources. In May 1828 the academy voted a sum of ten thousand rubles for a project advocated by Stroyev, who visualized the assignment somewhat as follows. The time required, approximately three years, would be divided into three stages: first, a thorough examination of all archival and bibliographical collections in ten provinces; second, a search through twelve central provinces of a similar nature; third, similar explorations in nine western, Ukrainian, and central Russian provinces. An additional two years was considered necessary to examine and accurately describe the uncovered material.

The project went into effect in 1828, and the expedition lasted for nearly six years. During this time some two hundred libraries, monasteries, and other institutions were explored throughout fourteen northern and central provinces. The mission rendered an astounding result: it uncovered nearly three thousand acts, covering a period of four centuries (1340-1700), numerous chronicles, geographic descriptions, and other materials. The entire bulk came to constitute the initial basis on which the Archaeographic Commission began to operate. Much of the discovered material served for the composition of a bibliographic dictionary or guide to all literary works of the period.

Needless to say, the exploration also revealed sources never used, or even suspected as existing, and offered opportunities for a much broader interpretation of history. It enabled historians throughout the century to enrich their narratives and substantiate interpretations, and it also added new and manifold aspects to events of former centuries. The remarkable contribution of P. M. Stroyev was perhaps best described by N. P. Barsukov, who regarded the nineteenth-century archivist as the founder of modern historical research in Russian history.[12]

Since 1829 the archaeographic work had been headed by Stroyev. During the first three years of his guidance twelve provinces were searched and hundreds of libraries, archival depositories, and monasteries or ecclesiastical schools were examined. The men gathered nearly three thousand records. After combing the country for that length of time, the men ran into serious opposition everywhere, which could be overcome only slowly and painfully. Owners, fearful of losing the treasured rarities, objected to any methods of taking inventories; they suspected that criticism might be made. In 1834 came the first positive result, despite all the difficulties—the first publication by the Archaeographic Commission.

The entire expedition represented a semiprivate, semistate undertaking, and as such operated under various handicaps. Nonetheless, the story of the expedition is a dramatic tale in itself, with a record of which Stroyev and his colleagues could be justly proud: after years of travel throughout the vast country in search of historical documents in many libraries and archives, the men brought back some three thousand copied records.[13] The accumulated mass of materials came to constitute the foundation for voluminous publications that were to appear throughout the nineteenth century in Russia. The quantity of unearthed material compelled the government to pursue the work further, and in December 1834 the Ministry of Education was instructed to form an Archaeographic Commission to be placed in charge of the publication of materials gathered by Stroyev. This task was successfully carried out in 1836, and a year later the commission became a permanent institution with a regular annual budget.[14] The Archaeographic Commission led virtually an independent life until 1922, when by government decree it became a division of the Academy of Sciences of the USSR.

Each set of documents published by the Archaeographic Commission is supplemented by a detailed place and subject index. The bulk of the historical material covers the thirteenth through the seventeenth centuries. It includes numerous charters, various legislation and judicial acts, ecclesiastical commentaries, and regulations regarding trade and industry, growth of towns, fiscal laws, budgetary problems, military and foreign affairs. Simultaneously, the Archaeographic Commission undertook the enormous task of publishing the entire collection of Russian chronicles. Armed with experience and aided by a legion of experts in various fields, the commission could not handle these valuable sources more scientifically. The publication, which began in 1841, continued throughout the century. During this period revisions and new editions were issued; to date, the latest edition includes thirty-one volumes of the chronicles, published by the Institute of History of the Academy of Sciences.

The Archaeographic Commission also sent out a number of scholars to gather all materials to be found in foreign archives. The result of this expedition was the publication of archival material found abroad. One set includes much of the source material found in the Vatican Library, covering the period 1075-1719. Another ten-volume set covers the subject of Russian relations with the Western European countries.[15]

Like many of his contemporaries, Rumyantsev was interested in the origins of the Russian people; unlike others, however, he looked deep into the past, which included the history of the Near East, the Byzantine Empire, and Arabian medieval trade routes. He hoped to trace the ultimate key to early Russian history not only in his own country, but abroad as well, and for this reason he sought the assistance of many foreign authorities in Byzantine and Oriental history. For the same reason he dispatched a number of men to Germany, Italy, England, and Poland to explore the archives of these countries and to copy from them all the important documents relating to Russia[16]

Thus, Rumyantsev saw to it that every document bearing any relation to Russia's past would find its place in the collection to be published.[17] "The fuller and better this collection appears," he wrote to one of his assistants, "the more it will bring honor to you and pleasure in executing this enterprise to men. And whatever sums the expenses of its publication may require, I am ready to make sacrifices to supply them."[18] Rumyantsev remained faithful to his promise, contributing his time—especially after his retirement from office in 1812—his money, and his energy. As a collector of sources for later historians, and the person financially responsible for their publication, he occupies a prominent place in the dramatic tale of Russian historical research.[19]

From this brief survey it can be safely assumed that the Archaeographic Commission accomplished a monumental work in the field of Russian historiography. Nor must the student of history neglect the publication of the *Complete Code of Laws.* At the head of this enormous project was the eminent statesman M. M. Speransky, who was assigned the task of collecting all laws from 1649 to the time of the reign of Nicholas I. Beginning in 1830, when the first volume made its appearance, the publication continued throughout the rest of the century until the end of the empire. The *Complete Code of Laws* (*Polnoye sobraniye zakonov*) added another principal source of historical information for subsequent scholars.[20]

The ever-increasing outpouring of published documentary records inspired the founding of provincial societies with similar purposes, notably at Kiev, Vilna, Tiflis, Voronezh, and Odessa.[21] Accounts of travels in Siberia, local official records, and diaries of native and foreign travelers in the particular provinces found their way to publishing houses. In this connection must be mentioned the important contribution that contemporary periodicals made to history by publishing newly found sources from time to time. A valuable index to the scattered material in periodical literature was compiled by S. R. Mintslov.[22] He was also responsible for the compilation of the bibliographies of writings on Russian history in foreign languages, one entitled *Russica*, the other *Peter the Great in Foreign Literature.* As the volume of historical writings increased, bibliographical literature grew proportionately. In 1861 the two Lambin brothers began a ten-volume Russian historical bibliography that still stands as one of the most notable contributions in its field.[23]

The work undertaken by the Lambin brothers was continued by another distinguished bibliographer, Vladimir Izmaylovich Mezhov (1831-1894).[24] During the 1880s he published a six-volume historical bibliography covering the period 1800-1859. Three volumes of this projected work appeared; his death precluded the completion of the plan. During his lifetime, however, Mezhov succeeded in compiling a three-volume bibliography on Siberia and two volumes on central Asia.

In 1866 the Imperial Russian Historical Society was founded. This organization began to publish documents related to the eighteenth and part of the nineteenth century in Russian history. Although much criticism had been heaped on the society for its careless editorial work and, what was worse, for its arbitrary textual "amputations" before publication, nonetheless the collected materials represent a valuable aggregate of sources. Altogether the society published 146 volumes of extracts from foreign and Russian archives. These included the valuable papers of the Great Legislative Commission summoned by Catherine II in 1766; the correspondence between Catherine II and Frederick II as well as Voltaire, D'Alambert, Grimm, and others; documents pertaining to Poland and Russian financial policies during the eighteenth century; sources relating to the War of 1812; diplomatic correspondence with Napoleon; the exchange of letters between Constantine and Nicholas I; and a multitude of others.

The student of history must not neglect the published family archives that began to appear by the end of the nineteenth century. The archives of the Vorontsov, Rayevsky, Mordvinov, Vyazemsky families shed much light on various aspects of Russian cultural, economic, financial, and political history.[25] Nor must the historical journals such as *Russky arkhiv* [Russian Archive] or *Russkaya starina* [Russian Antiquity] be overlooked. The former, published by P. Bartenev, and the latter, by M. I. Semevsky, contain invaluable source materials on the preceding two centuries of Russian history.

Needless to say, the extraordinary interest in history during the past century proved helpful in the development of many of the sciences allied to history: paleography, metrology, genealogy, numismatics, sphragistics, heraldry, historical and economic geography, economic history, and statistical science. In addition, interest was awakened in regional history, notably concerning Siberia and the Ukraine. A cult of historicism seemed to have enveloped an entire generation. Looking back, one can safely say that by the end of the last century Russian historiography demonstrated a record of accomplishment of which the nation can be rightly proud. The extensive publication of sources enabled a legion of historians to delve into the past with greater enthusiasm and with a firmer faith that their labor was bound to be rightly rewarded. Historical science came of age.

Karamzin

The true heir of the eighteenth-century historians was Nikolay Mikhailovich Karamzin (1766-1826). Son of a Simbirsk squire, he was sent to Moscow to receive his education at a private school and at the university there. In his younger days he associated himself with the distinguished publisher N. I. Novikov; was on friendly terms with some of the leading Freemasons such as I. P. Turgenev, A. M. Kutuzov, or I. V. Lopukhin; favored Masonic liberal ideas, and for a while even toyed with the ideas of Rousseau. From May 1789 to September 1790, Karamzin toured Western Europe, including England, and recorded his impressions in his widely read *Letters of a Russian Traveler.*[26] He closely observed the life of Western Europe, chiefly from the point of view of a philosopher and *literatus*. His first impressions inclined him to a great admiration for Western civilization. England failed to arouse the enthusiasm of the "Russian traveler," and except for a warm appreciation of the Anglo-Saxon judicial genius he left the British Isles "as cold as the English themselves." But Paris made an overwhelming impression on him and nearly converted him to cosmopolitanism.[27] This city, the pulse of European political and social life, made him believe that nationalism must eventually yield to universalism. One must be a man first and a Slav after. What was good for mankind was good for Russians.[28] After his return the "Russian traveler" assumed the editorship of the *Moscow Journal*, which represented the current sentimental school in literature. A few years later he became editor of another periodical, the *Herald of Europe* (*Vestnik Evropy*). But a history of the country must have been on his mind for some time.

While in Paris, Karamzin already bemoaned the absence of an adequate interpretive history of Russia written in the style of a Tacitus or a Gibbon. He resented any suggestion that Russia had no past. On the contrary, he argued, Russia had a glorious history, which she could proudly present before Western Europe; all she needed was a Russian Tacitus or a Michelangelo to demonstrate her greatness. Russia, Karamzin wrote in one of his letters from Paris, "had her own Charles the Great—Vladimir; her own Louis XI—Czar Ivan III; her own Cromwell—Godunov, while such an Emperor as Peter I Western Europe had never seen."[29] In later years Karamzin, after regretting the absence of a Russian Tacitus or a Michaelangelo, probably realized that it might be presumptuous to assume the role of the latter, and seems to have at least reserved the role of a Russian Tacitus for himself.

Karamzin's spontaneous outbursts of poetic enthusiams about the West proved of short duration. Even during his journey in Western Europe, Karamzin cautioned against rash adoption in Russia of outside ideas, for fear that it might do violence to entrenched traditions and ancient customs indispensable to a nation. Such violence, Karamzin warned, in the end led to nothing but ruin. Later he began to discard other vestiges of cosmopolitanism that he had come to cherish for a brief spell in his earlier years, exchanging it for conservative nationalism. Jacobinism, the Thermidorian events, followed by the ascendancy of Bonapartism—Karamzin watched all this with absorbing interest and considerable trepidation. The events in France forced Karamzin to recoil from many of his recent political notions, though he was inclined to believe that Napoleon was destined to restore law and order to France. But the path of developments left him trembling at its implications, particularly in view of the wars that followed soon after.

Slowly but surely Karamzin began to revise his earlier ideas. By 1811 he vacillated no longer, for his political faith was crystallized and best expressed in the well-known memorandum he presented to Alexander I, in which he proved himself *plus royaliste que le roi*. In the document, entitled *Memorandum on the New Russia*, his former enthusiasm for Peter's reforms now underwent a more "rational" reevaluation. He began to regard the changes as an unhappily forced breakdown of old institutions, leading to a crumbling of valuable customs and morals or manners. He blamed his former idol for interfering with the natural course of national history and for undermining the spirituality of the Russian church. He criticized Peter for curbing the privileges of the nobility, for without that class the monarchy itself was inconceivable. He warned that the nobility and the institution of serfdom were the two pillars on which autocracy rested.

The inchoate Decembrist ideology could be nothing but a condemnable idea bound to lead to chaos and ruin. In short, the course of events gradually led Karamzin to the acceptance of *ancien régime*. Thus, already in 1803, in his essay on Novgorod published in the *Herald of Europe* (*Vestnik Evropy*), he stated that autocracy was inevitable. His belief, even at that time, emanated from his philosophical view that human progress had been attained only by way of eminent personalities and not by mass movements. It is from this point of view that one must approach and understand Karamzin's reasons for opposing even mild reforms such as those suggested by Speransky. Bearing this in mind, we can have a clearer comprehension of the spirit in which he sat down to present his *History of the Russian State*.

Casting aside his former cosmopolitanism, Karamzin came now to base his new views on historical precedents as he saw them, or, shall we say as his generation, under the pressure of events, saw them. If Peter I, he said, had made Russians citizens of the world, he also contributed to their neglecting to be citizens of their own country. His relentless drive, continued Karamzin, forced Peter to employ tyrannical methods. He uprooted the traditional old capital of Moscow and exchanged it for the swampy northern city of St. Petersburg. He tampered with hereditary privileges of the new gentry and thereby imperiled the social structure; he modified the status of the church and thereby stripped the faith of spirituality. After Peter's death, political pygmies, according to Karamzin, replaced the giant and proved instrumental in further weakening Russian autocracy.

Catherine II saved the monarchy from an oncoming catastrophe: though her reign was not entirely free of blemishes, her brilliant rule restored the prestige of autocracy. Here, incidentally, Karamzin and Shcherbatov seem to meet on common ground, though reaching each other by rather devious paths. Their common link was the tender subject of the place of nobility in Russian society, a subject on which both writers could see eye to eye. Karamzin reprimanded the enlightened Empress for the notorious favoritism at court, which in the end was bound to have a demoralizing effect on the prestige of the Russian nobility. In the reign of Catherine II he detected "more glitter than efficacy," and though appreciating the accomplishments of the period, he concluded that there was another side to the picture that Russia must blushingly admit, a deterioration of morals. The ghost of Shcherbatov must have smilingly nodded when Karamzin recorded his views. And after the unhappy rule of Paul, came Alexander I, whom Karamzin urged to learn his lessons from history and under no circumstances to consent to any form of limited monarchical government. "Autocracy founded and resurrected Russia; any change of the established political order was bound to lead to complete ruin."[30] Such is briefly, the political physiognomy of Karamzin. We must now turn to the subject that concerns us most, Karamzin the historian.

For some years Karamzin continued to be an observer while leading an easygoing life, occupying himself chiefly with literary writings, sentimental novels such as *Poor Liza* or *Natalie, the Boyar Daughter* (*Natalya, boyarskaya doch*). With the passage of years his interest in history increased. What made him popular at court was his panegyrics to Catherine II and his well-known ode dedicated to Alexander I on the occasion of his accession to the throne, not to mention his frequent articles in the *Herald of Europe*, which Karamzin published and edited. He had already sufficiently demonstrated his reverence for the monarchical regime and his belief that all virtue radiated from the purple robe.[31]

In 1803 Karamzin petitioned Alexander I to grant him an allowance so that he could devote himself entirely to the writing of history. By imperial decree on October 31, 1803, the state granted Karamzin the title of Historiographer and allowed him an annual pension of two thousand rubles on condition that he write a complete history of Russia. The following year he retired as editor of the *Herald of Europe* and began to write his *History of the Russian State*, a work that gave him wide publicity and initiated the legend of his being the "First Russian Historian."[32] The work appeared in 1816 in eight volumes; it was followed in 1821 by the ninth and in 1824 by the tenth and eleventh volumes. In 1826 he died without completing the twelfth volume, which appeared posthumously, leading up to historical events to the year 1611.[33]

The work initially enjoyed considerable success. Karamzin had derived his general thesis from his nationalistic philosophy as well as from his belief that mankind's progress was universal. Its basis was the constant struggle of enlightenment versus darkness, of justice versus inequity, of literacy versus ignorance. The guiding factors in progress are leading figures, men of integrity with leadership qualities. Basically these were the beliefs professed already by men like Tatishchev or Shcherbatov. But Karamzin had witnessed the turbulent era of the French Revolution and other events closely related to the developments in the French capital; therefore he was inclined to consider historical progress in the light of universal struggle between good and evil. In other words, history can and must serve as a moral and political factor, as a contributing force to higher moral standards.

In his Memorandum of 1811 and later beliefs, autocracy represented the constructive force in history. Without it, Karamzin could envision nothing but total chaos. Karamzin was unable to perceive even the very "beginning of history" without autocratic rule. And although Karamzin began his history with a geographical account and general conditions of the state in the earliest times, the initial step toward the "Russian history" he viewed had been initiated with the so-called invitation of the Varangians. Henceforth he followed basically the course of Russian history, in very much the same path as his preceding historians, Tatishchev and Shcherbatov. To both of them, as to Karamzin, the history of the state and the history of autocracy coincide. The chronological order of each might be slightly altered, but the basic principles of the two are identical.

Karamzin was able to employ a wider base of resources during his years of writing than his predecessors had utilized. He was able to utilize many of the recently uncovered chronicles, the charters, Codes of Laws, accounts of foreign travelers in Russia. His references to these sources become even more valuable in light of the regrettable fact that some of his utilized records are no more in existence, since most of them, such as the *Troitsky Chronicle*, perished in the Moscow fire in 1812. Furthermore, Karamzin, in a literary sense, was one generation removed from his precedent historians: his literary style was more readable, more intelligible to many readers, making his work more popular than any previous historical account.[34]

Having said all this, we may now take a closer look at the *opus magnum* of Karamzin. The title of Karamzin's history is in itself revealing: it is a history of the Russian state, not a history of the Russian people. It is not even a history of the state—it is a rhetorical, penegyrical narrative that endeavors to prove that autocracy alone has bestowed all the blessings that the Russian Empire ever enjoyed; it is an album of sovereigns accompanied by descriptions in a most florid style. The author's approach to his subject encompassed, no doubt, a gigantic sweep, but he was badly handicapped by his monarchistic blinders. Besides, Karamzin began his history without experience or training in this field; critical history was totally alien to him. His contemporaries, Schlözer and Niebuhr, had no influence whatever on him. Being more a representative of sentimental romanticism in fiction than of scholarly writing, he was naturally inclined to consider history as in large part a beautiful narrative, in which the characters were either heroes to be worshipped or villains to be deplored. The masses did not count; everything emanated from a single source—strong government—while justice "radiated from the purple robe."

Such an outlook was not unexpected, since already during his journey abroad Karamzin's ideas had been influenced by events he observed in France and elsewhere. Furthermore, his observations had inspired him with the idea that the history of Russia could be turned into a beautiful dramatic narrative. All that one must possess, Karamzin thought, was "mind, taste, and talent"; once equipped with such gifts one could "select, inspirit, and illuminate," and the reader would be amazed to see how, for instance, a *Nestor Chronicle* could be transformed into something attractive, powerful, worthy of the attention not only of Russians but also of foreigners.[35]

Equipped with such armor, not to mention a generous state pension, Karamzin could now give free reign to his artist's pen, his poetic vision, and his political philosophy. In 1816 the crusade started in earnest.

Naturally, Karamzin could not avoid discussing the question that had already occupied or baffled others since the times of Lomonosov—the origins of the Russian state, in short, the notorious Norman theory. Karamzin went back to the early Greek writers, chiefly Herodotus, glided hastily over the confusing morass of ancient references to a legion of tribes in the north and the south, and—for fear of bogging down—conveniently accepted the Scythians as the most logical precursors of Russian history. Karamzin circumvented the Norman theory, with its legend of the "invitation" extended to the Varangians "to come to rule and reign over the Slavs"; he dismissed the entire story as of no importance, by giving the general impression of a Varangian admixture in the early Kievan state and nothing more.

According to Karamzin, early Kievan Russia reached a high degree of development because of its strong monarchical government. The downfall of old Russia was explained by the established political custom of dividing the state among the royal heirs and by the bitter rivalry among the princes, which in the end contributed to the triumph of the Mongols. As for the princes, in Basil III Karamzin saw an extremely colorful figure; without him history would have looked like a "peacock without a tail." But of all the Muscovite grand princes who built the future state of Russia, Ivan III was considered by Karamzin as the greatest of them all—the true founder of the national state and also the father of Russian autocracy. This was the traditional "Great Russian" interpretation, the theory that the entire historical process was centrifugal rather than centripetal, a theory later to be vigorously opposed by the "Federalist" historians, particularly by the Ukrainians such as M. Hrushevsky.

There is, however, another side to the entire narrative. In fairness to Karamzin, it must be stated that his *History of the Russian State* is not without weighty merits, in spite of its pontifical presentation of the monarchy and obvious political slant. Throughout all the volumes there was a novel unity in his narrative that made the course of Russian history seem meaningful. It is not an aimless stream without source or destination. The fact that Karamzin was primarily a literary artist with no pretense to scholarship had one positive result: his manner of writing. His florid literary style tended to liberate Russian writing from the antiquated Old Church Slavonic terminology that was greatly admired by members of the old school and to introduce a style more elegant, vigorous, and flowing—even though rhetorical—a style that appealed to the literary aesthetes of his time.[36] Many people compare Karamzin's writings with those of Sir Walter Scott, while some detect a definite influence of the latter upon him. Undoubtedly, as the volumes began to make their appearance, they awakened an unprecedented interest in national history.[37] To Pushkin, Karamzin was the "Columbus of Russian history."

Even more worthy of note is the significance of Karamzin's "Notes," or appendices, that accompanied the volumes. These included an extraordinary number of references to various rare sources formerly unknown or previously not utilized. Here, it can be said most assuredly, the author accomplished a prodigious feat. The value of these "Notes" became even greater when during the Moscow fire of 1812 many of the cited sources, including Karamzin's private library and the state archival depositories, completely and irretrievably perished. The nature of the lost documents is known to us only through Karamzin's voluminous references.[38] Altogether, Karamzin's *History of the Russian State* contains no less than 6,538 references, a veritable history in itself!

Karamzin enjoyed the rare privilege of access to many private and state archives. He utilized the private collection of manuscripts of Musin-Pushkin and the equally valuable library of the synod. He familiarized himself with numerous chronicles: the *Ipatiev*, the *Laurentian*, the *Troitsky* (which, incidentally, perished during the Moscow fire), and others. He consulted the various Codes of Laws of the fourteenth and fifteenth centuries and the medieval literary writings, such as *The Lay of Igor's Raid;* he read the early accounts of foreign travelers in Eastern Europe. No preceding writers could claim more extensive consultation of sources than Karamzin; to date he crowned all efforts whether in literary style or in historical synthesis.

Despite these merits, his work is a mere curiosity rather than an authoritative study or even good reading material. It totally lacks historical perspective, since Karamzin could not conceive of a historical process; like the eighteenth-century rationalist, he saw in history only evil or benevolent sovereigns who led the country either to disaster or to glory. It is very doubtful that Karamzin was even able to examine sufficiently the sources to which he refers in his footnotes, though the archives were at his disposal and he was generously aided by high officials and learned friends, among them M. Muraviev, the Assistant Minister of Education; Count N. P. Rumyantsev; A. Malinovsky, head of the archives; and his close friend, A. I. Turgenev, who gathered and copied documents for him abroad, particularly at the Papal archives. It was a physical impossibility within the comparatively short period of time, interrupted by frequent illnesses, for him to go over the voluminous amount of material referred to; and though he never mentioned them, Karamzin relied in great part on references cited in secondary authorities, thereby creating an impression of extraordinary erudition.[39]

Of the secondary authorities that greatly aided Karamzin, Schlözer's edition of the *Nestor Chronicle* must be mentioned for the earlier period of Russian history, and Shcherbatov's history for the later. The history that Shcherbatov had written served not only as a ready pattern for the literary embroidery of Karamzin, but also as the most helpful guide to the sources. Professor P. N. Milyukov, by comparing page after page, has shown quite convincingly how closely Karamzin followed Shcherbatov's general outline.[40] To Shcherbatov's bulky work and inelegant literary style Karamzin had to add stylistic refinement and poetic imagination, precisely the qualities Prince Shcherbatov had lacked, and the history was indeed bound to become "selected, inspired, and illuminated." A single citation from Karamzin, describing the eve of the historic battle of Kulikovo of September 8, 1380, will prove better than any lengthy discourse the accuracy of this statement.

> The noise of arms had not quieted down in the town, and the poeple looked with emotion at the grave warriors ready to die for the Fatherland and the Faith. It seemed as if the Russian people had awakened after a deep sleep: the long terror of the Tartars had vanished from their hearts as if removed by some supernatural power. They reminded one another of the glorious Vozhsk battle; they enumerated all the evils they had suffered from the barbarians during the hundred and fifty years and wondered at the shameful patience of their forefathers. Princes, boyars, townsmen, peasants, all were fired with equal enthusiasm, for the tyranny of the khans oppressed all equally, from the throne to the hut. What was more just than the sword at such a noble and unanimous call?[41]

Patriotic? To this skeptical query Karamzin's simple and disarming reply was that where there is no love, there is no soul. He never shrank before such accusations. "I know that I need the impartiality of a historian; forgive me, but I was not always able to conceal my love for the Fatherland."[42] It was this very "soul" that made his history so popular; the first edition of three thousand sets, at the prohibitive price of fifty-five rubles a set, was sold out within twenty-five days.[43] But the very qualities that made Karamzin's history popular undermined its validity among critical scholars.

Even in Karamzin's lifetime his work drew fire because of its patriotic tone and its questionable interpretation of the past.[44] As a precursor of Slavophilism, the work was bound to be criticized by the Westerners, or "skeptics" as some of them were called in Russian historiography, who were under the influence chiefly of Schlözer and Niebuhr.[45] Polevoy considered Karamzin's *History of the Russian State* an outdated piece of work before it was produced; for Pogodin, even the title of the twelve-volume work was a mistake and Karamzin himself was as far from Gibbon as intellectual England was from Russia.[46] In 1818 M. Kachenovsky, editor of the *Herald of Europe*, wrote a review in which he described Karamzin's *History* as "a chronicle masterfully recorded by an artist of superb talent, but not a history." The poet Vyazemsky called Karamzin the Field Marshal Kutuzov of History, for he saved his country from the "invasion of oblivion"; in the field of history he demonstrated to the world that the Russians had a fatherland much as Kutuzov did on the battlefield in 1812.

Most of the Decembrists condemned Karamzin for his panegyric presentation of autocracy. Nikita Muraviev disapproved of it on the grounds that "history belongs to the people and not to czars"; M. Fonvizin thought Karamzin concealed the political freedom that the Russian people had enjoyed in their earlier period of history, and instead forced Russian autocracy to the footlights of the national scene. N. Bestuzhev lamented that thus far, all that people wrote about was czars and heroes, but few mentioned the sufferings and needs of the people. M. S. Lunin declared that autocracy was immoral and that God alone was entitled to the power claimed by autocracy. A. I. Turgenev in his diary of 1818, after he read Karamzin's history, wrote that the record of the past was the possession of the people and not of the czars and that Karamzin's account concealed despotism from the eye of the reader. A. Pushkin, though considering the history a "creative work of a great writer" and referring to Karamzin as the "Columbus of Russian History," nonetheless discerned the weakness when he added the following four-line biting epigram:

> In his history, beauty and simplicity
> Prove without bias
> The necessity of Autocracy
> And the charm of the whip.

Among Karamzin's critics may be mentioned the later historian N. G. Ustryalov (1805-1870). He expressed his view in an historical essay in which he credited Karamzin with much that was due him, yet cautiously added a few subtly formulated notes to his praises.[47] History, he stated, is not a gallery of princes and czars, but a chain of interlocking events. The purpose of the historian is to show pragmatically the gradual changes that the state had undergone and to explain how the state came to be what it is. Karamzin's *History of the Russian State*, Ustryalov declared, failed completely to come near such an accomplishment; Karamzin crowded his pages with accounts of royal persons and failed in the end to reveal the genuine moving forces in Russian history.

But these were only isolated voices drowned by the general hosannas to the author; "Old Russia" extolled Karamzin as the first national historian, and his twelve-volume work remained for some years to come the official history of Russia, approved particularly by officialdom or those who shared the views of the author of "Old Russia."

Polevoy

Among the earlier successor of Karamzin who undertook the reinterpretation of Russian history was Nikolay Alekseyevich Polevoy (1796-1846). Born in the distant Siberian city of Irkutsk, son of a merchant, he was a typical self-made man and representative of the rising "classless intelligentsia." In his early youth he read Golikov's work on Peter I and was fascinated by it to such a degree that he decided to devote himself to history. He read voraciously, but failed to attend the university or to receive any regular academic training. Material circumstances compelled him to assist his father in business; but in 1822 the death of his father freed him from the tedious chores of business, so that three years later he was able to settle down permanently in Moscow.

Once in Moscow, Polevoy plunged into literary activity and became associated with the most prominent writers of the time. His chief interest was journalism, and Polevoy soon assumed the editorship of one of the most progressive magazines of the time, the *Moscow Telegraph*. A man of undoubted literary talent, endowed with a native critical capacity, Polevoy nonetheless lacked the refinement of Karamzin.[48] His disapproval of Karamzin's *History* caused Polevoy considerable difficulties; his friends, among them some of the most influential literary men of the time, such as the poets Zhukovsky, Vyazemsky, and Pushkin, left him. It was not long before his journal ended entirely. In 1834 the *Telegraph* was closed down for an article that did not meet with official approbation. The action caused Polevoy endless financial embarrassments and eventually undermined his moral and physical strength. "To become silent in proper time is a great achievement: I should have remained silent in 1834," Polevoy wrote later.

From his early days and intensive reading, Polevoy had been an enthusiastic admirer of Guizot, Thierry, Schelling, and particularly of Niebuhr, whose philosophy inspired him to engage in historical writing, and to whom he dedicated his history, calling him "the First Historian of Our Age." The title of Polevoy's six-volume work, *A History of the Russian People*, is in itself self-explanatory, indicating the basic idea of the author and his reaction to Karamzin's *History of the Russian State*. Nor does it require much speculation as to Polevoy's real motive for beginning to write history.

In 1828 Polevoy contributed a critical review of Karamzin's *History* to the *Moscow Telegraph*. The essence of the review was that, though only currently completed, this work could already be regarded as an entirely obsolete work. Karamzin's work, Polevoy believed, was essentially devoid of any philosophical content, while the entire course in Russian history, as presented by the author, had no relevance to world history. Furthermore, Polevoy added, unless national history is narrated within the orbit of universal history, its true purpose was bound to fail. The historian, he argued, who was not capable to present the past objectively, free of verdicts, emotional or prejudicial, fails in his basic assignment.

Though essentially Polevoy was never a cosmopolitan, he saw things differently when it came to discussions of the writing of history. Certain historical "processes," Polevoy argued, were bound to be universal in nature, and Russian history, as any other national history, was intelligible only within the frame of world events. Postulating his views, Polevoy based his comments exclusively on the philosophy of Schelling—seeing native history in the light of universal developments. This spelled serious problems in the 1830s, shortly after the Decembrist fiasco and the establishment of the autocracy of Nicholas I.

Polevoy also tried to fit Russian history periodization into universal or at least into Western patterns. Thus he regarded the opening phase in Russian history as the "Norman-Feudal Period, 862-1054." The period to follow, according to Polevoy, was the "Family Feudalism, 1053-1224," since Prince Yaroslav had initiated the practice of partitioning among his heirs the land he ruled. Feudalism to Polevoy signified not an economic, but a politico-judicial system. In a strict sense, he thought, the birth of Russian statehood could not be traced until after the overthrow of the Mongolian dominance.

When Polevoy reached the fourteenth and fifteenth centuries, his narrative began to assume an increasingly national interpretation, which he disapproved in the writings of others, while the state began to assume more and more the focal point in his own history. It seems as if the dynamism of the people had suddenly dissipated and the force of the state assumed priority, particularly when he reached the period of Ivan III. In short, initially Polevoy set out as a firm opponent of Karamzin; as he progressed he kept moving into the opponent's camp; the former strength of his arguments seemed to have been sapped and his will to challenge recent opponents was emasculated.

Following his difficulties with officialdom, and the closing of his publication, the *Moscow Telegraph*, he decided to devote his writings to a history of Peter the Great. In the end the study essentially differed little from the ideology he had recently so militantly attacked. For this reason Polevoy was subjected to severe criticism during his lifetime. Foremost among his attackers was the eminent literary critic V. G. Belinsky, who noted that Polevoy had no comprehension of what Russian history was all about, and that all his models—Herder, Guizot, or Shelling—only led him to total confusion. Another of Polevoy's critics, Professor M. T. Kachenovsky, expressed his doubts about the actual value of the chronicles and frankly expressed his view that the distant past is bound to remain a mystery accompanied by futile interpretations.

Polevoy dedicated his history to B. G. Niebuhr.[49] One of his cardinal points was the suggestion to follow the school of Western historians, to narrate without bias the past of the people, to show the part the Russian nation played in the general course of history. Polevoy's intention was aimed at the presentation of the people and not at picturing a gallery of sovereigns.[50] Moreover, Polevoy was not content with the humble role of a chronicler; to him history was a "practical reevaluation of universal philosophical concepts of past events, their analytical study in order to arrive at a sound philosophical synthesis." For this reason he hoped to write a national history not from a local point of view, but to interpret it in the light of world developments.[51] In this respect Polevoy ventured far beyond his successors in the field of history. Unfortunately Polevoy himself was neither equipped with the necessary academic training nor the discipline such assignment called for. His formulation of purpose was too far removed from his time as well as his ability. All in all, the task Polevoy visualized for himself proved far beyond his capacity.

The six-volume work of Polevoy represents a valorious intellectual effort that reminds one again that despite noble intentions, without adequate intellectual equipment such a venture was destined to fail. Polevoy's extensive reading in the field of philosophy and history, as well as his eclectic search for some acceptable formula, in the end led to confusion and faulty construction of a basis on which he hoped to interpret national history. At best it could be said that Polevoy's endeavor represented a healthy reaction to fallacious concepts in historiography, a valorous attempt to place the entire field on a much broader and more meaningful level whence the past might become a truthful panorama. The sad part was that Polevoy never understood how woefully backward he was for the undertaking of such a mission, particularly in view of the Hegelian tide that soon swept through the entire generation. Loyally adhering throughout his lifetime to the views of Schelling and remaining an admirer of his, he thereby brought upon himself the fate of being cast by the wayside of history during the later and most matured years of his life.

Soviet historians regard Polevoy in their glib manner as the historian who favored bourgeois ideas and expected bourgeois developments in Russia. To support this view these writers cite his sympathies with the July monarchy in France, in which Polevoy detected a model form of political order. This oversimplification needs elaboration. Nevertheless Soviet historians come closer to factual circumstances when they temper their verdict and admit that Polevoy did advocate economic and cultural changes in Russia way before his time, opposed the reactionary forces that blocked such changes, or severely criticized the idolatrous presentation of the state in historical writing.[52]

Polevoy's weakness, however, emanated from other sources. The thesis originally undertaken by Polevoy was noble in intention, but far too general in content, and for that reason proved weak and unconvincing. Polevoy challenged Karamzin's thesis of the superiority of the state and its priority over the people. He argued further that Karamzin was first a philosopher and a man of letters and last a historian. In this respect Polevoy was far ahead of his generation, while Karamzin was a generation behind his own. Unfortunately Polevoy lacked the intellectual force to prove his stand, defend his posture, or drive his convictions effectively home.

According to Polevoy, a genuine history must not only incorporate philosophical principles, but base its interpretation on universal concepts. History, as Polevoy envisioned it, was an enormous area in which all nations, states, or faiths were encompassed. He therefore suggested that true history must not be occupied with individual episodes, or cast flippantly liberal interpretations, unless they are within the universal orbit. A narrative of the past should not include moral judgment, it should state objective truth.

Though Polevoy insisted on some kind of universal interpretation, as he kept writing Russian history his loyalty to cosmopolitanism seemed to have wavered, while his adherence to patriotic principles strengthened. From this seemingly inconsistent presentation one derives the view that perhaps Belinsky was right when he concluded that Guizot, Thierry, or Niebuhr, whose works Polevoy carefully read and admired, instead of being enlightened, become more confused in the end. In his enthusiasm Polevoy expanded the field too far, became lost, and remained what he was at start—a provincial writer, despite his progressive views.

Pogodin

Though a contemporary of Polevoy, the next personality we wish to introduce to students of Russian historiography, Mikhail Petrovich Pogodin (1800-1875), is a totally different character from that of Polevoy. Pogodin reflects far more the past midcentury than Polevoy. Pogodin is the academician of his age, the historian-politician wrapped in one, the product of his era par excellence.

The name of M. P. Pogodin is closely linked with the so-called official school, since these historians were the staunchest supporters of the national policy of the administration of Nicholas I.[53] At the outbreak of the Crimean War Pogodin cried out for nothing less than Constantinople. Threats of revolution, he wrote, cannot intimidate Russians, for Russia is not the West. When, however, the prospects of victory were dimmed at Sebastopol, he played a different tune: now motivated by fear of a complete collapse of the political order, Pogodin began, in his famous *Historical-Political Letters*, to urge reforms. "We do not fear a Mirabeau," he declared; "what we fear is a

Yemelka Pugachev."[54] During his lifetime he advocated ideas that some-times coincided with Slavophile and Panslav philosophies; on other occasions he seemed to have taken the side of the opposite camp, the "skeptics" or those noted for their Western proclivities.

Like Polevoy, Pogodin was descended from a humble family; his father was a serf, belonging to Count Saltykov. But, living in Moscow, the boy by sheer good fortune came into contact with university life; and after being graduated, he joined the faculty. Karamzin and Schlözer were his great heroes, though strictly speaking he was a follower of neither. He worked out his own method of writing, his own interpretations, though the conservative era through which he lived deeply stamped its imprint upon his work. Thus in 1830, as a result of the revolt in Poland, Pogodin wrote an essay, "Reflections on Russo-Polish Relations," which pleased the Third Division (Intelligence Department) so much that it paid the author an honorarium. Yet when he applied for permission to go abroad, the government refused him the privilege, announcing the "present circumstances make it futile to send this master to foreign lands to complete his studies; it is more useful to offer him in the university that kind of education which the government would consider profitable." It was not until 1835 that Pogodin made his first journey abroad.[55]

Like many of his contemporaries, Pogodin was interested in early Russian history, and especially in the Varangian or Norman problem. His master's thesis of 1824, "Concerning the Origins of Russia," was highly praised by Karamzin; the thesis was instrumental in opening the doors of his alma mater to his academic career.[56] Ten years later he published his analysis of the *Nestor Chronicle*, a study that is still considered an important contribution to the research in annalistic literature. On his second sojourn in Western Europe Pogodin visited Paris in 1839, met some of the eminent scholars of his day, including the Slavicist P. J. Safarik and the French historian F. P. G. Guizot, and came into closer contact with Western thought. Upon his return from abroad there followed the decade of his fruitful period of writing and of collecting valuable sources.

His association with the University of Moscow dates to 1835, when he was appointed professor of Russian history, taking the place of his former teacher, M. T. Kachenovsky. The appointment was well fitted to the general policy of the current administration, for Pogodin had no sympathy with the beliefs of the "skeptics" any more, particularly their belief in a "universal philosophical synthesis"; anything even remotely related to "universality" was frowned upon, regarded as perilous, a threat to the three pillars—autocracy, orthodoxy, and nationalism—on which the entire social structure rested.

In 1884 Pogodin resigned his professorship at the University of Moscow in order to devote himself entirely to the editing of the journal *Moskvityanin* and to his government position with the Ministry of Education. The vacated chair was shortly afterward given to his opponent, S. M. Solovyev, about whom more will be said later. Though Pogodin entirely severed his relations with academic life, he never abandoned the field of history. In his seven-volume *Early History of Russia* Pogodin reveals an amazing acquaintance with the early historical sources available during his time. It is an enormously detailed study, though it sadly lacks both historical synthesis and any consistent architectonic pattern. For this reason Pogodin's seven-volume history can be more aptly described as a voluminous compilation of source information than a synthesized history.

According to Pogodin the two forces instrumental in the molding of the Russian state were Greek and Byzantine Christianity coming from the south, and Slavic learning penetrating from the southwest. Since the strength of Russia emanated from these two mighty sources, Pogodin never hesitated for a moment, as did others, to acknowledge the existence of Norman influence in early Russian history. The foundation laid by the Normans was unstable—witness the ease with which the Mongols overthrew the entire structure. It was only with the rise of Moscow that a true national state had emerged and was given ultimate expression by Peter the Great. Much of this hypothesis Pogodin borrowed from Schlözer, but he added to it a strong national tinge, a touch of providential destiny to the general picture that he drew of the past.

It was in the doctoral dissertation, his analysis of the *Nestor Chronicle*, that Pogodin made a real contribution. The thesis constitutes a superb supplement to Schlözer's study. Here Pogodin analyzed quite ably the chronicle as a historical document and discussed at great length the style of the author as well as the biographical and chronological data implied; he made a skillful comparison between the *Nestor* and other preceding chronicles of foreign origin, showing the influence of the latter on the contents of the Russian documents. Schlözer was interested in presenting the original text, freeing it from all foreign sources that were incorporated by the author. Pogodin was more interested in the sources that influenced Nestor and in this respect considerably advanced the method of study of annalistic literature.

But even here Pogodin did not fail to add a touch of the national sentiment that characterized all of his work. His reverence for Nestor stands out quite conspicuously. Pogodin urged the Russian people to "proclaim his eternal memory and to worship him so that he may grant us the spirit of Russian history, for the spirit alone, my friends, uplifts, while the letter alone kills." Such lines could have been written only by a native "soul-searching" historian of the era of Nicholas I and not by a "Euclidian-minded German academician of the Era of Enlightenment." There is a breath of *Zeitgeist* in the statement![57]

Though Pogodin was fond of citing similarities between Russian and Western European history, he was equally emphatic in stressing the vital differences. Some of these parallels are of the nature of sweeping generalities and therefore are extremely problematic. He interpreted the conquests of the Normans in early Russia and in Western Europe as of identical character; in both cases the conquests led to the foundation of states. The appanage system in Russia was similar to the Eastern feudal system. The crusades and the Mongolian invasion resulted, in both cases, in the undermining of feudalism and were instrumental in establishing or consolidating absolutism. The Reformation and the reforms of Peter I, according to Pogodin, accomplished similar changes—secularization of the state. Having acknowledged such similarities, Pogodin then continued, as if by lapse of memory, to draw vital differences that are equally sweeping and even more problematic. In Western Europe he saw only wars, conquests, division, class struggle, social antagonism, and revolution, while in Russia none of these could be found. The spirit of Slavophilism was already hovering in the air. The reason for this was, as Pogodin explained it, that Russian statehood was based on a peaceful agreement between the people and the government, best illustrated by the "invitation of the Normans to come and govern." To soften the injury that this might cause to sensitive national pride, Pogodin hastened to add that, naturally, even if the Normans had never been invited, the course of history would still have been the same. Be that as it is, the Norman theory thus was dismissed with no offense to national feelings. If the first contention, stressing the similarities between Russian and Western history, delighted the Westerners, the second one, minimizing the historical significance of the Normans, pleased the Slavophiles. Pogodin could truly pride himself as the proverbial merchant, being ready to serve all alike.

On occasion Pogodin found himself tied up by contradictory theories of his own creation. A single illustration will suffice. Pogodin asserted that a mass revolt for people's sovereignty was inconceivable because of the "uniqueness" of Russian history. Revolutions in Russia, if they occur, are initiated from above and not below, as in the case of the reforms of Peter I. Russian authority rested on a totally different principle from authority in the West. In Russia the people "invited" the government, made a contract between themselves and the ruler, and consented to be ruled by the chosen prince. The deduction one could naturally draw was that if the same people happened to be displeased with the sovereign, they had the right to nullify the contract and choose a more suitable ruler. But this was a dangerous doctrine, too strongly flavored with the spirit of the American Declaration of Independence. Therefore Pogodin hastened to add, almost in the same breath, that once the power to rule was granted, it was irretrievable and the people had nothing more to say about it. The Slavophiles seized upon the "uniqueness" of political development in Russia; the Westerners deduced the theory of government by consent of the people as a traditional institution. In short, every party was given, or thought it was given, something to use for its own ideology.

Though Pogodin received a far broader education than Polevoy, he set sail on shallower waters. With Pogodin it was almost axiomatic that Russia was destined to defend and maintain peace and social order on the continent and that, as a historian, he must clarify that mission for the public. He predicted that the destiny of Europe and mankind might be determined by his country. Though no admirer of the philosophy of the Westerners, he had some praise for Peter I as he saw his place in history. Pogodin considered that rebel Czar as presenting the most unique illustration of a nation where profound revolutionary changes emanate from a lawful source rather than from mob action. To Pogodin this was one of the vital differences between Russia and Western Europe.

Pogodin's reverence for Russian antiquities in the strictest orthodox sense suited the prevailing philosophy during the reign of Nicholas I. As lecturer in the University of Moscow, as member of the Ministry of Education, as editor of the *Moscow Messenger* (1827-1830) and subsequently of the *Moskvityanin* (1841-1856), he consistently followed an extremely nationalistic line. How he could embrace both the broad principles of Schlözer and a homespun patriotism was a mystery even to his contemporaries, but that was the mystery also of his time.[58] Had not even Polevoy, crushed by many reverses, become, according to A. Herzen, "within five days a loyal subject"? Pogodin's duality allowed both Westerners and Slavophiles to cite his writings in order to prove their contentions.

Pogodin's contribution to historiography has been recognized mainly for the following. He carried on further studies of the chronicles that proved of great aid to subsequent scholarship in the field of earlier Russian history, particularly his publication of several volumes of hitherto unknown chronicles. Pogodin collected many valuable manuscripts, which subsequently became the property of the Leningrad Public Library and are known as the Pogodin Collection. He revived the publication of the long forgotten two-volume work of I. T. Pososhkov, *On Wealth and Poverty*, written during the reign of Peter I. Pososhkov's purpose was to present an extensive project for economic reforms in Russia based on the mercantilist philosophy of the time. Though not an advocate of the emancipation of the serfs, Pososhkov urged the restraint of the nobility in their rights over the peasants and recommended the summoning of a legislative assembly and the adoption of appropriate legislation to carry out the projects elaborated. Instead of becoming a national hero, Pososhkov ended in 1725 as a prisoner in the Peter and Paul Fortress, where he died a few months later. The new edition of Pososhkov's writings by Pogodin was to pay honor to an overlooked work as well as to a martyr historian-economist.

In one of his essays on the origins of serfdom in Russia entitled "Is Boris Godunov to be Considered as the Founder of Serfdom?" Pogodin argued that the state was in no way responsible for the introduction of that institution; the government cared only for the welfare of the peasants and was indirectly involved in the approval of serfdom.[59] Serfdom, Pogodin concluded, came not through some single legislative action, but in a gradual development, the initiative resting exclusively with the landlord class. Such was the new interpretation as presented by Pogodin in 1858, on the eve of the collapse of the entire medieval order of society that prevailed in Russia. By then it did not matter much what theory of the origin of serfdom one might suggest; the most essential issue at that time was how to end serfdom. For nearly two decades Pogodin was destined to witness the crumbling of the social order which he so vainly either defended or hoped to interpret publicly. One is inclined to wonder if the two different phases of history through which Pogodin lived may explain at least in part the duality of Pogodin, the two contradictory points of view that are frequently found in his writings.

The Turbulent Midcentury Decades

Westernism and Slavophilism constitute a complex phenomenon, which can be referred to here only as far as the immediate subject is concerned. Nicholas I's policy of isolating Russia from the revolutionary contagion that plagued Western Europe stimulated thinking concerning Russia's past as well as her destiny; whatever subsequent discussions followed involved the use and often the abuse of history. They also accelerated the process of sharper demarcation between schools of thought, Western and Slavophile.[60] The two diverged markedly in their interpretation of Russian history and accordingly a literary struggle unfolded over a wide range of subjects involving historical interpretation. Various ideologies had been fermenting quietly until 1836. when the entire issue violently burst open. The occasion was caused by Peter Y. Chaadayev.[61] The tenseness of the arguments led to an agitated exchange of extreme views, often totally devoid of reality. Nonetheless, the opinions involved in the conflict must be briefly considered to show how each side employed history as its ideological weapon either in defense or offense against its opponents. Needless to say, the impact on the writing of history or its interpretation was profound and lasting.

CHAADAYEV

The Slavophiles held the view for some time that Russia had a great history but lost its continuity or national destiny with the ascendancy of Peter I; the Westerners professed the belief that Russia's past was unworthy of anything until the arrival of Peter I on the national scene. Out of the blue came Peter Yakovlevich Chaadayev (1796-1856) to declare that Russia had no history at all of which she might be proud, at any time in the past. With this sweeping assertion Chaadayev plunged into a flood of controversy in which he was nearly drowned, while the others were stunned and left to defend themselves the best they could. The dikes had gone down before the battering waves of bitter debates that continued throughout the entire generation between the two schools of thought, and in some milder forms continued long after the generation of the midcentury was removed from the national scene.

Peter Chaadayev represented what might be called the theocratic wing of Russian Westernism; in the historical past he traced three stages: "at first savage barbarism, then primitive superstition, followed by brutal, humiliating foreign oppression, characteristics inherited afterward by the national government.''[62] Chaadayev showed an ill-concealed sense of contempt for Slavophile jingoism and was equally skeptical about the philosophy of its opponents. He was depressed by the sorrowful state of *spiritual isolation* of his country and turned to history only because, as he said, the past alone was able to explain a people.

The first tragic development in Russian history, according to Chaadayev, was the fact that while in search of a new religious faith Russia, as if impelled by a fatal destiny, turned not to Rome, the genuine source of Christian teaching, but to Byzantium. And this had happened at a time when the Byzantine church, led by an egotist, Patriarch Photius, broke away from ''universal brotherhood.'' Thus a religion distorted by human passion made its initial appearance in Russia. Instead of embracing the faith that emanated from the Western brotherhood of Christendom, Russia became Christianized and civilized by the renegade faith of Byzantium. To this Chaadayev wryly added that the Abyssinians had also done so. The sad fact remained, Chaadayev observed further, that though Christianized, Russia remained a spiritual and cultural vacuum.

Russia's geographic position offered unusual opportunities, Chaadayev continued. ''Resting with one elbow on China and with the other on Germany, we should have encompassed the two great fundamentals of knowledge—imagination and reason—and correlated in our civil education the history of the entire world.'' Nothing of the kind happened; Russia remained immune to both and let opportunities pass by. At one time Peter I had every noble intention and ''threw the mantle of civilization'' to his people. In fact, what happened was that the Russians ''picked up the mantle and left the civilization untouched.'' Alexander I later led Russia in triumph across the continent of Europe, but when the armies returned they brought back a smattering of inspiration and a few ideas that ended with a tragic fiasco—the Decembrist revolt—and thereby set the clock of history back half a century.

The deduction Chaadayev arrived at was easy to guess: to take the road to Rome. In the Roman church Chaadayev saw the foundation of Christian civilization and the genuine cohesive force of Western society. Chaadayev considered the Reformation as the most deplorable event in modern history; it resulted in the tragic demolition of Christian unity and a division that had prevailed ever since.

Chaadayev reminds one of the characters in M. Gorky's *Lower Depths* who "came, stirred everything up, and then disappeared." The figure of Chaadayev is as mysterious as it is provocative; like Pushkin's prophet he pressed "a coal of living fire" in the quaking heart of the generation of Nicholas I. He keenly sensed the national crisis and desperately sought solutions. The old order, he felt, was trembling under his feet, while he was not able even dimly to visualize the new one. He looked with disdain on the Slavophiles and the Westerners and thought of his own remedy—the path to Rome. From all we know, however, he never took the road himself. The sad fate of Chaadayev was that he stood at the very threshold of a new chapter in Russian history; he was the symbol of a tantalized generation and his lot seems even more sad when one thinks that he died almost at dawn, when Russia awkwardly turned a page in her history and emancipated herself of medieval vestiges.

WESTERNERS

Those who advocated a Western national orientation did not share the dim view of Chaadayev, nor did they let themselves be swayed by the Catholic romanticism of the time. Though not seeing eye to eye with Chaadayev on many issues, they did agree with him in their negative opinion of Russia's past. They envisioned national salvation, not in mystical religious revival, however, but in political and economic emancipation of the masses, as it had been attained in Western Europe. They saw a higher stage of development in parliamentary government based on a Western model, which Russia could not neglect if she expected to move forward.

The Westerners could also agree with Chaadayev on the question of the historical significance of Peter I; both regarded his reforms as the initial step toward change. Chaadayev was disheartened by what had happened, but the Westerners refused to be swayed by his melancholy reflections; they considered the reign of Peter I as the true Age of Enlightenment in Russian history. They rejected other arguments such as that Petrine reforms constituted a violation of the natural evolution of national progress. The Westerners branded this idea as crude homespun patriotism, which served no other purpose than to perpetuate Asiatic despotism.

In the summer of 1847 the famed literary critic and leading figure among the Westerners, V. G. Belinsky, was provoked by the publication of Gogol's

Choice Passages from Correspondence with Friends. He wrote a review of this book in the form of a letter to the author. Though the occasion bore no direct relation to the ideological battle presently to be discussed, the letter can be justly regarded as the first salvo fired by the Westerners. The document contained all the accumulated wrath and revulsion against Slavophile piety in whatever form it might appear. Gogol's morose religiosity only antagonized the militant ranks of the Westerners; behind the glabrous, seamless front of Christian morality was hidden a defeatist spirit.

Russia's salvation, declared "Raging Vissarion" (Belinsky), was not in mysticism and prayers, "but in awakening among the common folk a sense of human dignity (for so many ages have been lost amid the mire of garbage) and rights and laws." What the country needed most was abolition of serfdom, introduction of justice, and restraint of the unbridled tyranny of the administration. In essence, glorification of Orthodoxy signified blind praise of Cimmerian darkness and Mongolian morals. It was a voice of outrage, or, as Belinsky stated, "one cannot keep silent when, under the cover of religion and the protection of the knout, falsehood and immorality are preached as truth and virtue."[63]

Centuries of cultural isolation, the Westerners asserted, served to perpetuate the harmful legacies of Byzantium and Tartar domination. Many of the worse characteristics were engrafted on the national character: mental sloth, a sense of inferiority, widespread illiteracy and superstition, cunningness, and evasiveness. These were not inherent traits, only influences absorbed during forced association with the Mongols while they dominated the country.

Peter smashed all barriers that stood between the West and his country; for the first time, through the crashed "window," came a gust of fresh Western air. Catherine II assured further benefits from contacts with Western Europe forced by Peter I. A close relationship did not mean that the Russians would turn into slavish reflectors of Western culture; rather, it would make them European Russians. From Western experience Russians could gain much: they could dissociate genuine cultural values from false appearances; they might avoid all the faults of capitalism and ensure a pattern of social and economic development more advanced than that of the West. Furthermore, it should be borne in mind that institutions that collapsed in the West were destined to meet the same fate in the East. Contrary to Slavophile allegations that Western Europe represented a decaying civilization, the westerners urged that Russia take cognizance of the enormous progress the continent had attained and that Russia must overtake. They advised their opponents to lay aside their Oriental yardsticks and admit that the West remained a great reservoir of vitality that nourished much of the world.

The frequent rebuttals carried one feature particularly worthy of notice: both sides used history as their chief weapon. Seldom had the past been studied more intensively in order to illustrate the points each ideological camp wished to drive home. Whatever ends each side pursued, history meanwhile made gains, being widely studied, written, rewritten, interpreted, and reinterpreted by an agitated generation.

SLAVOPHILES

Chaadayev's savage criticism, which stripped his country of its history, and the philosophy of the Westerners, which shared to a degree the views of Chaadayev, aroused the ardent nationalists. In self-defense they elaborated a curious thesis of their own: a mixture of sentimental patriotism and a romantic interpretation of history, known generally as Slavophilism. Slavophile opponents of the West asserted with adolescent zeal that the Russian people were in possession of a civilization of their own and needed no imitation of others. Russia, they said, was a world in her own right, to which Western yardsticks were totally inapplicable; her stability was due to the social and political institutions the country had enjoyed.

The course of Russian history, the Slavophiles continued, is refelcted in the two capitals of the land, Moscow and St. Petersburg. These cities are uniquely symbolic, one representing the epoch of traditional relationship between the people and their government, a time when a genuine bond of common interests prevailed between the two; the other representing a later period when the authorities, motivated by a foreign spirit, established a government apart from the people and alien to their true national aspirations. "You [Peter I] have detested Russia and all her past," wrote one of the Slavophile champions, Constantine Aksakov. "For this reason a seal of malediction is imprinted on all your senseless work. You heartlessly repudiated Moscow and went to build, apart from your people, a solitary city, the reason being that you and the people could no longer dwell together." The reforms of Peter I, so highly glorified by the Westerners, were anathema to the Slavophiles; all the violent changes of Peter I were considered as some sort of blundering Teutonic intrusions of national life, for they superimposed on the nation a philo-European form of government and legislation historically, traditionally, and spiritually alien to the people. Though the Slavophiles admitted that the country was at a critical turning point, their remedies could hardly be accepted as a solution to the problem since they sought an answer, not in the future, but in the past, which they idealized as totally "unique" and apart from the Western world.

Slavophilism thus can be regarded as a conservative, romantic nationalism that sensed the urgent need for reforms. However, these reforms could be enforced peacefully by a national assembly that would curb, if not abolish, the institution of serfdom and partition the land, though preserving the revered institution of the village commune. Thus far there was nothing that would radically differ from any program of a bourgeois Western European party. Yet there was a difference in the Slavophiles' approach to history distinct from that of the West in that Russia's future as well was to be gloriously unique. To uphold their views the Slavophiles searched through history and discovered three bases on which to build their philosophy; Orthodoxy, autocracy, and the commune.

The first, Russian Orthodoxy, represented to the Slavophiles more than a Western form of religious organization; it was a truly spiritual bond that held men together in a common loyalty to God and to each other. No other religious organization allowed the individual member a greater degree of freedom than Orthodoxy; no other had managed to preserve the qualities of the original founders of the church as had Orthodoxy. Roman Catholicism is based on the authoritarian despotism of one man, Protestantism on an unprincipled revolt and a book; but Orthodoxy is based on free unity, on a genuine spirit of freedom and Christian love.

The second and peculiarly Russian institution, autocracy, was as unique as the first. Autocracy in early Russia represented patriarchal authority and had nothing in common with other autocratic governments, which were usually based on physical compulsion and therefore violently opposed by their subjects. In Western Europe the state is based on sheer force and thus rests, according to the Slavophiles, on artificial unity and internal contradictions. The Western state, then, is bound to witness revolts of those coerced to accept imposed authority. But upon Russia, a nation of a different political complexion from the dawn of history, autocracy never imposed itself; it had been "invited" by voluntary consent of the people. Here authority was based on persuasion, unity, communal interests, and genuine spirituality, according to P. V. Kireyevsky. For this reason Russia had no need of the Western type of democratic institutions, which resulted only in political and social strife, sharp economic rivalry, and class antagonisms.

Finally, there was the commune, the symbol of a truly "moral union of men," a "fraternal triumph of humanitarian spirit." The Slavophiles interpreted this institution as an answer to the Western utopian ideals cherished by socialists. According to the Slavophiles the commune practiced socialism long before the socialists in the West conceived their economic doctrines; in Russia socialism operated without the political convulsions manifested elsewhere in Europe. Moreover, whereas in the West socialism had been enforced from above, in Russia the organically Christian commune had applied social and economic justice voluntarily through its local members. The fact explained the absence of class struggle and of a proletariat, the class that constituted a constant revolutionary peril and contributed to the decline of European society.

While challenging this idyllic interpretation of the past, the Westerners, as well as later critics of Slavophilism, had erred on one point particularly; they identified Slavophilism with the absolutism of the period of Nicholas I. This was either a deliberate distortion or an unconscious misconception of their views. There was one cardinal difference between autocracy as the Slavophiles envisioned it historically and as it existed in Russia. In the past, the Slavophiles pointed out, the people played a different part in relation to the state: the latter was the creation of the people, the instrument chosen and accepted by themselves. Sovereignty of the people was the *raison d'être* of the state in early Russian history, that state being a party to a contractual agreement that served the interests of the masses. On this score the Slavophiles and official authorities disagreed, for, in the opinion of the latter, admission of such a precept might lead to perilous political deduction such as the need of a national assembly or the principle of inviolable rights of the people that the state was bound to honor under any circumstances. The Slavophiles, at the same time, cannot be regarded as opposing absolutism in a Western sense, for they merely represented a political concept that endeavored to delineate more clearly the interests and rights of the state and those of the people. How the two could be kept apart without fundamental political changes, the Slavophile exponents never succeeded or even tried to explain. Because of this lack of clarity on such a vital point, the government looked upon Slavophilism with misgivings, while the Westerners came to interpret it as another disguised device to perpetuate "Byzantine autocracy" in Russia.

While envisioning reforms, the Slavophiles could not accept the measures advocated by their opponents; and it is here that they revealed their ideological vulnerability. The Slavophiles were essentially retrogressive in their aspirations, insisting on a restoration of the status quo of bygone days when true Christian freedom prevailed, and harmony between the people and sovereign served as the basis of "unique" Russian government. This presentation of history irked even such a poised historian as S. M. Solovyev, who caustically dismissed it as the Buddhist concept of Russian historical thought. The Slavophiles asserted that the old harmony between faith and politics, between church and state, was destroyed by the devastating policies of Peter I. This destruction was bound to lead, they thought, to the creation of a westernized minority and an unaffected majority, thereby alienating the leaders from the masses, the majestic imperial state from the Russian people. Peter's reforms introduced an air of artificiality, of aping alien culture while casting overboard traditional institutions and the national way of life. Slavophile interpretation of Russian history represented a curious mixture of idyllic loyalties to institutions and traditions that had never existed, and negation of the obvious realities of political life that stubbornly kept staring the nation in the face.

SUMMARY

The intellectual conflict that raged in Russia during the middle of the nineteenth century was part and parcel a reflection of the German romantic movement and of the outburst of Slav nationalism in central and southeastern Europe during the same period. The idealization of traditionalism, of early national institutions, and the worship of the "national and cultural spirit" characterized the generation of the mid-nineteenth century. The idealization of the past can be regarded as an escape from the sordid present. Perhaps, to use the apt observation of Sir John Maynard, all of them had a tendency to mix their wish with its fulfillment. And yet, as one contemplates this turbulent period retrospectively and tries to summarize the intellectual tempest, certain facts stand out significantly. The verbal encounters between the opposing camps of Slavophilism and Westernism were not without some salutary effects. On the ideological battlefields were tempered a number of eminent national figures: liberals like Herzen, literary critics like Belinsky, famed pedagogues like Granovsky, and writers and publicists like Yury

Samarin, A. S. Khomyakov, the Kireyevsky brothers, or K. S. Aksakov. The conflict stimulated an unprecedented interest in ethnography, Russian folklore, and particularly Russian history, since each camp cherished a majestic sense of destiny and sought in the past a revelation of universal reason on which to build its philosophy. Seizing on the ideas of Hegel and Schelling concerning the successive ascent of nations with historic missions for mankind, they tried to find justification for their hopes that the next message to the world would be delivered by Russia.[64]

Those who took sides in these disputes—and it was difficult to remain passive—turned not only to national history but to Eastern European history as well. Young men absorbed themselves in the writings of the French Encyclopedists and were fascinated by the philosophies of Kant, Fichte, Schelling, and Hegel. Whereas the Slavophiles remained basically loyal to Schelling, the Westerners came to idolize Hegel, read his works voraciously, and make appropriate deductions to support their own philosophy. The intellectual fever of the middle of the nineteenth century brought forth a series of brilliant scholars, whose names, with only a few exceptions unfortunately, mean little to Western readers. Suffice to mention A. N. Popov; I. Y. Zabelin; I. D. Belyayev, known for his studies of earlier periods of Moscow life, chiefly concerning the peasant problem, communal landownership, and conditions of the Slavic tribes before the coming of the Varangians; K. D. Kavelin; I. I. Dmitryev; later to be followed by that prolific scholar, A. N. Pypin, noted for his works on recent political and social history, Russian Freemasonry, Slavic literature, and Russian ethnography; or V. I. Sergeyevich, the distinguished student of legal history, whose *Antiquities of Russian Law* remains to this day a distinguished contribution to scholarship; or B. N. Chicherin, Hegelian jurist and philosopher, whose chief contribution was in the field of Russian local government of the eighteenth century. The list could be greatly augmented, but the limited scope of this study does not permit a detailed account of this period of "storm and stress" in Russian history. Since the survey can include only the pillars of modern historiography, produced by the intellectual fermentation of the time, the most imposing of them must be considered next.[65]

Notes

1. *Ocherki istorii istoricheskoy nauki v SSSR* [The History of Historical Science in the USSR] (Moscow, 1955), Vol. I, Chapter 11.
2. E. Shmurlo, *Mitropolit Yevgeny kak uchenyi* [Metropolitan Yevgeny as a Learned Man] (St. Petersburg, 1888); N. V. Zdobnov, *Istoriya russkoy bibliografii do nachala XX veka* [A History of Russian Bibliography Until the Beginning of the Twentieth Century] (Moscow, 1955).
3. I. L. Mayakovsky, *Ocherki po istorii arkhivnogo dyela v SSSR* [A History of Archival Development in the USSR] (Moscow, 1941), Part 1, pp. 222-23.
4. V. S. Ikonnikov, *Opyt russkoy istoriografii* [A Study of Russian Historiography] (Kiev, 1891), Vol. 1, Book 1, pp. 297-99.
5. Ikonnikov, *Opyt russkoy istoriografii*, 1: 135 ff. A graphic account of Rumyantsev's role in collecting national sources may be found in *Sobraniye gosudarstvennykh gramot in dogovorov* [Collection of State Charters and Treaties] (Moscow, 1813-1828) 5: ii-xiii. For a more detailed study, see A. A. Kochubinsky, *Admiral Shishkov i Kantsler gr. Rumyantsev. Nachalniye gody slavyanovedeniya* [Admiral Shishkov and Chancellor Count Rumyantsev: Initial Years of Slavic Studies] (Odessa, 1887-1888); *Vestnik Evropy* 10 (1888): 703 ff.; N. L. Rubinstein, *Russkaya istoriografiya* [Russian Historiography] (Moscow, 1941), pp. 212-22.
6. *Sobraniye gosudarstvennykh gramot i dogovorov* [Collection of State Charters and Treaties], 4 vols. (Moscow, 1813-1828); a fifth volume appeared in 1894.
7. Ikonnikov, *Opyt russkoy istoriografii*, Vol. 1, Book 1, p. 150.
8. Ibid., pp. 149-50.
9. The Codes of Laws of the fifteenth and sixteenth centuries were republished by the Academy of Sciences in 1952. These include the Codes of 1497, 1550, and 1589. See *Sudebniki XV-XVI Vekov*, ed. B. D. Grekov (Moscow-Leningrad, 1952).
10. P. M. Stroyev, *Opisanie letopisey Volokolamskogo, Novy Yerusalim, Savvina-Storozheskogo i Pafnutieva-Borovskogo.* (St. Petersburg, 1889).
11. See M. T. Kachenovsky, "Parallelnye mesta v russkikh letopisyakh," *Vestnik Evropy*, No. 18, 1809.
12. N. P. Barsukov, *Zhizn i trudy P. M. Stroyeva* (St. Petersburg, 1878).
13. S. F. Platonov, *Lektsii po russkoy istorii* [Lectures on Russian History] (St. Petersburg, 1913), pp. 34-35. See also *Ocherki istoricheskoy nauki v SSSR* [Studies of the Historical Science in the USSR], (Moscow, 1955) 1: 553-56.
14. During the long stretch of years the Archaeographic Commission amassed and published a large number of volumes containing sources of various nature. To mention only some of them published by the commission: *Akty, sobranniye v*

bibliotekakh i arkhivakh Rossiiskoy Imperrii Arkheograficheskoyu Ekspeditsieyu [Documents Gathered in Libraries and Archives by the Archaeological Expedition of the Russian Empire], 4 vols. (St. Petersburg, 1836); *Akty yuridicheskiye ili sobraniye form starinnogo deloproizvodstva* [Juridical Documents or Collection of Old Forms of Procedure] (St. Petersburg, 1838); *Akty otnosyashchiesya do yuridicheskogo byta drevney Rossii* [Documents Pertaining to Judicial Conditions of Early Russia], 3 vols. (St. Petersburg, 1857-1884); *Akty istoricheskiye* [Historical Documents], 5 vols. (St. Petersburg, 1841-1842); *Dopolneniya k Aktam istoricheskim* [Supplements to the Historical Documents], 12 vols. (St. Petersburg, 1846-1872); *Akty, otnosyashchiesya k istorii zapadnoy Rossii* [Documents Pertaining to the History of Western Russia], 5 vols. (St. Petersburg, 1846-1853); *Akty, otnosyashchiesya k istorii yuzhnoy and zapadnoy Rossii* [Documents Pertaining to the History of Southern and Western Russia], 15 vols. (St. Petersburg, 1863-1892.

15. *Akty istoricheskiye, otnosyashchiesya k Rossii, izvlechenniye iz inostrannykh arkhivov i bibliotek* [Historical Documents Pertaining to Russia Drawn from Foreign Archives and Libraries], ed. A. I. Turgenev, 2 vols. (St. Petersburg, 1841-1842); *Dopolneniya k aktam istoricheskim . . .* [Supplements to the Historical Documents . . .] (St. Petersburg, 1848); *Pamyatniki diplomaticheskikh snoshenii drevney Rossii s derzhavami inostrannymi* [Documents Concerning Diplomatic Relations of Early Russia with Foreign Countries], 10 vols. (St. Petersburg, 1851-1857).

16. Ikonnikov, *Opyt russkoy istoriografii*, p. 164.

17. The nature of these sources is discussed by A. Starchevsky in *Zhurnal Ministerstva Narodnogo Prosveshcheniya* 49 (1846): 14-40.

18. Kochubinsky, *Admiral Shishkov*, pp. 70-75 (see note 5, above); also Appendix, pp. *vii* ff.

19. A. Starchevsky, "O zaslugakh Rumyantseva, okazannykh otechestvennoy istorii" [Concerning the Services Rendered by Rumyantsev to National History], *Zhurnal Ministerstva Narodnogo Prosveshcheniya* 49 (1846): *i* ff., 51-56; Kochubinsky, *Admiral Shishkov*, Part 2, pp. 37 ff.; P. N. Milyukov, *Glavniye techeniya russkoy istoricheskoy mysli* [Main Currents in Russian Historical Thought] (Moscow, 1898), pp. 204-42.

20. Marc Raeff, *Michael Speransky* (The Hague, 1957), Chapter 11.

21. A. N. Pypin, *Istoriya russkoy etnograffii* [History of Russian Ethnography], (St. Petersburg, 1890-1892) Vol. 4, Chapter 7.

22. S. R. Mintslov, *Obzor zapisok, dnevnikov, vospominanii, pisem i puteshestvy, otnosyashchikhsya k istorii Rossii i napechatannykh na russkom yazyke* [A Survey of Memoranda, Diaries, Reminiscences, Letters, and Travels, Pertain-

ing to Russian History and Published in Russian] (Novgorod, 1911-1912) (three issues).

23. Pyotr i Boris Lambiny, *Russkaya istoricheskaya bibliografiya* [Russian Historical Bibliography], 10 vols. (St. Petersburg, 1861-1884).

24. V. I. Mezhov, *Bibliografiya Azii* [Bibliography of Asia], 6 vols. (St. Petersburg, 1891-1894); *Krestyansky vopros v Rossii. Polnoye sobraniye materialov dlya istorii krestyanskogo voprosa na yazykakh russkom i inostrannykh napechatannykh v Rossii i za-granirsey, 1764-1864* [The Peasant Problem in Russia: Complete Collection of Sources Concerning the History of the Peasant Problem in Russian and Foreign Laguages, Published in Russia and Abroad, 1764-1864] (St. Petersburg, 1865); *Russkaya istoricheskaya bibliografiya za 1865-1876 vklyuchitelno* [Russian Historical Bibliographical for the Years 1865 Until 1876 Inclusive], 8 vols. (St. Petersburg, 1882-1890); *Sibirskaya bibliografiya. Ukazatel' knig i statey o Sibiri na russkom yazyke i odnyekh tol'ko knig na inostrannykh yazykakh* [Siberian Bibliography: A Guide to Books and Articles in Russian and to Books Only in Foreign Languages], 8 vols. (St. Petersburg, 1891-1892).

25. *Arkhiv knyzya Vorontsova*, ed. P. Bartenev, 40 vols. (Moscow, 1870-1897); *Arkhiv grafov Mordvinovykh*, 10 vols. (St. Petersburg, 1901-1903); *Ostafievsky Arkhiv knyazyey Vyazemskikh*, 5 vols. (St. Petersburg, 1899-1909); *Arkhiv Rayevskikh*, 5 vols. (St. Petersburg, 1908-1915); *Arkhiv knyazya F. A. Kurakina*, ed. M. I. Semevsky, 10 vols. (St. Petersburg, 1890-1902).

26. N. M. Karamzin, *Pisma russkogo puteshestvennika* [Letters of a Russian Traveler], 2nd ed., 2 vols. (Moscow, 1864); *Briefe eines reisenden Russen*, 6 vols. in 3 (Leipzig, 1801-1803); *Travels from Moscow Through Prussia, Germany, Switzerland, France and England*, translated from the German, 3 vols. (London, 1803); *Lettres d'un voyageur russe en France, en Allemagne, et en Suisse (1789-1790)* (Paris, 1867); *Izbrannye sochineniya* (Moscow, 1964). A late edition of Karamzin's *Letters* was published by the Columbia University Press, 1957.

27. M. Pogodin, *N. M. Karamzin, po ego sochineniyam, pismam i otzyvam sovremennikov* [N. M. Karamzin, According to His Work and Letters in the Opinions of His Contemporaries] (Moscow, 1866), 1: 139-44.

28. V. V. Sipovsky, *N. M. Karamzin, avtor 'Pisem russkogo puteshestvennika'* [N. M. Karamzin, Author of "Letters of a Russian Traveler"] (St. Petersburg, 1900), pp. 416-17; *Russkaya Mysl'* 7 (1891): 22-23. See also *Starinaya novizna*, (St. Petersburg, 1897-1917) 1: 60; *Pisma Karamzina k I. I. Dmitrievu* [Letter of Karamzin to I. Dmitriev] (St. Petersburg, 1866), pp. 248-49.

29. A. N. Pypin, *Istoriya russkoy literatury* [History of Russian Literature] (St. Petersburg, 1913), 4: 222-23; M. O. Koyalovich, *Istoriya russkogo samosoznaniya* (St. Petersburg, 1893), p. 143; Pogodin, *N. M. Karamzin,* 2: 1-2.

30. N. M. Karamzin, *Zapiska o drevney i novoy Rossii* [Memorandum on the Old and New Russia] (St. Petersburg, 1914).

31. See, for instance, N. M. Karamzin, *Istoricheskoye pokhval'noye slovo Yekaterine Vtoroy* [A Word of Praise for Catherine II] (Moscow, 1902).

32. Pogodin, *N. M. Karamzin,* 1: 396-97 (see above, note 27).

33. N. M. Karamzin, *Istoriya gosudarstva rossiiskogo* [History of the Russian State], 12 vols. (St. Petersburg, 1816-1829); another edition, Moscow, 1903; French translation by St. Thomas and Jauffret, 11 vols. (Paris 1819-1826); German translation, 11 vols. (Riga, 1820-1833).

34. See Pogodin, *N. M. Karamzin,* Vols. 1-2 (see above, note 27); K. Bestuzhev-Ryumin, *Biografii, kharakteristiki* [Biographical Essays] (St. Petersburg, 1882); P. N. Milyukov, *Glavniye techeniya russkoy istoricheskoy mysli* [Main Currents in Russian Historical Thought] (Moscow, 1898); N. L. Rubinstein, *Russkaya istoriografiya* [Russian Historiography] (Moscow, 1941); *Ocherki istorii istoricheskoy nauki v SSSR* [Studies of the History of the Historical Science in the USSR] (Moscow, 1955), vol. 1.

35. Pogodin, *N. M. Karamzin,* 2: 2 (see above, note 27).

36. See *Zhurnal Ministerstva Narodnogo Prosveshcheniya* 134, (1887): 20 ff.

37. *Chteniya v Imperatorskom Obshchestve Istorii i Drevnostey Rossiiskikh pri Moskovskom Universitete* 3 (1862): 23.

38. *Zhurnal Ministerstva Narodnogo Prosveshcheniya* 133, (1867): 17-18.

39. Compare the different views of M. I. Koyalovich, *Istoriya russkogo samosoznaniya* [History of Russian Self-Realization], pp. 143 ff.; P. N. Milyukov, *Glavniye techeniya,* pp. 152 ff. (see above, note 27).

40. Ibid., pp. 161-63; also pp. 187-90.

41. Karamzin, *Istoriya gosudarstva rossiiskogo,* 5: 64 (see above, note 33).

42. Pypin, *Istoriya russkoy literatury,* 4: 224 (see above, note 29).

43. *Russky istorichesky zhurnal* 1 (1917): 14.

44. *Zhurnal Ministerstva Norodnogo Prosveshcheniya* 133 (1867): 47.

45. On the "School of Sceptics," see V. Ikonnikov, *Skepticheskaya shkola v russkoy istoriografii i eë protivniki* [The Sceptical School in Russian Historiography and Its Opponents] (Kiev, 1871); Rubinstein, *Russkaya istoriografiya,* pp. 233-41 (see above, note 34); *Ocherki istorii istoricheskoy nauki,* 1: 334-38 (see above, note 1).

46. N. Barsukov, *Zhizn i trudy M. P. Pogodina* [The Life and Works of M. P. Pogodin] (St. Petersburg, 1889), 2: 333. See also E. Kovalevsky, *Graf Bludov i ego vremya* [Count Bludov and His Time] (St. Petersburg, 1866), p.

232; *Dekabrist N. I. Turgenev. Pis'ma k bratu S. I. Turgenevu* (Moscow, 1936), p. 349; Bestuzhev-Ryumin, *Biografii*, pp. 205-30 (see above, note 34); Rubinstein, *Russkaya istoriografiya*, pp. 166-88 (see above, note 34).

47. N. G. Ustryalov, *O sisteme pragmaticheskoy istorii* [About the System of Pragmatic History] (St. Petersburg, 1836), pp. 21-22, 40-48 passim.

48. A. Borozdin, "Zhurnalist dvadtsatykh godov" [A Journalist of the Twenties'], *Istorichesky vestnik* 63 (1896): 946-59. Interesting material may also be found in M. I. Sukhomlinov, *Issledovaniya i stati* [Studies and Essays] (St. Petersburg, 1889), 2: 367-431; Rubinstein, *Russkaya istoriografiya*, pp. 242-54 (see above, note 34).

49. N. A. Polevoy, *Istoriya russkogo naroda* [A History of the Russian People], 6 vols. (Moscow, 1830-1833); *Istoriya Petra Velikogo* [A History of Peter the Great], 2nd ed. (Moscow, 1899); *Obozreniye russkoy istorii do edinoderzhaviya Petra Velikogo* [A Survey of Russian History to the Absolute Reign of Peter the Great] (St. Petersburg, 1846).

50. Pypin, *Istoriya russkoy literatury*, 4: 471-72 (see above, note 29).

51. *Istorichesky vestnik* 63, (1896): 958; *Russky biografichesky slovar*, 14: 299-300.

52. *Ocherki istorii istoricheskoy nauki v SSSR*, 1:331.

53. M. P. Pogodin, *O proiskhozhdenii Rusi* [About the Origin of Rus'] (Moscow, 1825); *Issledovaniya, zamechaniya i lektsii o russkoy istorii* [Investigations, Annotations, and Lectures on Russian History], 7 vols. (Moscow 1846-1857); *Drevnyaya russkaya istoriya do mongolskogo iga* [Early Russian History to the Time of the Mongolian Period], 3 vols. (Moscow, 1871); *Istoriko-politicheskie pisma i zapiski v prodolzhenii Krymskoy voyny, 1853-1856 g.g.* [Historical-Political Letters and Memoranda During the Crimean War, 1853-1856] (Moscow, 1874); N. Barsukov, *Zhizn' i trudy M. P. Pogodina* [The Life and Works of M. P. Pogodin], 22 vols. (St. Petersburg, 1888-1910); Milyukov, *Glavniye techeniya* (see above, note 34); Rubinstein, *Russkaya istoriografiya* (see above, note 34); *Ocherki istoricheskoy nauki v SSSR*, vol. 1 (Moscow, 1955); G. V. Plekhanov, "Pogodin i borba klassov" [Pogodin and the Class Struggle], in his *Complete Works* (Moscow-Leningrad, 1926), Vol. 23.

54. M. P. Pogodin, *Istoriko-politicheskie pisma*, 2: 187, 202, 261-62.

55. *Entsiklopedichesky slovar* (Brockhaus-Efron), 24 (1): 32. See also, Rubinstein, *Russkaya istoriografiya*, pp. 254-70 (see above, note 34).

56. Bestuzhev-Ryumin, *Biografii*, pp. 235-36, 239-40 (see above, note 34).

57. *Russky bibliografichesky slovar*, 14: 159-60.

58. Barsukov, *zhizn' i trudy*, 4: 252-53 (see above, note 53).

59. Pogodin, *Istoriko-kriticheskiye otryvki* [Critical Essays], 2: 197-257.

60. P. V. Annenkov, *Literaturniye vospominaniya* [Literary Reminiscences]

(Moscow, 1960); A. V. Nikitenko, *Dnevnik* [Diary], 3 vols. (Moscow 1955-1956); *T. N. Granovsky i ego zapiski* [Granovsky and His Memoranda], 2 vols. (Moscow, 1897); C. Vetrinsky (V. E. Cheshkin), *T. N. Granovsky i ego vremya* [T. N. Granovsky and His Time] (Moscow, 1897); C. Vetrinsky (V. E. Cheshkin), *V sorokovykh godakh* [During the Forties] (Moscow, 1899); F. F. Nelidov, comp., *Zapadniki 40kh godov* [The Westerners of the Forties] (Moscow, 1910); G. V. Plekhanov, "Zapadniki i Slavyanophily," in *Istoriya russkoy obshchestvennoy mysli* ["Westerners and Slavophiles," in his History of Russian Social Thought], *Complete Works* (Moscow, 1926), vol. 23; G. A. Maksimovich, *Ucheniye pervykh slavyanofilov* [The Teachings of the First Slavophiles] (Kiev, 1907); N. L. Brodsky, *Ranniye Slavyanofily* [The Early Slavophiles] (Moscow, 1910); A. N. Pypin, *Kharakteristiki literaturnykh mneny ot 20kh do 50kh gg.* [Characterization of Literary Opinions from the 1820s to the 1850s] (St. Petersburg, 1906); P. Linitsky, *Slavyanofilstvo i liberalizm* [Slavophilism and Liberalism] (Kiev, 1882); P. K. Christoff, *An Introduction to Nineteenth Century Russian Slavophilism. Vol. I. A. S. Khomyakov* (The Hague, 1961).

61. P. Y. Chaadayev, *Sochineniya i pisma* [Works and Letters], 2 vols. (Moscow, 1913-1914); see also *Literaturnoye nasledstvo* [irregular periodical] (Moscow, 1935), Nos. 22-24; G. V. Plekhanov, *Sochineniya* [Works] (Moscow, 1925), Vol. X.

62. P. Y. Chaadayev, *Sochineniya i pisma*, 2: 6-7.

63. V. G. Belinsky, "Letter to Gogol," *A Treasury of Russian Literature*, ed. Bernard Guilbert Guerney (New York, 1943), pp. 241-250.

64. The literature on the subject is vast. The following may be suggested: A. S. Khomyakov, *Polnoye sobraniye sochineny* [Complete Works] (Moscow, 1900), of which Vols. 1 and 3 are of special interest; I. V. Kireyevsky's and S. T. Aksakov's essays dealing with the basic tenets of Slavophilism may be found in *Moskovsky Sbornik*, particularly vols. 1 and 3 (1852), and *Moskvityanin* (1845 and 1847). Also, Peter K. Christoff, *An Introduction to Nineteenth Century Russian Slavophilism: A Study of Ideas* (The Hague, 1972); Peter K. Christoff, *The Third Heart: Some Intellectual-Ideological Currents and Cross-Currents in Russia in 1800-1830* (The Hague, 1970); see also S. T. Aksakov, *Sochineniya istoricheskiye* [Historical Works] (Moscow, 1889); M. Gershenzon, *Istoricheskiye zapiski* [Historical Notes] (Moscow, 1908); Michael B. Petrovich, *The Emergence of Russian Panslavism, 1856-1870* (New York, 1956), particularly Chapters 1 and 2; G. A. Maksimovich, *Ucheniye pervykh slavyanofilov* [Teachings of the First Slavophiles] (Kiev, 1907).

65. A. N. Popov, *Materialy dlya istorii vozmushcheniya Stenki Razina* [Sources Concerning the History of the Revolt of Stenka Razin] (Moscow, 1857);

Poslednyaya sud'ba papskoy politiki v Rossii, 1845-1867 gg. [Papal Policy in Russia, 1845-1867] (St. Petersburg, 1868); *Russkoye posol'stvo v Pol'she v 1673-1677* [The Russian Legation in Poland in 1673-1677] (St. Petersburg, 1854); I. Y. Zabelin, *Domashniy byt russkikh tsarey v XVI i XVII st.* [Domestic Lives of Russian Tsars During the Sixteenth and Seventeenth Centuries] (Moscow, 1872); *Istoriya goroda Moskvy* [A History of Moscow], 2nd ed. (Moscow, 1905); *Opyt izucheniya russkikh drevnostey i istorii* [A Study of Russian Antiquities and History], 2 vols. (Moscow, 1872-1873).

I. B. Belyayev, *Zemskiye sobory na Rusi* [National Assemblies in Russia] (Moscow, 1867); *Idem., Krestyane na Rusi* [Peasantry in Russia] (Moscow, 1891); *Otnosheniye pridneprovskikh gorodov k varyazhskim knyazyam do vzyatiya Kieva v 1171* [Relations Between the Dnieper and the Princes Prior to the Capture of Kiev in 1171] (Moscow, 1848); *O russkom voyske v tsarstvovaniye Mikhaila Feodorovicha i posle ego, do preobrazovany sdelannykh Petrom Velikim* [Russian Armed Forces During the Reign of Michael Feodorovich Until the Reforms of Peter the Great] (Moscow, 1846).

A. N. Pypin, *Istoriya russkoy etnografii* [A History of Russian Ethnography], 4 vols. (St. Petersburg, 1890-1892); *Istoriya russkoy literatury* [A History of Russian Literature], 4 vols. (St. Petersburg, 1902-1903); *Histoire des littératures slaves* (Paris, 1881); *Geschichte der Slavischen Literatur*, 2 vols. (Leipzig, 1800-1884); *Russkoye masonstvo XVIII i pervaya chetvert' XIX v.* [Russian Freemasonry of the Eighteenth and First Quarter of the Nineteenth Centuries] (Petrograd, 1916); *Obshchestvennoye dvizheniye v Rossii pri Aleksandre I* [Social Movement in Russia During the Reign of Alexander I] (St. Petersburg, 1900).

[4]

The Second Half of the Nineteenth Century

Introduction

The second half of the nineteenth century can be considered as a period in Russian historiography that stands apart from the preceding decades—a period during which we notice the emergence of a new kind of historian, whom we may call the professional historian, in contrast to the "amateur school"; these men devoted their lifetime to the narration of "events of bygone years." In the past we met men who employed history to express their personal admiration of some prominent historical figure, such as in the case of I. I. Golikov, who revered the memory of Peter the Great. The aristocrat M. Shcherbatov was moved to write history because he feared there was a decline of morals in the country. General I. N. Boltin wrote history because he was outraged by some French amateur, LeClerc, who misinterpreted Russian history. Many others turned to history because they were provoked by some writings or interpretations, as in the case of M. V. Lomonosov, who was aroused by his German colleagues and their Norman theory. We have N. M. Karamzin, the romantic sentimentalist, superpatriot, and man of letters, who fused his patriotic loyalties with historiographic tasks. We have seen men such as P. Y. Chaadayev, who detected in Russian history a regrettable course, the erroneous choice of a path that led to Byzantium instead of taking the righteous road to Rome, for which the nation, according to Chaadayev, paid dearly. There were others who, under the influence of Guizot or Schelling, vainly endeavored to rewrite Russian history, touching up the narrative with personal views, accompanied by challenging interpretations and short-lived studies. Such was the case of N. A. Polevoy or M. P. Pogodin. These were either accompanied or followed by the Westerners and Slavophiles who, by reason of "philosophical fury" and in the midst of heated debates, resorted to history as a means of defense.

By the middle of the past century there began to appear a new kind of historian in Russian historiography. He can best be defined, once again, to employ the descriptive terminology of Schlözer, as the new *Geschichtserzähler* and particularly the *Geschichtsmaler*. Among these stand out two particularly eminent figures, S. M. Solovyev and V. O. Klyuchevsky. These two men, who dedicated themselves to the teaching as well as to the writing of history, came to offer original interpretations of history in addition to the gathering of materials. Their mission was, to use Frederick Jackson Turner's description, "to preserve the consciousness of the past," to uncover meaningful narrative in the "bygone years," to present a millennium of national life not merely as a vacuous flow of events, but as a purposeful process of growth, of state and empire expansion, of national self-realization and cultural advancement. Such is the outstanding character of the forthcoming decades leading to the year 1917. We must begin with the figure of S. M. Solovyev.

Solovyev

Sergey Mikhaylovich Solovyev (1820-1879) appeared at a time when Russian historiography was in need of a writer who could amalgamate all the theories that had emerged through the preceding decades into a single synthesized narrative. This was no simple task for any man, but Solovyev assumed it and carried it an almost unbelievable distance, to hand it over to a successor who crowned the undertaken assignment with unbelievable success.

Solovyev was born in Moscow and, until he was fourteen years old, received his education at home. His father was a priest and teacher, and the young man inherited a profound religious faith, which subsequently influenced his entire philosophy of history. In 1838 Solovyev entered the University of Moscow, where he was a pupil of both M. P. Pogodin and T. N. Granovsky. The former did not seem to have impressed him very much, but to Granovsky Solovyev felt deeply indebted for the rest of his life. The historical synthesis presented by Granovsky at once fascinated young Solovyev.[1] In 1845 Solovyev completed his master's thesis, "The Relations Between Novgorod and the Grand Princes," and two years later successfully defended his doctoral dissertation, "A History of the Relations Among the Russian Princes of the Ryurik Dynasty." In the latter Solovyev stressed the internal rather than external factors that contributed to the consolidation of the Russian state. Later the idea was developed further when he brushed aside the Norman as well as the Mongolian theories. He came to regard both as inconsequential compared to the facts of internal political development.

Like many young people of his day, Solovyev had to sail toward intellectual maturity between the Scylla and Charybdis of Westernism and Slavophilism. For a time he leaned toward Slavophilism, until, by careful reading of Russian history, he was "cured." But the "cure" was evidently not thorough: Solovyev retained a dim faith in the religious and political messianism of Russia; he continued firmly to believe in a monarchical form of government, though in time this faith was tempered by the acceptance of a provision that the monarch must be attentive to the opinion of the "better portions of the nation." Among the historians who proved of lasting influence on Solovyev and who undoubtedly helped to crystallize his view was J. P. G. Ewers, whose studies in early Russian history profoundly impressed Solovyev during his student days.[2] Later, recalling his training, Solovyev wrote: "From Karamzin I gathered only facts; Karamzin stimulated my feelings, but Ewers stimulated my thinking and compelled me to contemplate Russian history."

During the years 1842-1844 Solovyev traveled abroad as tutor in the family of Count Stroganov and made wise use of every available hour. In Paris he audited the lectures of the French historians Jules Michelet, Edgar Quinet, Charles Lenormant, successor of Guizot, and Victor Chasles; here he also made the acquaintance with the widely recognized poet, Adam Mickiewicz, In Prague he met the leading philologist and Slavophile, Pavel Josef Safarik; in Berlin he audited the lectures of Leopold von Ranke, Karl Ritter, and the eminent church historian Johann August Wilhelm Neander.

During his short sojourn in Western Europe he also familiarized himself with Western historical literature and was fascinated with the writings of Henry T. Buckle. He returned to Russia with warm reverence for Giovanni Vico as the great thinker of the eighteenth century and for François Guizot as the eminent historian of his own time.[3] The breadth of Solovyev's interest is characteristic. Unlike many historians, especially of the later generation, he demonstrated an amazing knowledge of universal history. He was also excellently versed in European history and culture, in the broadest sense, and was a keen student of ancient civilization.

On his return from Western Europe in 1844, Solovyev was appointed to the faculty of the University of Moscow to teach Russian history, a chair formerly held by his recently retired teacher, Pogodin. As lecturer and writer, Solovyev stood forth as the champion of the theory of national development as an "organic whole"; he was a determined opponent of the old periodizations in Russian history, whether Norman, Mongolian, appanage, or any other. All "epochs," "periods," and "eras," he maintained, were misleading, artificial, and only obscured any view of the organic unity of historic events. The first obligation of historical science, he taught, was to cast overboard all notions of epochs; instead of dividing history, one should stress continuity throughout the centuries of national development. "People live, develop according to certain laws, and pass certain ages as individuals, just as all living organisms do." In recording the past, Solovyev insisted, one must show how the separate components of the past came together to form the organic present. History is never aware of beginnings and ends; every event is rooted in the past and projects into the future. There was no "Norman period" because the Normans were soon absorbed by the Slavs; there was neither a "Mongolian" nor an "appanage" period because the process of organic growth never ceased.

This new view was bound to leave indelible marks on the development of Russian historiography. The historian was warned never to overlook the dramatic unity in the course of past events. With such a design, Solovyev set out to rewrite history, and in 1851 the first volume of his famous *History of Russia from Earliest Times* appeared. In the next twenty-eight years there followed volume after volume, twenty-nine altogether, ending with the date 1774. His original project was to lead up to the nineteenth century, which would have required at least six more volumes; death, interrupting the author in the middle of a sentence, prevented the completion of the plan.[4]

As the immense tapestry of Russian history is unrolled, Solovyev does not limit the pattern to simple recording of events but tries to elucidate these by tracing their origins and linking their correlations, then derive plausible conclusions. According to Solovyev three conditions mold the history of a people: the character of the natural environment in which the people settle; the character of the people, or the "national physiognomy"; and the external pressures to which the people are subjected. He made an analysis of the social, economic, and political forces and of the geographic environment that contributed to the changes in society, beginning with the time when ancient Slavic tribes lived, as he thought, along the Danube; then he proceeded with the development by which the Slavs were forced eastward by some other people to a totally bare and inhospitable territory, later to become known as Russia, and left behind them the fertile and strategically more convenient lands.

Scattered along the Dniester, Dnieper, and Oka rivers, they required a long time for readjustment, while constant invasions of Asian hordes from the east and bitter rivalry with Poland and Lithuania along the western frontiers made progress difficult and slow. Whereas in Western Europe nature served as the mother of the people, in Eastern Europe nature was destined to be their callous stepmother. Herein lay the main reason for Russia's backwardness and her desperate need for centralized authority to control the "fluid condition." The more favorable geographic position of the Muscovite principality aided its political growth. Being farther away from immediate danger and exploiting every occasion for consolidating its power at the expense of its weaker neighbors, this principality gradually laid the foundation for the future Moscow state, from which the Russian Empire was eventually to arise.[5]

Moscow's destiny was shaped not only by exceptionally able leaders, but also by strategic advantages and favorable material resources. Personalities interested Solovyev only to a small extent, for he could never admit that history stemmed solely from the operation of personal force; nor did he believe that the dynamics of national history involved either blind force or destiny, for only human will added shape and meaning to the course of national life. The so-called era of Peter I therefore becomes only an accelerated course of events derived from preceding developments. The new course is determined by pressure forces of an internal and external nature. Nothing is accidental, since no historic event begins suddenly or ends abruptly; the new begins at a time when the old is still continuing. Ivan IV was instrumental in delivering a fatal blow to the old Boyar class that had already been receding from the scene of national history. Circumstances forced Peter I to leadership in a struggle for a cause already determined before his ascendancy.

Solovyev developed his thesis concerning the rise of the Russian state somewhat as follows. State and nation, he explained, are inseparable, the one deriving from the other; the history of Russia is a history of its government. National leaders do not rise by accident, since they are products of their times and social environment: their caliber is measured by the nation they stem from, and the nation by the part it plays in history. The influence of Hegel and Ranke is obvious; Solovyev read Hegel's *Philosophy of History* avidly, absorbing every thought, and later incorporated it as part of his entire outlook on history. In the presence of the broad conception and logical deductions Solovyev had made, the works of the earlier writers were bound to be superseded by the new pattern of interpretation. Solovyev boldly attacked Karamzin at a time when his nine-volume work was still considered officially as the last word in Russian historiography. Nor did he ingratiate himself with the Slavophiles when he warned against their idealization of the past, defined it as "Buddhism in the science of history," and described it as philosophical stagnation.

It was the first time that a history of Russia had been conceived on such a scale, with the narrative based always on the authentic source and held fast to the principle of pure, objective truth. In this comprehensive conception both of history and of the nation in all aspects of its life, Solovyev emphasized three main factors—political, religious, and cultural—and found their expression in "loyalty to the state, devotion to the church, and struggle for enlightenment." Peter I, that "rebel on the throne," fascinated Solovyev on account of the reforms he himself had witnessed during his own lifetime. As he observed the oncoming reaction to the reforms of the 1860s and compared Alexander II with Peter I and other historical personalities, Solovyev commented: "Fate did not send Alexander II a Richelieu or a Bismarck, but it is doubtful that he would have been capable of using a Richelieu or a Bismarck. Alexander had pretenses; he was a weak man who feared to appear weak or dependent. Compelled by fear, he would, one beautiful morning, have expelled both Richelieu and Bismarck." All in all, to Solovyev Russian history seems to have appeared as a linear process. There is almost a touch of historical fatalism in this process. By an additional stretch one could even trace a touch of mechanical materialism in the picture. Environmental conditions had eliminated man from social change.

Furthermore, Solovyev's emphasis on cultural development was in accordance with the prevailing tendency of historical writing in Western Europe. His main thesis of depicting Russia's history against a background that ranged beyond mere national limitations also brought him closer to the philosophy of the westerners. At the same time his broad knowledge of his subject and his strictly critical approach to every problem of his work won respect even among those who could not agree with his contention. Yet even Solovyev himself never considered his work, to which he had devoted his whole life, as final; he regarded it only as a tool to be used in clearing the future way for a closer, fuller, and perhaps more penetrating study of Russian historical development.[6]

Solovyev's last volumes particularly are based on sources obtained in the St. Petersburg and Moscow archives that were either unknown or not previously utilized. In many respects the voluminous work represents an encyclopedia of the nation's growth rather than a "narrative of bygone years." In this fact lies its merit as well as its weakness. One of its shortcomings is that, notwithstanding the author's insistence on "organic unity," his twenty-nine-volume work, not to mention other studies, constitute amassed material laced with Hegelian design without adequate integration. Solovyev himself had described his work as only a tool for later scholars, and we may add, it still offers enough raw material to be well worth consulting. The numerous documents cited by Solovyev and formerly unpublished are of considerable value to this day. Solovyev was not gifted with a speculative mind: whatever was obscure he omitted, and he never indulged in hypothetical interpretations. This is the main reason, says Klyuchevsky, that Solovyev's history contains so little "learned trash" and may explain also why the author has been labeled a "dry historian."[7]

Solovyev lacked the literary gift and the architectonic skill of Klyuchevsky, nor did he have the time to be concerned either with style or with design; he was occupied with "pick and shovel" labor, composing largely for the student of history rather than for the average reader. Solovyev is truly a historian's historian, for how else could he have produced a twenty-nine-volume historical account, several extensive monographs, and numerous essays? He never dwelt in an ivory tower but always responded to current issues, lectured, and contributed numerous articles during the agitated period of reforms. "Life," he said on one occasion, "has its full right to present questions to science and science has the obligation to answer questions of life."

After his death Solovyev left a mass of raw material with numerous threads dangling at loose ends. It became the task of his pupil and successor, the true *Geschichtsmaler*, Klyuchevsky, to weave these threads together into an original design, embodying in his historical writings of supreme excellence a summary of all the efforts of Russian historians, beginning with Tatishchev in the eighteenth century. It fell to the later generation of writers to utilize the broad outlines of Solovyev's philosophy for further studies comparing Russian and Western European institutions, such as serfdom and feudalism. The greatest contribution Solovyev made to historical science was to map the road for those who detected in history a universal design. The path of development, as Solovyev saw it, was not a regular one, to be sure: at times it followed zigzags, sometimes it simply kept retracing itself, occasionally it either retreated or advanced, but in the end it always demonstrated a relentless surge forward. Solovyev's pilgrimage through the maze of materials set to work for Klyuchevsky, Pavlov-Silvansky, and others who with greater success sought the pattern of events rather than accepting history as simply a "tissue of disconnected accidents."[8]

The Juridical School

Before we take up the next eminent figure in Russian historiography, we might pause for brief mention of two writers connected with the so-called Juridical School. This school played a vital part in crystallizing the historical consciousness of the time, contributed to the vital debates conducted during the period, and helped to answer the frequent query "What is history?"

K. D. Kavelin and B. N. Chicherin can be considered the founders of the Juridical School. The main view of both men can be summarized as the belief that the masses played either no part or only a minor role in the shaping of history. Historical processes were in fact shaped mainly by the state; the state represents the force behind history and stands above all classes. Acting in the interests of all classes, the Juridical School argued, the state is compelled to use power as it considers wisest or most necessary for the sake of society's welfare. Accordingly, history is a continuous transformation of juridical forms and social changes. Hence the main change such as from the most primitive social existence to a more modern state system is the natural course of history.

In 1846 appeared the work of K. D. Kavelin, an analytical study of juridical conditions in early Russia. The study came to serve as the theoretical background of the forthcoming Juridical School among historians. In 1856 followed the thesis that further elaborated the subject, by B. N. Chicherin, stressing mainly the subject of regional institutions during the eighteenth century in Russia. Two years later his work on Russian law appeared and, finally, a decade later, his interpretation of "popular representation." The combined work of Kavelin and Chicherin formed the basis of what came to be known as the juridical point of view in Russian historiography.

The juridical philosophy left a definite mark, first, on Solovyev, as can be seen in the extensive writings in which he interpreted the entire process as a natural legal development with the state as the most decisive central factor. The same school left a noticeable impact on other prominent writers such as V. O. Klyuchevsky, V. I. Sergeyevich, A. D. Gradovsky, throughout the second half of the nineteenth century. It was for this reason that we pause shortly for a reference to Kavelin and Chicherin, the founders of the juridical interpretation of history, before we continue with the successor of Solovyev, V. O. Klyuchevsky.

KAVELIN

Konstantin Dmitriyevich Kavelin (1818-1885) has been justly considered as one of the founders of the Juridical School in Russia. Soviet historiographers regard him as the historian, jurist, sociologist, publicist, and bourgeois-liberal ideologist. In his earlier years he favored the philosophy of the Westerners, was a friend of A. Herzen, and in the fifties advocated emancipation of the serfs.[9] He published his views in the currently liberal magazine, *The Contemporary* (*Sovremennik*) and for this his professorship at the University of St. Petersburg was terminated. With the advance of years Kavelin began to shed his former "radicalism," to the distress of Herzen.

In his earliest work, *A Survey of Political Conditions in Early Russian History*, published in 1846, Kavelin already expressed some views that strongly influenced historical writing of his day, including that of Solovyev. The essence of it was that all historical processes result from the cumulative and communal efforts of preceding periods of a nation's past. National development is in essence an organic process based on relentless, immutable laws that neither the individual genius nor historical incident is able to offset. Only the genius of the people can ultimately shape the destiny of a nation—never a national leader. Very much as the *Iliad* and the *Odyssey* represent products of the collective genius of the Greek people, so is social life the product of the collective rather than of the individual effort, no matter how preeminent the individual may be.

With the advance of years Kavelin began to show signs of retreat from his former views. Thus in 1862 Kavelin published a pamphlet in which he expressed strong support for the monarchy and opposition to any form of constitutionalism. He favored the preservation of the peasant commune, valued the benefits rendered by the Orthodox faith, and showed militant opposition to nihilism or any other form of materialism.[10] A clearer statement appeared in 1867 concerning Kavelin's philosophy of history. The essay appeared in the form of an article in the *Herald of Europe* (*Vestnik Evropy*), in which Kavelin expounded his Hegelian view of the nature of the state. The state represented, according to Kavelin, the symbol of national evolution, of peaceful advancement. In essence it constituted the heart and core of the "juridical" interpretation of history. Bearing this in mind, we can now proceed with the philosophy of the Juridical School and see what influence it had on many historians and their writings.

Kavelin placed little stress on economic or cultural aspects of national growth. The emphasis of his interpretation was on the "immutable laws" that control the historical process or changes that a society is bound to undergo.[11] The fundamental law of history, Kavelin believed, was the organic growth and transformation of a community from a loosely knit tribe into a modern state. The reign of Ivan IV, according to Kavelin, heralded the rise of the Russian state, while Peter I expressed its final form. To use Kavelin's formula, Ivan served the state as the poet, Peter as the practical statesman. In its development toward the highest form of social organization, society must go through three stages: the tribal, the patrimonial, and finally, the institutional form. To Kavelin the first symbolized the primitive step, leading to the family, while the last marked the formation of the modern nation.

In brief, the history of a society is entirely a part of the history of the state; only in the latter can one find the key to an understanding of the hidden forces that mold a nation. The process naturally has its ramifications, but historical law relentlessly drives society toward its goals; resistance to this law explains the social unrest that occurs from time to time in history. It was

иноталь платити, чемлибо҃е. А ги҃ вꙋ хоꙋфіе понꙗ же, или
оꙋрекше. иного офеннаго тали не гоꙋ штинеꙗ. гоꙋ штꙗ от всего городꙋ ть.
землꙗ оꙋ нанаꙗ пашнꙗ крони је омефꙋ. А что оꙋ ретым мефꙋ.
нани галинис еꙗе. из великих боꙗ ке Землꙗ, боꙗ рꙗ нанꙗ мꙗ наст нꙗ ꙗ или
боꙗ рес сон. нꙗ моꙗ на ест писсꙗ он. от селꙗ на сих ꙗ Землꙗ н. или вꙗ бꙗ лꙗ сон,
нꙗ монасты сꙗ он на бꙗ менꙗ. или бꙗ лꙗ рес сꙗ он монꙗ на ест писꙗ ꙗ. ни то
мефос оꙗ га, при гꙗ линис с вꙗ. или то ки тꙗ писꙗ нꙗ стꙗ лꙗ. А лиса вꙗ зꙗ
тꙗ на нем вꙗ оꙗ ꙗ. А хенꙗ ст пꙗꙗ не Про мефꙋ ꙗ е бꙗ помꙗ н поꙗ ест нꙗ. или
се лꙗ ть. к тꙗ бꙗ гꙗ на гꙗ ме фꙗ ги ресꙗ е. или ти пересꙗ есꙗ, или не поꙗ л оꙗ ст нꙗ лꙗ ꙗ,
нани то селꙗ сꙗ он. или мꙗ тꙗ нꙗ тꙗ ꙗ м за бꙗ гꙗ по сꙗ дꙗ лꙗ тꙗ нꙗ. или вꙗ оꙗ гꙗ нꙗ ꙗ
Пом сꙋ дꙋ ꙗ по смотꙗ тꙗ ꙗ почꙗ нꙗ. и по сꙗ лꙗ нꙗ тꙗ и по рꙗ лꙗ с оꙋ ꙋ фꙗ енꙗ ꙗ о. о зꙗ
мꙗ дꙗ сꙗ оꙋ. А. азꙋ нꙗ щꙋ стꙗ бꙗ ꙗ гꙗ нꙗ кꙗ а бꙗ менꙗ гꙗ. нꙗ ни мꙗ на ест писꙗ ꙗ ꙗ мꙗ
на ест писꙗ ет. нани бꙗ лꙗ рес сꙗ он нꙗ мꙗ на ест писꙗ ет. или мꙗ на ест пꙗ сꙗ он нꙗ ꙗ ꙗ
дꙗ ренꙗ. или но сꙗ тꙗ нꙗ за тꙗ нꙗ гꙗ дꙗ ꙗ. А дꙗ лꙗ ст пꙗ гꙗ одꙗ нꙗ ес сꙗ пꙗ нꙗ. или зꙗ
цꙗ е чꙗ нꙗ он нꙗ чꙗ нꙗ он мꙗ. нани тꙗ мꙗ ст писꙗ нꙗ с нꙗ по Пꙗ м оꙗ чꙗ ни ꙗ е. за сꙗ тꙗ пꙗ ꙗ
зꙗ мꙗ лꙗ нꙗ гꙗ лꙗ нꙗ оꙗ кꙗ и ꙗ. или нꙗ тꙗ е мꙗ он, нани сꙗ ꙗ сꙗ он. к а пꙗ мꙗ е чꙗ нꙗ е. или нꙗ тꙗ о
мꙗ чꙗ нꙗ вꙗ нꙗ а чꙗ ернꙗ ꙗ, у на с лꙗ е с с с кꙗ ꙗ мꙗ. и но сꙗ тꙗ нꙗ по томꙗ за тꙗ пꙗ ен гꙗ одꙗ ꙗ.
А дꙗ лꙗ ст пꙗ гꙗ одꙗ нꙗ ес сꙗ пꙗ нꙗ. А азꙋ нꙗ щꙋ нꙗ а бꙗ менꙗ гꙗ нꙗ ть. нани ни мꙗ онꙗ нꙗ ꙗ сꙗ тꙗ ꙗ
рꙗ нꙗ се лꙗ нꙗ оꙗ кꙗ нꙗ а бꙗ менꙗ гꙗ нꙗ. или но сꙗ тꙗ нꙗ за щꙗ е ст пꙗ лꙗ ꙗ. А дꙗ лꙗ нꙗ ес сꙗ ꙗ пꙗ нꙗ.
А по тꙗ е бꙗ е зꙗ мꙗ лꙗ нꙗ за пꙗ ен ст пꙗ гꙗ о се бꙗ ꙗ ть. и пꙗ тꙗ зꙗ мꙗ лꙗ нꙗ ресꙗ омꙗ фꙗ ꙗ пꙗ ꙗ тꙗ нꙗ
дꙗ Пересꙋ чꙗ нꙗ цꙗ, пересꙗ ꙗ. или мꙗ тꙗ нꙗ нꙗ а нꙗ нꙗ о а пꙗ тꙗ мꙗ ꙗ чꙗ сꙗ тꙗ нꙗ нꙗ. А мꙗ е шꙗ ꙗ
е вꙗ тꙗ лꙗ ꙗ Пересꙗ кꙗ а нꙗ вꙗ оꙋ тꙗ ꙗ. А се пꙗ нꙗ е нꙗ сꙗ е гꙗ оꙋ нꙗ ꙗ о. не хꙗ а лꙗ опꙗ а не вꙗ земꙗ лꙗ нꙗ

in accord with this law that Kavelin conceived the rise of the Muscovite state. So far his views coincided with those of Solovyev; thereafter, however, Kavelin formulated an independent idea that became basic to the Juridical School. Whereas Solovyev believed that the centralized Russian state had evolved largely because of a number of favorable historical coincidences, Kavelin insisted that a state had to emerge as a historical inevitability, since society cannot escape the prescribed course "from the tribal stage with its form of communal ownership, to the family with its patrimonial estate or separate ownership, to the individual within the modern state."[12]

One more detail is perhaps worth noting. The rise of the state in Russia, as Kavelin saw it, differed from the ascendancy of the state in Western Europe. Whereas in the West the process emanated "from below," in Russia it had emerged "from above." Though in both Western and Eastern Europe the state arrived at the same goal, their historical paths differed. Here Kavelin's view coincided with that of Chicherin. Kavelin accepted the contention that Russia was a "peasant state"; yet his faith in the peasant masses had always been thin, gnawed away by skepticism. To Kavelin the peasantry was nothing but an "ethnographic protoplasm" that held out no more than a promise of national life. For this reason Kavelin favored a strong, centralized, monarchical authority as the only form of government capable of preserving national life.

Kavelin's interpretation seemed too dogmatic to many students of history. The Slavophiles frowned on a philosophy that professed little faith in a communal form of social organization. Later, V. I. Sergeyevich carried the theory farther by maintaining that the state came into being, not because of historical laws, but by virtue of a civil contract between the prince and the assembly, or *veche*.[13] He defined two stages in the development of the state: in the first, individual will was supreme, and in the second stage, sovereignty of the state superseded individual free will. Sergeyevich was followed later by Klyuchevsky and Kostomarov; whereas Sergeyevich approached the problem with an eye mainly on the socioeconomic aspects, the latter two concentrated on its ethnography, and thus, little was left of Kavelin's laboriously erected theory. Whatever the validity of each of the philosophical contentions, cumulatively they stimulated historical research, tempered the will to scholarly pursuits, aroused curiosity about the past, and compelled many to publish what was considered to be newly discovered historical truth. This development barred any static faith in "eternal verities" and agitated a cultural alertness in the country as never before.

CHICHERIN

Hegelian philosophy and the German school of Ranke, Niebuhr, Eichhorn, and Savigny influenced many historians in Russia. The writings of Boris Nikolayevich Chicherin (1828-1904), a contemporary of Solovyev, may be cited as the best illustration of this influence. The stress on the role of the state, in the development of a nation, could already be noted in the writings of others. It gave rise to the trend in Russian historiography known as the Juridical School, as we have already seen. The basic idea of this school, as we pointed out, was that behind the entire historical development of the nation had always been the state. The state, accordingly, represents "the highest form of national life" or national development; the obscure concept of nationality assumes concrete form in the embodiment of the state. The most prominent member of this school, besides Kavelin, was Chicherin, author of numerous works all of which contain some aspect of the same thesis.[14]

Chicherin was a cultured man who had a keen interest as well as knowledge in many fields. He was an eminent jurist, a political scientist, a philosopher, and a historian. He favored constitutional monarchy and was an outspoken opponent of Marxism. He favored peasant emancipation and all the reforms derived from such legislation. It was his theory of the state that made Chicherin the leading figure in the Juridical School. His central theme was that the beginning of the Russian state marked the beginning of history; the formation of the state came while the people represented nothing but a "lonely, wandering face" and played only a passing or opposing part in the process.

From the day of the Muscovite Principality and throughout subsequent events the initiative always emanated from the center, from the sovereign authority that acted as the moving spirit of national will and unity. The role of the middle class, according to Chicherin, was to serve as the ballast to keep the ship of state on an even keel. It was this class that acted as an instrument of social leveling, a factor evenly distributing wealth within the nation and thereby precluding extremes of either wealth or poverty. The strength of the state was determined by the role the masses played; the less they interfered in public affairs, the more chance there was for the state to fulfill its mission.

Developments within a society were determined not by economic production and class rivalry, but by the actual needs of the state. Chicherin even traced the origin of the institution of serfdom directly and exclusively to the interests of the state, while the privileges of the landed aristocracy came as a by-product and were entirely accidental. The dominant fact was service of *all*, in whatever form it might be, to the state. The conclusion was that the parent of all institutions within a society was the state; it was within the power of the state to retain, alter, or abolish any institution it chose.

At times his philosophy led Chicherin to rather curious generalization, which tested the patience of the rising liberal elements in the country. He explained the "invitation" of the Normans or Varangians, for example, by the fact that the Slavs were always noted not only for their inability to get along among themselves but also for their readiness to sacrifice themselves for their land and sovereign. Needless to say, the view was not a palatable one to the younger generation of his later life. On the other hand, as a mild liberal—though of a proud, old aristocratic family—he came to be regarded by the authorities as politically "unreliable." In 1868 he resigned as professor of history of law at the University of Moscow in protest against the policy of the administration and returned to his native estate in Tambov, where he devoted most of his time to local administration. In 1881 he was elected mayor of the city of Moscow, a post that proved of short duration: by an order of Alexander II he was dismissed two years later after he assumed office. The reason for this curt action was a speech that Chicherin delivered at a gathering of city mayors in which he urged the "united action of all local governments to assure the welfare of Russia." The career of Chicherin manifested the plight of even the mildly liberal elements, the anguish of inner conflicts that the Russian intelligentsia had suffered during the last decades in the past century; men were torn between lingering and deep-seated loyalties to the past and budding enthusiasm for the future.

The period dealt with last coincides with the "Era of Great Reforms" in Russia. It was a time when the study of law and institutions in the nation was stimulated by manifold developments. This was a period that subsequently produced a legion of scholars of history, men such as A. D. Gradovsky, N. M. Korkunov, M. A. Dyakonov, A. V. Romanovich-Slavatinsky, or B. E. Nolde, who investigated Russian institutions; others, like M. F. Vladimirsky-Budanov or S. B. Veselovsky, who made a comparative study of Russian public law and financial legislation; a third group, typified by A. S. Lappo-Danilevsky, who distinguished themselves in the field of diplomatics; and still others, such as M. K. Lyubavsky, who contributed to the

… всѣх доли. Але полна со всемъ по госпожею. Ле писанъ об офни надоло пол летписма натца дру. И но по томъ пере сроу. А тшаонъ сии пра па по де се миа д

…ет А ни матиннинна пла топре. А наис по го годь бу въ веде на ни тни кв. и лн на поло сти да сь поло стисл. и ни вни датти по шли нни по семстей сисъ. иъ за и нмо та на мъ тинни. Ле тип соо но мти, за и но тип добна. нин сети да ель по по винна, о полнои грамо тпе. Попо нон гра мотти холоп. По тпи сеа ме стиа о. И пи ли чю по селе скем холи о. за р кла мон ки дро сла дъ. нс бо рое нои не въ тпи. ко тороге са иного дрру. Хипо рое иие сей бе даръ пои гу иите. Напсе бу чи мъ фн тпи, топе холо тни. А по торе щио иу клю чено холоп. По сак холо, По холоп тъ воеду. Пен д мои холотй. Под хо снои холоп, А по се буду, И ни по сла ще ети нетъ. А пел пои про сии ннех, По тпо томъ дъ на мо сии тъ. Ко виет Тогорд те ме си осей о земли. И ни по ло боющи се земли. И по пе т во лости за по те дра лети. Летп вои нре мъ ни поу тни сие. со дия мъ ви пен стиа о. посе важ не соа ни ли пе даръ. А посе лу ха мъ вне пи дру ни по слу ще ети по дрти. А ни дру тъ и се сти за тпи по ла дъ. А посе лу ще ети под посе ла кло фни се не пцад ъ. Хи ви ще тпелтпо ши по се елтъ. И но на по томъ по се ло хе пь Пь ве лни це сио нсл, не то Го тип ои о об торе пои по ши нну, А по ли пеи тре сио нни чен, ико тъ но со кни чем пру дру. А ве тре ои нсе се. И нъ сеи ни нь тпи нно. Кпо за нни мие тер лу тпи чен, И по дру нни вы, ни во бо сиа фо у тпъ за со ко во стери чн. И пору чни ко. Нн мъ тпъ ем Ле сел ва тпи ни под дтпи. А дрети хъ на дрениио. И не холо по сти те дру тпи нмъ И пору чни но о у ве бъ ме дсф тпи.

field of historical geography, particularly with regard to the formation of the Muscovite state and its relations to the medieval Grand Duchy of Lithuania. In the field of historical science they marked a vibrant era in Russia.

The towering figure among these writers was Alexander Dmitriyevich Gradovsky (1841-1889), who through his interest in Western political institutions came to advocate the principles of legality and political liberty.[15] To Gradovsky history was mainly a matter of legal development; he viewed Russia's past largely through the development of local institutions, as their functions coordinated or conflicted with those of the national agencies. As a professor at the University of St. Petersburg, Gradovsky left a considerable following among the former students; of these some were destined to become world-renowned jurists, like N. Tagantsev in the field of criminal law and F. Martens in international law.[16]

Bestuzhev-Ryumin

The list of nineteenth-century historians would be incomplete without the names of Bestuzhev-Ryumin and one of his pupils, S. F. Platonov. Konstantin Nikolayevich Bestuzhev-Ryumin (1829-1897), pupil of Pogodin, Granovsky, and Solovyev, and great admirer of Karamzin, was among the first to steer an independent course through the stormy sea created by the Slavophiles and Westerners of the 1840s and 1850s.[17] He was more of a critic than a historian, more of an eclectic idealist than an original thinker, an observer rather than a warrior—and therefore a less colorful figure than his teachers. Conservative, noncommittal, scholastically sterile, adhering to no particular school, he naturally had no historical Pleiad of his own and his disciples were not many; among them, the most distinguished was the late S. F. Platonov, of whom more will be said later.

Of noble birth and refined education, Bestuzhev-Ryumin entered academic life with an impressive intellectual baggage, though, as he himself humbly stated, it was rather "chaotic," or in the words of Pushkin, he had learned "something and somehow." His knowledge was not limited to history alone, but embraced also the fine arts, literature, theology, and philosophy; and he possessed no meager knowledge of the Russian chronicles. Bestuzhev-Ryumin matured amid the restless decades of the era of Nicholas I, when Westernism and Slavophilism were in full armor against each other. He absorbed much from both camps, though for the rest of his life he sentimentally leaned toward Slavophile nationalism.

As professor of history of the University of St. Petersburg and member of the Academy of Sciences, Bestuzhev-Ryumin always maintained that the historian must be impartial, giving nothing but the facts.[18] The duty of a historian, he taught, must be to gather carefully verified factual material and put it together without embellishments of "social processes." The basis of national history, he further taught, was the "complex phenomenon called society." To present it accurately one must be objective about the social components of society and the factors that held the community together: social authority, government, judicial institutions, social classes, religion, cultural standards, trade industry, and the institution of the family. Platonov recalled that Bestuzhev-Ryumin particularly endeavored to impress this principle on his pupils. The insistence on complete objectivity at times involved Bestuzhev-Ryumin in incidents not much to his credit, such as in the case of Semevsky, to be discussed later. It all indicates how precarious such an attitude may become when applied without either imaginative daring or a sense of humor.

Bestuzhev-Ryumin was a true product of the early Germanic school of Schlözer, in which authenticity and unbiased narration of the past were the highest arts of historical writing. It can be truly said that before Bestuzhev-Ryumin "every bird lay unfeathered." Is it any wonder that he was over-shadowed by such a giant as Solovyev and such an artist as Klyuchevsky? Today Bestuzhev-Ryumin is a half-forgotten man, an object of curiosity to the student of Russian historiography, or a symbol of his time. Yet, in all fairness, the student of history must pay due tribute to Bestuzhev-Ryumin for his able analysis of the chronicles and biographical sketches of Karamzin and Pogodin, which, though written in a panegyric vein, characterize the political milieu of the author as well as the climate of the time.

In his *Russian History*, Bestuzhev-Ryumin endeavored to follow the pattern he taught his students; he emphasized methodology and authenticity of utilized sources and refrained from delivery of a "message" or of philosophical summations. Klyuchevsky's amazing skill at painting on an immense canvas was alien to the nature of Bestuzhev-Ryumin. Yet his cold-hearted objectivity or callous detachment gave way before sentimental loyalty to admired personalities, manifested best in his *Biographical Sketches*. His two-volume history of Russia, leading up to the death of Ivan IV, is an incomplete work that he planned to extend through the nineteenth century. He also translated Henry T. Buckle's master work, *The History of Civilization in England.* Of all his works the *Biographical Sketches* is the most quoted, while all other seemed to rest in oblivion in historical literature.

Klyuchevsky

Karamzin was the first historian to present a portrait of Russia on a grand scale and in an imperial style. By the end of the last century Karamzin's grandiose work was in the dustbin of history. After more than three decades Solovyev's massive work began to emerge, more suitable to students of history than to the general reader. Neither Karamzin nor Solovyev was endowed with the rare gift, or even with the depth and "rational enthusiasm," to turn out national history in the fullest sense. Solovyev simply plowed a fertile field, but the sowing and particularly the reaping of the harvest were left for someone else. Karamzin's history was flashingly patriotic. Solovyev's literary style was not his forte, nor did he have the time to polish it. His patriotism was rational, his method as cool as a scalpel. It took another decade before Klyuchevsky came to the scene to enrich the field with a general history of Russia as well as with a variety of monographic studies. All of these revealed a literary gift hardly found previously in historiography. Klyuchevsky presented the past in poetic prose; he represented a rare combination of critic, pragmatist, and artist all wrapped in one. He had a genius to extract from the past fascinating contents, pragmatic interpretation, national valor or individual eminence, all presented in an artistic style.

The name of Vasily Osipovich Klyuchevsky (1841-1911) is a landmark in Russian historiography. He was born on January 16, 1841, in the small village of Voskresenskoye, near the town of Penza. As the son of a parish priest, it was only proper that his initial education would be mainly reading the Bible and mastering Church Slavonic. Klyuchevsky's ancestry is traced to a long line of churchmen. His father, a village priest, managed on a very modest annual income. When the future historian was hardly nine years of age, his father was killed in an accident. Later, Klyuchevsky, referring to his childhood, retrospectively considered it a mere "irrevocable flicker" in his life.[19] The shock must have been so profound that, as Nechkina plausibly presumes, the episode caused the young lad to have a lifelong stammer.

It may also be noted that Klyuchevsky's youth was spent mostly in rural communities. The villages of the Penza district were noted neither for their affluence, nor for adequate living conditions among the peasantry. In his youth Klyuchevsky saw areas where the soil was exhausted, the tilling primitive, the toil often unrewarding, and the combination hardly afforded the peasantry more than a bare existence. This milieu also included the parish priest. This is where the historian was to obtain his firsthand knowledge of the economic plight of the Russian peasantry, of rural realities.

In the 1850s, when Klyuchevsky witnessed the tragedy in his family, the decay of serfdom, and the Crimean disaster, the events must have cumulatively left the sensitive youth with lasting impressions of rural poverty and national humiliation. Then followed the "Era of Great Reforms," creeping industrialism with all its political and social implications, the gathering storm within and without, conflicts in the Near East, and eventually the fiasco in the Far East, not to mention the gathering storm in the west—such was the drama Klyuchevsky had experienced, had observed with an uneasy premonition.

In many ways Klyuchevsky was the product of his time, of his family sorrows, and of the national critical decades. As he himself once remarked in one of his lectures: "I am a man of the nineteenth century by sheer chance; fate erroneously forgot to remove me in proper time."[20] But Klyuchevsky was by no means a mere nineteenth-century "leftover": he was an intellectual of his time par excellence. In addition he was excellently versed in theology, but by nature somewhat skeptical on various occasions and more often a loner. Though he spent most of his life in Moscow, by heart he was more at home in rural Russia; though a *popovich*, that is, the son of a priest, one often senses in him a member of the Third Estate. Klyuchevsky could not help observing the encroaching changes in Russian society, at times with academic detachment, occasionally with ill-concealed fear.

Klyuchevsky entered the ecclesiastical seminary in Penza in 1856. Here, aside from such required fields as Greek, Latin, Hebrew, he studied modern history. Russian history was simply a narrative "from czar to czar and war to war," while other events were barely touched upon if mentioned at all. Yet Klyuchevsky had a special interest in history, while theology and related subjects seemed to him of relatively small importance. After some agonizing contemplation and weighing, he determined to drop out of the seminary and go to Moscow to study history. Having overcome some serious obstacles to depart from the seminary, he finally succeeded in wresting permission to withdraw and left for Moscow.

At the University of Moscow Klyuchevsky was fortunate in finding a few remaining academic luminaries of the old guard, but above all, Professor S. M. Solovyev, who was at that time in the prime of his popularity. The man deeply impressed young Klyuchevsky, and it was through this teacher that Klyuchevsky arrived at his broad vision of history, learned the necessary skill of mastering sources, and gained a sense of purpose in the historical process that did not permit the past to turn into an aimless flow of events as it seemed in so many other accounts.

Klyuchevsky found Solovyev most absorbing, and the teacher left a deep imprint upon his pupil. What impressed young Klyuchevsky most in the course offered by Solovyev was the "wholeness," and the flowing continuity in his presentation of the past centuries. To Klyuchevsky the student Solovyev was the man he longed for. Later Klyuchevsky described him as the lecturer who neither moved nor fascinated the audience, neither stirred nor stimulated, but the historical embroidery was unforgettable. Each of his lectures was an audible thought, a visualized picture that would run through the mind of every listener for a long time. The merit of Solovyev, according to Klyuchevsky, was the rare pedagogical gift, possessed by few lecturers, not of stimulating by didactics or methodology, but of inspiring by a method derived from some deeper subconscious source.

At the suggestion of Solovyev, Klyuchevsky came to consider several projects, including a study of the accounts of foreign travelers in the Muscovite state. Another, his master's thesis, was on the lives of early Russian saints as a source of history. A third project dealt with the Solovetsky monastery as a factor in the economic development of northern Russia, a study that later confirmed the expected results of Solovyev.[21]

We must mention, albeit briefly, some of Klyuchevsky's more notable studies, before taking up his general history of Russia. One is the *Lives of Early Russian Saints as a Source of History*. Perhaps the greatest value of this study of early religious personalities is to be found in the voluminous biographical data as well as in the newly uncovered documentary materials extracted from private depositories in Moscow and elsewhere, particularly the library of Count A. S. Uvarov. Furthermore, the study also included the interpretation of the inner national forces that lay behind the surge toward expansion. Klyuchevsky maintained that it was mainly population growth and environmental condition that acted as the dynamic forces to territorial expansion.

The second monograph that deserves mention is Klyuchevsky's *Accounts of Foreigners Concerning the Muscovite State*. This impressive study stands out for its systematization of widely scattered material, for the uncovering of previously neglected details all ably utilized for a synthesized narrative. It also represents an innovation in Russian historiography as one of the first studies to present a modern interpretation, casting aside the early romantic style of Karamzin and the lifeless matter-of-fact presentation of Solovyev. Not only was the work written in an attractive literary style, enriched by the colorful "Penza manner of speech," but it is supported throughout by firsthand source material. The integration of massive material in the essay within the limited period of time allowed represents a monument to the author's efficiency. Finally, it could be added, from a historiographic point of view, Klyuchevsky introduced into Russian historical literature a subject that would hardly be considered proper either by his predecessors or his contemporaries—the economic aspects of national history, including trade, finance, population, national production, and the rise of towns.

Another of Klyuchevsky's notable monographic works is that on the Boyar Council in early Russia. This is a masterfully synthesized account of that political body from the tenth century, gradually leading up to the end of the seventeenth century. This study includes an extensive discussion of agricultural development, particularly in the South, as well as of trade expansion in the Northwest. The author also examined the Muscovite administration, the status of the prince, and the special Princely Guard made up mainly of the Boyar class and the "City Eldermen." It is a superbly synthesized survey, traced from the origin of the Boyar Council to its decline and total eclipse. The Juridical School considered the prince as the "sole moving power in national life"; Klyuchevsky gave the reader a different impression: the prince appeared at a time when the social order had already been crystallized by popular action prior to the establishment of princely authority.

While Klyuchevsky worked on these different monographic themes, he never overlooked the main theme of his interest, the overall story of Russia. He wanted to paint a broad design on a national canvas rather than concentrate on local details. Endowed with the vision and temperament of an artist, he was able only by self-discipline and determination to complete the studies originally undertaken—accounts of some old monasteries that bored him. Yet the tedious work was not wasted: it developed in Klyuchevsky qualities indispensable to historical research, infinite patience and analytical ability to scrutinize numerous sources, to sift much sand for a few grains of gold, as well as the capacity to take advantage of access to source materials never before utilized. It also enabled him to familiarize himself with a field rarely delved into by scholars—the relations between church and state in the realm of economic expansion of the Russian Empire.

We must return to the initial stages of Klyuchevsky's academic career. He began his academic advancement at the Alexandrian military school and at the University of Moscow for Women. It was here that he first demonstrated at once his exceptional ability as a lecturer, an aesthete, and a man with an unusual vision in presenting events or personalities emerging from dusty archival records. Within a few years Klyuchevsky had become known to such an extent that when his former teacher, Solovyev, became gravely ill in 1879, Klyuchevsky was given the chair in the field of Russian history. Many students at the University of Moscow at first looked askance at this young appointee, this teacher from a military school and a woman's university! Quickly, however, as one of his pupils recalls, his lectures became so popular that it was futile to offer anything else at the hours when Klyuchevsky lectured: he would simply empty all other auditoriums.[22]

What was so fascinating about this new faculty member? It was the breadth of his historical presentation, the wealth of his information, the lucid delivery of the lectures, the subtle humor he demonstrated occasionally. His broad cultural interests led him to a variety of activities. Klyuchevsky was an active member of the Moscow Archaeological Society. After continuous and persistent urging, he consented to lecture in 1900 at the School of Fine Arts, where he remained to his last days. His addresses on Fonvizin, Pushkin, and Lermontov, later published in the form of essays, bear witness to his profound familiarity with literature.[23] His essay on Lermontov, entitled "Melancholy" (*Grust'*), appeared in one of the leading periodicals, *Russkaya mysl'*, and did not bear his name, but Klyuchevsky's style was so characteristic (that rich, colorful Penza tongue!) that it betrayed the author quickly.

Our interest, however, must be focused on Klyuchevsky the historian, particularly on the *Course in Russian History* he had delivered at the university. The *Course* immediately revealed the genius of the lecturer and his gift to bring history alive to an auditorium. To this day it remains a monument to the art of both historical writing and Russian letters. He toiled over every single lecture with rare perseverance. On one occasion a group of students asked Klyuchevsky to deliver an address on the poet Nekrasov. He accepted the invitation; yet when he discovered that the address was to be delivered within a month, he withdrew his consent, explaining that one could not prepare himself within such a brief period. "It takes little time to deliver a lecture," Klyuchevsky explained, and "it does not take much time to write it either; but it takes a long time before the theme begins to 'nibble.' " He would not even think of less than six months' preparation.[24]

As stated above, the *Course in Russian History* is the result of Klyuchevsky's lectures delivered at the University of Moscow. As one reads the *Course*, as well as his other independent studies, the personality of the author stands out more fully. The general impression one gathers from this monumental work can be seen in the following fact. The author was neither a Westerner nor a Slavophile; he resolutely opposed blind Western imitation and would not accept the rather crude chauvinism of the opponents. His analytical evaluation of Peter's reforms is too well known and only confirms that Klyuchevsky was first, last, and always a historian. He did not merely derive from the distant and recent past "bygone events" in the sense of the old chronicler, but considered these as vital elements that molded the Russian nation. Klyuchevsky examined each process with the eye of a historian in order to fit it into a meaningful narrative of the course of Russian history. Though a severe critic of Peter I, he soberly evaluated the compelling reasons for his reforms while often questioning his alien, arbitrary conduct accompanied by the unbearable tax burdens and compulsory services in order to enforce modernization. He frankly exposed the thesis that princely as well as czarist authority and legislation often led to the enslavement of the peasantry in order to compensate the state-serving elements. He disliked and often lashed out against the artificial implanting of alien culture or foreign institutions that satisfied a minority and left out the vast majority, leaving the latter indifferent if not hostile to the edifice of the state.

Klyuchevsky came at a time when Slavophilism, Westernism, and Hegelianism were beginning to fade; the old feudal order was definitely passing and there was no lack of evidence that a new Russian was emerging from the recent profound changes the nation was undergoing. Thus

Klyuchevsky was in the advantageous position of one who could look back on time and on schools of thought that emerged and faded, and he made the best of his opportunity. In his work he considered the social strata of the past ten centuries of Russia horizontally: at the bottom, the "dark" peasant masses; at the top, the gentry nurtured physically by the peasantry and intellectually by French culture; while in between were the two other social groups that depend on both. These social layers were now antagonistic, now allied, as circumstances dictated. In his description of the process of social formation, certain concrete factors stand out: struggle for national unity, demands of national defense, longing for cultural development, or strife for economic security.[25] These factors make his narrative systematic, unique, and meaningful. The only criticism one can make is that the author gave little space to Russian foreign policy, emphasizing mainly the internal development of the empire; the Foreign Office occupies no place of prominence in Klyuchevsky's history. Even the Mongolian invasion is presented as an incidental experience in Russian history, a brief nightmare rather than a period of the nation's past. Nor did Klyuchevsky show any interest in problems of national minorities incorporated within the empire, not even the Ukrainian people. Klyuchevsky, we may say, was truly a "Great Russian" historian.

Klyuchevsky's approach to any past event was never that of the old logician-scientist with lancet poised to probe, but rather that of the keen, sympathetically intuitive psychologist; yet never did his rich and fertile imagination betray the scientific accuracy of his observation or his judgment. Therefore his generalizations remain usually sound, his characters emerge from the distant past clothed in flesh and blood, and the whole process of historical development becomes a vivid, integrated panorama. His striking accomplishment is his harmonization within himself of the qualities of an erudite historian, a sociologist, an artist, and a teacher. As the reader turns the pages of Klyuchevsky's *Course*, he can but marvel at the living figures that step out of the pages or the lucid revival of the past before him. How can one forget the artist-historian Klyuchevsky's presentation of Ivan III, of Ivan the Terrible, of Boris Godunov, of Patriarch Nikon, or of Peter I and Catherine II? The masterful metaphors and characterization of personalities, once read, cannot be erased from the student's memory. Many of his portrayals give one the impression not so much of an individual as of an alloy that served to temper the national character. Klyuchevsky compared, for instance, Patriarch Nikon to a sail—magnificent in stormy weather, but in the calm air an ordinary cloth pitifully hanging from the mast. Or the picture of Peter I, the epitome of an elemental fury that combined the dynamism of his people with personal fanatical allegiance. In Catherine, Klyuchevsky brings out the fusion of French culture, boundless feminine vanity, stately imagination, and personal voluptuousness. As an illustration of his mastery in describing an era in history, let us take his characterization of the Time of Troubles.

> As in time of storm trees cast high their leaves showing their reverse side, so violence of this Period of Troubles destroyed the old pillars and revealed what was able to survive. . . . This was basic to political thinking, to popular revolution. It was bound to alter political life in Muscovite society. If formerly the Czar was regarded as the land proprietor of the state and the subjects as his servants, now emerged the more modern concept of a state. After the nation had experienced short intervals during which sovereigns were absent, and particularly when the population was forced to elect a sovereign, the old Autocracy could never be brought back to life. It was realized that the sovereign and the state are transient whereas the people are eternal.[26]

Not only students of history learned from Klyuchevsky, but accomplished artists like Feodor Chaliapin as well. Before he undertook the difficult part of Boris Godunov, Chaliapin had a long session with Klyuchevsky, seeking counsel on the character of Godunov's personality. Later the great opera singer recalled "with grateful pleasure the marvellous pictures he [Klyuchevsky] painted of Boris, his times and environment." Recalling his visit, Chaliapin wrote: "An artist in words, and gifted with a most powerful historical imagination, Klyuchevsky was, in addition to being an historian, a most remarkable actor."[27] If one may once more plagiarize Schlözer's classification, it can be truly said that Klyuchevsky was the rare phenomenon, the incorporation of both the *Geschichtsschreiber* and the *Geschichtsmaler* into one.

No previous general course in Russian history had given so much space to the peasant problem. The peasant of Kievan Russia in all his multiple appearances—the frontiersman, tradesmen, the tiller of the soil, whether free or enslaved, in field or factory, whether groaning under the burden of crushing taxes, submissive and downtrodden at the feet of his master, or great and terrifying in the reawakened spirit of his frontier ancestors of the wide Eurasian plains of Russia—this peasant occupies a prominent place in Klyuchevsky's history. For the historian realized that it is only by the systematic analysis of the peasant himself as well as the agrarian problem in general that Russian history may be fully grasped. Yet, for some strange reason, though deeply sympathetic with the peasant masses and profoundly aware of the hidden reservoir of social explosives, he hardly devoted any space to such mass rebellions as those led by Stenka Razin or Yemelyan Pugachev.

Though Klyuchevsky greatly revered his teachers, Solovyev and Chicherin, he left them far behind.[28] Solovyev, like Buckle, later emphasized the influence of "spiritual forces" on history; his pupil turned more to the political, social, and economic spheres. Of real importance were the material rather than the moral forces, those that manifested themselves in social phenomena. And if to Chicherin institutions meant everything, to Klyuchevsky they were simply mechanical devices shaped by the sociological process of a nation. Among the works that display this conception are the analytical study of the Council of Boyars, which remains to this day a classic piece of historical literature; the study of the ruble from the sixteenth to the eighteenth century; and finally, the essay on the origins of serfdom, a reply to J. Engelmann's book, *Die Leibeigenschaft in Russland* (The Institution of Serfdom in Russia), in which Klyuschevsky endeavored to prove that peasant indebtedness was the main condition that led to the establishment of serfdom.[29] This view, though questioned by present-day scholars, who are inclined to attach more importance to direct state legislation than any financial involvements, has seriously challenged Engelmann's thesis.

Klyuchevsky destroyed many of the happier notions of the past, notably those held by the Slavophiles. For instance, Slavophiles were fond of pointing out that in the early days Russia was governed by a limited monarchy, the agency to limit its powers being the *Zemsky Sober* or National Assembly. Klyuchevsky exploded that theory by proving that so far as the assembly of the sixteenth century was concerned, it never constituted any limitation on the monarch's powers, for the simple reason that that chamber of loquacity never constituted an elective body but was appointed by no other than the sovereign himself.[30] Klyuchevsky masterfully explained the origin of the autocratic state and the rise of the military landowning gentry mainly by two factors: continuous territorial expansion and the urgent necessity of defending the frontiers of the far-flung state. Precisely the same motives dictated the reforms of Peter I.[31] To the delight of the Slavophiles, Klyuchevsky painted the stormy Petrine years in the most unsparing light. But he also incorporated pages that equally delighted the Westerners: descriptions of ruthless, petty dynastic wrangles and quibbles, the oppression and exploitation of the peasant in a truly Asiatic manner, with little concern for individual rights. The reason for the satisfaction in both camps is that Klyuchevsky never wrote "patriotic" history in a Karamzin style, though he was a Russian from top to toe. He hated national glorification no less than national debasement. He felt with equal sting of conscience the heartrending ruthlessness of Ivan the Terrible and of Peter the Great, the bigotry of Boyar pettiness, the snobbery and class selfishness of the later gentry, and the brutality and blind hatred of the anarchic peasantry toward any form of social discipline.

Klyuchevsky understood the Russian character as few did. He saw the causes lying behind the blood-stained pages of the past and therefore was able to draw from history, not embittered and distorted ideas, but wholesome lessons. It would seem as if he always bore in mind the words of Dostoyevsky who admonished "to judge the Russian people, not by the degrading sins it often commits, but by the great and holy things to which, in the midst of degradation, it constantly aspires. . . . Judge not the people by what it is, but what it would like to become."[32]

For a long time Klyuchevsky's lectures were known only through the notes of students. All attempts to persuade him to publish them in book form met with Klyuchevsky's categorical disapproval because he felt that they were far from being worthy of appearing in print or the last word on Russian history.[33] Finally, he yielded, when in 1904 there appeared the first volume of his popular *Course*, which was soon followed by three more; in 1921 there appeared posthumously the fifth and last volume, compiled from the notes by one of his former students, Y. Barskov.

Until recently few students were aware of Klyuchevsky as the pioneering scholar in the field of historical science. During the last decades of the past century Klyuchevsky had been offering a course designed for students specializing in Russian history. The course included such subjects as the terminology of the medieval chronicles, the nature of the preserved records, various charters, and other kinds of historical records. In a broad sense the course was in the field of historiography, leading up to the eighteenth century. Because of ill health Klyuchevsky was forced to drop the course and limit his lectures to the field of general Russian history. It was only in

1959 that the publication of Klyuchevsky's writings finally included his lectures on *The Study of Sources in History* (*Istochnikovedeniye*). These are enlightening lectures and are strongly recommended to students of history, for aside from being sound and lucid discussion, they offer contents rarely found in Russian historical literature.[34]

Platonov

Among the "old guardsmen" and pupils of Bestuzhev-Ryumin, Sergei Feodorovich Platonov (1860-1933) stands out as preeminent.[35] He succeeded his teacher to the chair of Russian history at the University of St. Petersburg. By his own admission two men primarily influenced his views, Bestuzhev-Ryumin and Klyuchevsky. Grandson of a serf and tutor of the royal heirs, a man of persistent energy and possessing a religious reverence for his country's past, Platonov eventually gained recognition as a man of scholarly integrity. His outstanding work, *A Study of the Time of Troubles*, is an extraordinary work of its kind. Steering cautiously through the feculent pool of politics and masterfully handling all the sources to be found, the author deduced convincing conclusions. With genuine talent and Olympian patience, Platonov examined the amassed sources pertaining to the most complicated period in Russian history (1598-1613), brushing aside biased versions and basing his thesis on more acceptable chronicles and accounts of contemporary writers. Nothing escaped Platonov's vigilant eye, and the concatenated forces lying behind the whole social and political upheaval, with all their consequences, are masterfully brought to light. Particular attention has been given to the tense class struggle between the old Boyar class and the rising nobility created by Ivan IV, on the one side, and the urban and rural classes on the other, with their interlocking interests, now coinciding, now in sharp conflict.

Platonov's approach to the concurrence of causes that led to the fifteen-year strife preceding the ascendancy of the Romanov dynasty, or the Time of Troubles, was somewhat different. Platonov kept the problem of foreign intervention and the wars with Sweden and Poland in the background; the main issue, as he saw it, was the internal condition, the conflict of class interests, which by the end of the period assumed the proportions of a national social revolution. This enormous conflict was interpreted in terms of a class war, not in the Marxian sense of a mass uprising from below, but rather as a revolution steered from above, gradually forcing the masses into the whirlpool of violence.

Only in the last stages of these national developments did the masses rise, as if against their will, under the leadership of Ivan Bolotnikov in a predominantly political struggle, while the social and economic aspects of the conflict were kept in the wings of the national stage. The theme thus centered on the struggle for political power, and for this reason the question of dynastic aspirations or the problem of restoration of the social order assumed prominence throughout the entire discussion. Yet Platonov could not avoid dwelling at considerable length on such critical issues as the entrenchment of the institution of serfdom, with all the interests and opposition it implied at this turning point in history. Nor could the author fail to bring in the role of the Boyar class, the collapse of parts of the system violently introduced by Ivan IV, such as the *oprichnina* (special bodyguard), and the appearance of the new tenant nobility. The work received the highest praise of such eminent scholars as Ikonnikov, Sergeyevich, and Klyuchevsky and was recommended for the much sought-after Uvarov prize.

Platonov lived long enough to get into serious trouble with the authorities after 1917. Conservative, reserved, and alien to the materialistic interpretation of history, he could hardly adapt himself to the newly forming society or escape a clash with Marxist historians. It was not surprising that his difficulties increased as time went on. Still he refused to leave his native land and loyally performed his duties as director of the library at the Academy of Sciences until he was forced to resign, shortly before his death, on a trumped-up charge of having concealed some historical records. He was exiled to Samara (presently Kuybyshev), where he died in 1933 in loneliness and great want.

Lappo-Danilevsky

Another member of the "Old Guard" was Alexander Sergeyevich Lappo-Danilevsky (1863-1919), who occupies a special place in Russian historiography because in the strict sense of the word he could hardly be called a historian.[36] Lappo-Danilevsky concentrated his lifetime of ardent labor, not on Russian history as such, but on archaeology, paleography, and methodology of history. His first work dealt with Scythian culture, and in 1887 he published *Scythian Antiquities*, followed by a study of seals of the period of the Galich and Vladimir principalities. Subsequently his interest was diverted to economic history, growth of towns in the seventeenth century, and the status of the serf peasantry. A work on the development of Russian society during the eighteenth century remains in manuscript form in the files of the Academy of Sciences to this day.

Whether Lappo-Danilevsky's project at any particular time happened to be of the broadest dimensions or only of microscopic nature, it was invariably subordinated to his main field of interest, the methodology of history. Yet it is noteworthy that in his voluminous work (which lists 172 titles) the treatment of each individual topic, despite the fact that it is part of a larger scheme, constitutes a complete piece of work in itself, and each is, moreover, a masterpiece. Such, for instance, is the monograph of the *Russian Industrial and Trading Companies in the First Half of the Eighteenth Century* or his thesis, "The Administration of Direct Taxation in the Muscovite State from the Time of Troubles to the Period of Reforms," which P. N. Milyukov considered as "the most wonderful phenomenon in Russian historical literature." It is to be regretted that Lappo-Danilevsky's writings lack the stylistic grace of a Klyuchevsky and the daring interpretive talent of a Milyukov. This can be explained tartly by the fact that the author was a solitary person and very little in touch with the younger generation. He remained, instead, under the influence of the Juridical School of A. D. Gradovsky and B. N. Chicherin long after it had been shelved by the advancing decades. Out of voluminous, hitherto unearthed sources he constructed a grandiose tower of antiquated architecture.

Lappo-Danilevsky focused his attention mainly on the seventeenth and eighteenth centuries, to him an absorbing epoch during which the crystallization of social and political Russia could be seen vividly.[37] The emergence of a society with a new cultural physiognomy, new forms of economic life and judicial institutions, and a new sort of social consciousness, fascinated him. Distinguished contributions from his pen include monographs on the attachment of the peasants to the soil, formation of peasant categories, and patrimonial estates (*votchiny*) of the sixteenth and seventeenth centuries, which constituted the basis of the later structure of Russian society. His course of lectures on the eighteenth century at the University of St. Petersburg was interesting particularly in its organization. He divided the century into four transitional periods: (1) consolidation of the state under Peter I; (2) consolidation of the nobility, with its asserted privileges, at the expense of the state; (3) the amalgamation of government and aristocratic interests, emancipation of the nobility, and early rise of public opinion; and (4) severance of the bonds between government and society, and a period of reaction.

Coincident with his enthusiastic research in this period, Lappo-Danilevsky also engaged in a work that would seem drudgery to others—the systematization of historical materials and their publication, including all the sources concerning Russia to be found in foreign archives. He maintained that for an understanding of the relations between the Eastern Orthodox and Western Roman Catholic churches, as well as of Moscow's role in the Near Eastern problem, the Italian archives were indispensable. It was because of this that the Academy of Sciences later dispatched a member to Rome. Simultaneously, Lappo-Danilevsky continued to conduct an extended investigation of all foreign residents in Moscow during the first half of the seventeenth century, studying their activities, the purpose of their journey thither, any service they might have rendered the government, or cultural influence they might have exerted. He wrote a notable essay on Peter the Great as founder of the Academy of Sciences, another on I. I. Betskoy and his system of education during the reign of Catherine II, and a third essay on German-Russian relations in the eighteenth century. To Lappo-Danilevsky the final synthesis of history was to be the synthesis of universal history. But this goal was not to be attained merely by coining *a priori* formulae similar to those of Spencer, Comte, Hegel, or Marx, not by intuitive, spontaneous thinking; it was to be gained by an orderly, methodical understanding based on an intimate knowledge of the various stages through which humanity has passed during its long course of history. This required a longevity that regretfully was not granted to Lappo-Danilevsky.

Lyubavsky

The heavy lot of Platonov during his later years fell also to his contemporary, the historian Matvey Kuzmich Lyubavsky (1860-1937).[38] Lyubavsky belonged to the senior group of Klyuchevsky's pupils, though for his studies he chose a field somewhat remote from that of his colleagues; his interest was concentrated chiefly on the past of Lithuania, a subject he selected for both his master's and doctoral dissertations. These two bulky works immediately assured the writer an eminent place in his field. Written in a somewhat pedantic style and lavishly supported by references from firsthand sources, they represent a laborious task of research in the archives of western Russia. The caution with which the author elaborated his thesis and the frequent citation of references rob it, however, of any literary charm. Like Bestuzhev-Ryumin, Lyubavsky left no school, only a few appreciative individual students.

The central theme of Lyubavsky is the geographic factor in the formation of the Russian state. This in turn led the author to a special study of peripheral Western history. The field was an original one, and Lyubavsky was the only historian to explore the subject with painstaking care. His research led him to the theory that Lithuanian Russia, like Moscow, arose as a direct offspring of Kievan Russia. He elaborated this thesis in his lectures on early Russian history to the end of the sixteenth century, which he delivered at the University of Moscow. The course served as a supplemental field to the general field offered by Klyuchevsky. If Presnyakov in his work, *The Formation of the Great Russian State*, felt that Lithuania had arisen as a consequence of political concentration, Lyubavsky, on the other hand, approached the same subject from its ethnographic and geographic aspects, which led him to emphasize territorial concentration. While Lyubavsky saw in the union between the two principalities, Vladimir and Moscow, underlying military and financial causes, Presnyakov interpreted the same phenomena as the outcome of a political tradition.

In his writings as in person, Lyubavsky was detached from surrounding realities. He was, in the full sense of the word, the academician, to whom politics and social activity were alien, his whole life being absorbed in his studies of the past and in his careful weaving of bygone events into a factual account. The revolution was to him, therefore, a fatal blow; the revolutionary period demanded partisanship, colorful narration of current history, not detached, objective accounts of seemingly nullified events with no bearing on current tumultuous events. It is, therefore, quite understandable that the oncoming period was to Lyubavsky a fatal blow, an alien atmosphere, being totally uprooted from his home environment. Small wonder that his opponents sought Lyubavsky's removal from his post (he had been rector of the University of Moscow since 1911), and it was not long before they succeeded in replacing him. Eventually he was banished to Ufa, where he died a lonely, heartbroken man, watching the familiar old order around him give way to a new one that he was never able to comprehend, and forced to remain an alien in his own society.

Presnyakov

Along with Lyubavsky, of the University of Moscow, stood the figure of Alexander Yevgneyvich Presnyakov (1870-1929), of the University of St. Petersburg. Though a pupil of Platonov, Presnyakov in his writings showed himself to have been strongly influenced by the Juridical School, particularly by V. I. Sergeyevich, whose ideas underlie his master's dissertation on the authority of the prince in early Russian history. Presnyakov expanded this into a study on a much broader scale than the topic might suggest. An analysis of the princely authority soon developed into an elaborate investigation of the social order of the period. The result was a pioneering work on a subject that became a popular theme shortly after—feudalism in Russia.

It was Pavlov-Silvansky, of whom more will be said later, who carried the subject to its logical conclusion; Presnyakov plodded in the same direction and tended to consider favorably the idea that Western European and Russian feudalism had originated under similar social and political conditions. The assertion seriously challenged the former theory, cherished especially by the Slavophiles, that Russian serfdom had developed in a peculiarly national environment, totally different from that in the Western world. It must be added that Presnyakov did not conclude with any degree of certitude that peasant bondage existed during the tenth through the twelfth centuries. At best it can be said that Presnyakov left the problem open whether it had been originated at that time.

Presnyakov's doctoral dissertation, *The Formation of the Great Russian State*, reveals an amazing knowledge of all the Russian chronicles and charters in the fifteenth and sixteenth centuries. The whole topic acquired a new significant aspect and was presented in an entirely different light from that shed by all previous writers.[39] Formerly, the rise of Moscow had mainly been interpreted, not as a result of national and state aspirations, but as either the outcome of the greed of the landowning nobility (Chicherin) or— virtually the same driving force (Solovyev, Klyuchevsky)—the logical consequences of economic development leading to expansion. Thus the

Muscovite prince was a mere tool of either individual landlords or economic circumstances, or both, and the state as such played only a subordinate part in national expansion.

Presnyakov, throwing all these theories overboard, presented his own view, namely, that beneath all the strivings for territorial expansion was not mere individual greed, but a conscientious national aspiration and a natural realization of the necessity to form a consolidated state. The internal conflicts between Moscow and the other principalities, such as Tver, Suzdal, Ryazan, and others, were not simply expressions of the inherent belligerent instincts of their respective princes, but rather the expressions of conflicting ideas concerning the policy to be followed in the formation of a centralized national state. In other words, the whole internal conflict represented not the rivalry of acquisitive instincts, but a national centripetal force seeking the best methods for its materialization. The soundness of the theory has been questioned by some scholars, but the originality of the thesis has not been denied; in fact it stimulated the revision of many theories formerly held unchallenged.

Presnyakov's other works deal clearly with more recent Russian history. Among them must be mentioned his two short monographs on Alexander I and his admirable presentation of the Decembrist uprising. Under the influence of the revolution he was inclined to dwell on the writing of more recent history, though even here he was careful to maintain the old standard and avoid flag-waving. He died on September 30, 1929. The Society of Marxist Historians, of which he became a member, casually mentioned his death in the official publication, *Istorik-Marksist* (of which, incidentally, he was one of the editors), and promised to publish in the forthcoming issue a detailed appraisal of his works; there has been no further reference to Presnyakov in subsequent issues.[40] One reason that might explain this neglect may be found in the *Great Soviet Encyclopedia* (*Bolshaya sovetskaya entsiklopediya*), which states: "After the Great October Socialist Revolution, Presnyakov tried to revise his theoretical position and actively participated in the work of soviet scientific institutions as well as in institutions of higher learning. However, he was unable to emancipate himself from bourgeois-idealistic methodology in his search for historical processes."[41] Obviously the verdict as cited in the encyclopedia must have had some relation to the absence of further tribute to the departed colleague and scholar, since such heresy as "bourgeois-idealistic methodology" is never forgiven or tolerated in Marxist circles.

Milyukov

Another "old guardsman," and student of Solovyev and Klyuchevsky, Pavel Nikolayevich Milyukov (1859-1943), ardent Westerner in the more modern sense, editor, lecturer, statesman, and author of a number of notable studies in the field of Russian history, logically follows the legion of historian considered.[42] His early works, which secured him a wide reputation as a historian, were his master's thesis, *State Economy in Russia During the First Quarter of the Eighteenth Century and the Reforms of Peter the Great*, followed later by an equally penetrating essay on the *Debatable Questions Concerning the Financial History of the Muscovite State*. Both studies embraced such a mass of new material extracted from the files of archives that they cast light on many questions other than the economic measures of Peter I. They opened the way to other scholars, notably to M. M. Bogoslovsky, whose dissertation entitled *Local Reforms of Peter the Great* may be rightly regarded as an outgrowth of Milyukov's pioneering work. Milyukov's stimulating essays on the history of the Russian intelligentsia, including one on the "Decay of Slavophilism," demonstrated his wide range of interest, while his later book on Pushkin demonstrated his impressive familiarity with Russian letters. Another work deserves mention, his *Main Currents in Russian Historical Thought*, which is regarded as one of the most original studies in Russian historiography. It is regrettable that the work was never completed; the first and only volume ends with Chaadayev and the influence of Schelling on Russian historical writing.

Milyukov's most outstanding work is his *Studies of Russian Culture*. This is neither a chronological nor a "scientific" work in the orthodox sense; yet it is a superbly refreshing study because of its scope, its critical, realistic vision, as well as its originality. It is an excellent supplement to Klyuchevsky's *Course in Russian History*: the two should be read together, since Milyukov filled in many of the gaps that Klyuchevsky left open. First the author deals with the rise of the state, population, economics, and social developments. The state in Russia, according to Milyukov, passed through three stages of development: tribal, feudal, and national, the last being strongly military in character. Feudalism affected only the southwestern part of the land, adjacent to Poland and Lithuania, with which Russia had close contacts. Because of the local peculiarities, the Muscovite state hardly knew feudalism; environmental conditions were instrumental in accentuating the military character of the state. Threats from the east and lack of natural lines of defense forced the government to resort to military policies that in the end gave rise to political institutions, financial needs and taxing methods, and the formation of social groupings.

The geographic factors were largely responsible for mobility of population or a "wandering peasantry," while national interests called for a stable society on which authorities could rely for manpower and revenue. This state of affairs caused the government to "attach" the peasants to the soil and the gentry to the state. The gentry managed eventually to free themselves from their obligations, while the status of the peasants remained unaltered: serfdom, formerly a public institution, thus became a legalized private privilege. The entire development, Milyukov stresses, emanated from state authority; whatever institution, class, or community entered national life was dictated or initiated mainly by the needs of the government. By the second half of the last century, however, conditions had been so altered that the government was forced to cast off the social and economic legacy and initiate a total reorganization of national life. Serfdom had to be cast overboard, and the former serf owners who depended on compulsory labor had to learn quickly to manage their estates within the newly introduced free economy. According to Milyukov, they failed dismally at this task, and the gentry soon found themselves in a serious economic plight, largely because of their inability to cope with problems derived from a free economy and the rising capitalistic form of production.[43] By the end of the century the state had had to rescue them from total bankruptcy on several occasions. The solution, as the author envisioned it, lay, not in cherishing these "social relics," which Milyukov considered terribly overestimated by false national pride, but in a nationally concentrated effort to build a freer community in harmony with more recent political and social ideals.

After Milyukov expounded the role of the state, he turned to the church, sectarianism, and education, or as he states, to the "spiritual" rather than the "material" aspects of culture. Once again Milyukov reached firm conclusions. As in the case of the state, here too the course of events developed differently from that in Western Europe. Russian culture found its beginning not "below" in the masses, but imposed from above. Cultural life descended from the church, supported by the state from the very start. Since the people were neither organized nor in any manner able to stand behind the ecclesiastical leaders, the church was soon enshrined to the will of the state. This caused immeasurable damage, forming a wide abyss between the people and the church, which resulted in sterility of the faith, emphasis on ritualism, and desperate efforts such as those of Patriarch Nikon to correct the situation, which in turn led to the sorrowful schism within the church. Education shared the same fate: it became a function of and for the government.

It seemed even more important to Milyukov that Russian nationalism became a state-sponsored ideology, initiated and promoted by the government and being subservient to it. A general consequence of this development was a division between government and a minority of intellectuals oon the one hand, and the vast majority of the people on the other. Nationalism thus did not depend on the people; it did not draw its vitality from the masses, but from the superstructure of society, which represented a small minority. Consequently, in the end it led to a confrontation of the two groups, the alienated minority and the sullen, passive, and inarticulate masses. A precarious situation thus developed subsequently whereby a native population was governed by a culturally alien administration. This isolation of national authority was climaxed by Peter I, whose westernization of the state, now accelerated to a dizzy speed, was truly a task of a single man. Milyukov was at heart a strong Westerner, and was the last to oppose, on general principles, the reforms of Peter I. What disturbed him was the manner in which these reforms were carried out and the negative consequences that were bound to ensue. The reforms of Peter I came, as Milyukov saw them, like a storm; the nation was caught unaware, totally unprepared for such changes; they were carried out by men who at best hardly comprehended what they were doing, and at worst were often hostile to the order of their sovereign. For this reason it could be said that the reforms were the work of a single man, or as Pososhkov correctly observed, "Peter alone pulled uphill, while millions were pulling downhill."

Milyukov stressed particularly the fact that, as in the past, so again during the Petrine period the reforms were a by-product of military necessity rather than a result of keen cultural perception. What was needed first and foremost was an up-to-date military force backed by economic resources, with all other things implied by these two closely related objectives. The sum total was the continuation of a tradition that began far back in history—a determined sovereign furiously trying to dislodge an obsolete order while the masses, for whose benefit the sovereign toils, resentfully bemoan their fate. With extraordinary lucidity and persistency Milyukov traced the formation of the breach between the masses and the handful of intelligentsia, first on religious grounds, later in other spheres. The ever-present necessity of "overtaking" the West only widened the gulf, since the vanguard of this drive left the rear guard of the nation to struggle far behind.

A good portion of the blame for this lamentable state of affairs Milyukov seems to ascribe to Orthodoxy, which had failed to become a powerful lever like the Protestant church in Western Europe and, particularly, in England. Milyukov neatly summarized the situation by stating that in England religion nourished the citizen and that culture developed there along with religious thought; hence the Englishman was still religious. In France the situation was different: religion took a definitely hostile attitude toward the development of modern scientific and philosophical thinking, and the national mind, advancing in spite of clerical opposition, left religion behind; consequently the Frenchman turned against religion. In Russia, Orthodoxy did neither one nor the other; it failed to keep pace with cultural development, and it did not establish an inquisition; therefore the Russian intelligentsia became traditionally indifferent toward any religion.[44]

Though a Westerner to the core, Milyukov by his bold interpretation of his history unwittingly delivered much ammunition to his opponents. However, a conscientious perusal of his writings leads one to conclude that the future of Russia depends on the success of her adaptability to the course of Western civilization. The process, begun in the seventeenth century, will proceed in spite of the frequent opposition it is bound to meet, since it will be aided by economic and military aggression from outside and by growing needs from within. As an *émigré*, Milyukov later undertook a revision of the *History of Russian Culture*, but he never completed the laborious task: the political activities into which he plunged headlong at the beginning of the present century seriously handicapped his scholarly pursuits. It is a pity that his energy was so much diverted to other channels. Scholars of Milyukov's caliber are rare, and his frequent absence from their ranks has been acutely felt on many occasions.

Semevsky

The peasant question in Russian history had always been a vital problem around which many national issues have revolved. A good many Russian scholars have extended their studies and research in the field of agrarian problems far beyond the confines of their own country: M. I. Rostovtsev has enriched historical knowledge with his investigation concerning the ancient world, particularly Greece and Rome; V. G. Vasilevsky and F. I. Uspensky, followed by A. A. Vasiliev, have done the same for Byzantine history; N. I. Kareyev and I. V. Luchitsky have made sizable contributions to the study of the French peasantry. The history of the Russian peasantry was a subject popularly explored by a legion of scholars, among them B. N. Chicherin, I. D. Belyayev, M. A. Dyakonov, I. I. Ignatovich, V. A. Myakotin, A. S. Lappo-Danilevsky, M. M. Bogoslovsky, B. D. Grekov, A. A. Kornilov, A. Y. Yefimenko, P. B. Struve, and a host of others who contributed to the field of Russian agrarian history.

However, almost all these studies have dealt with the earlier period of Russian history; few of the writers have gone beyond the eighteenth century, nor have they made any effort to embrace the vast field in its entirety. A task of this magnitude was undertaken and successfully carried out by Vasily Ivanovich Semevsky (1848-1916). This profound student and eminent authority on the history of the peasant was branded by his faculty colleagues as a "radical" and partisan unworthy to enter the teaching career; after his death his memory was bespattered by inferior Marxian writers who labeled him a "petty bourgeois lacking a knowledge of Marxian dialectic," and a "populist-historian" who could possibly write of labor but was incapable of comprehending the principle of class struggle in history.[45]

Whatever the partisan opinion concerning Semevsky may be, calmer judgment will consider his work among the most distinguished contributions to the agrarian history of Russia, from which both friends and foes will ungratefully draw material for years to come. It is indeed unfortunate that his works are not available in other languages: historical literature might have been spared many mediocre and repetitious accounts of a subject that Semevsky had long ago thoroughly explored. His life illustrates the bitter cup that is put to the lips of a man who dares to defy the conventional or domestic concepts of his contemporaries.

Semevsky was born in the province of Pskov, into the family of a poor squire; he was one of fourteen children and from an early age experienced want and struggle.[46] In 1866 Semevsky entered the St. Petersburg Medical Academy, where he spent two years and had the opportunity to study with such distinguished scholars as the physiologist I. M. Syechenov and the world-famed I. I. Mechnikov. The two years contributed much to his character and immunized his mind against the various forms of intellectual sluggishness that, years later, afflicted many members of the Russian intelligentsia. In 1868 Semevsky entered the University of St. Petersburg and devoted himself to studying peasant history as well as doing social work among the peasants, whose economic problems became of absorbing interest to him for the rest of his life.[47] "It is high time," Semevsky wrote some years later, "for our agrarian country, which has been maintained for a thousand years almost exclusively at the expense of the peasant, to pay due tribute to the class to which we owe everything."[48]

Semevsky spent ten years on his master's thesis, which he presented in 1881. Later he enlarged this work into two volumes, which were published in 1903 under the title *Peasants in the Reign of Catherine II.*[49] For the first time there was revealed to the public a subject that until 1861 had been completely banned, and which after the lifting of the ban was reluctantly handled because of its extremely complex nature and politically dangerous aspects. The warmest empathy with the peasantry did not hinder Semevsky from producing a work of singular merit, in which he demonstrated not only a phenomenal knowledge of archival material, but also a special talent for absorbing and properly synthesizing the amassed resources.

After that Semevsky began his short career as a historian. When the thesis was presented to the faculty, the candidate was immediately offered the bitter fruit of adverse criticism from university authorities. Bestuzhev-Ryumin, to whom we have made some previous reference, led the opposition against the acceptance of the thesis on the ground that the author had besmirched Russian history. He considered the conclusions tendentious and alleged that the thesis presented unfair criticism of official policy and generally discriminated in favor of the peasantry. By an unfortunate coincidence it so happened that Semevsky initiated his battle for the acceptance of his dissertation during the year of the assassination of Alexander II, which was followed by a strong reaction in the country at large against any adverse criticism of social conditions, particularly among the panic-stricken intellectuals in university circles. All the arguments against the guardians of "pure history" to the effect that the presented study was a scholarly achievement based on primary and previously explored sources proved totally futile: the thesis was rejected and Bestuzhev-Ryumin scored his triumph.[50]

Semevsky thereupon shifted his battlefield to Moscow, where, to his surprise, his thesis was finally accepted. Among those who approved it was V. O. Klyuchevsky.[51] With his degree now in hand, Semevsky returned to St. Petersburg to apply for a chair in Russian history, evidently with the intention of facing his recent opponents on an equal footing. Surprisingly, the chair was granted, but his victory proved of short duration. Three years later, through the same Bestuzhev-Ryumin,[52] Semevsky was forced out, despite the fact that he had become the most popular lecturer among the liberal students—and who was not a liberal student in those days? One of the main accusations leveled against Semevsky was that he presented Russian history in colors too black and dared to refer, though subtly, to such a touchy subject as the assassination of Paul, an ill chosen subject for discussion in a university auditorium.[53] Expulsion from the university was a hard blow to Semevsky, after having dreamt all those years of teaching. For a long time he was unable to reconcile himself with the idea of abandoning his chosen academic career. "Yes," he wrote in a private letter, "difficult and ungrateful is the work of an economist-historian!"

It would seem that there is no evil without compensating good. Deprived of his privilege of teaching, Semevsky was forced to concentrate his attention on research into fields of special interest. His acquaintance with the work of Georg Ludwig von Maurer and his "Mark Theory" was an incentive to Semevsky to make a similar study for his own country.[54] In 1888, his second capital study appeared, *The Peasant Question in the Eighteenth and First Half of the Nineteenth Century*, a continuation of his previous study, thought this time the reception was different. The author was highly praised, voted the Uvarov prize, and granted a gold medal by the Free Economic Society. In a short review an appraisal of this extensive work would render only a disservice to either the author or the true quality of profound study. It is a classic work, and it is most unlikely that much could be added to Semevsky's research in the field. Every aspect of the problem— legal, political, social, and economic—is minutely analyzed. The author's conclusion is that emancipation of the peasants was made inevitable not by the decision of the upper hierarchy in the capital, but by the pressure of the masses in cooperation with the liberal intelligentsia; if in 1861 the reforms proved inadequate, as he later tried to show they did, it was because of unwillingness on the part of the government to carry the program to its logical end. It may also be of interest to note that in this as well as in all his later works, Semevsky adhered to the belief that communal land ownership must be preserved, that its abolition would spell nothing less than economic disaster for the peasants.

For a long time Semevsky's attention was focused on Siberia, where he went in 1891 at the invitation of an eminent industrialist, A. I. Sibiryakov.[55]

His wide travels and personal observations of peasant conditions, reinforced by the use of local archives, enabled him to publish in 1898 a two-volume study of laborers in the goldmining industries of Siberia, a work equaling in thoroughness and empathy his preceding volumes. During the following years he turned his attention to another subject, the liberal movement in Russia. As a result, the last book published in his lifetime appeared in 1909, *Political and Social Ideas of the Decembrists*. For the first time the Decembrist movement was examined by court historians like N. K. Schilder or M. I. Bogdanovich, and by Westerners such as A. N. Pypin, and even by more conscientious writers such as M. V. Dovnar-Zapolsky. These studies were overshadowed by later writers such as V. I. Semevsky. He traced the rise of the Decembrist ideas from their earliest sources in the preceding century, from the increasing demand for reforms which were inspired from abroad and intensified from within. Semevsky did not touch upon the formation or organization of either the societies or the climaxing revolt of December 14, 1825. His cardinal interest was in the very origins, in the roots, of the entire drama. And this investigation, quite naturally, led him to further research in the radical or liberal ideas of the decades following the revolt, the 1830s and 1840s. The results of the latter research were presented in two essays that should not be overlooked: the story of the Petrashevsky circle and the origin of the Cyril-Methodius Society. Both essays occupy a recognized place in the historical literature of nineteenth-century Russian liberalism.

Aside from these works, Semevsky contributed numerous articles to various magazines, most of which deserve wide publicity and point to the urgent advisability of collecting his entire works for publication at the earliest possible time. In 1913 he became editor of a well-known magazine, *Golos minuvshego* (Voice of the Past), fulfilling an ambition he had dreamed of for many years; death prevented Semevsky from developing his editorial abilities to a fuller extent and as he had hoped. In an obituary notice one writer summarized Semevsky's accomplishment thus: barred from university lecture halls, this scholar could do nothing but transform his learning into ponderous volumes. These writings have proved a far more enduring monument to Semevsky than the lectures he hoped to deliver. His voluminous works will be read and consulted for many years to come and by many more students than any university auditorium could have ever accommodated.

Shakhmatov

The study of Russian sources continued throughout the entire nineteenth century, culminating with the research by Aleksey Aleksandrovich Shakhmatov (1864-1920), a most remarkable linguist and one of the greatest authorities on the language of the chronicles. Shakhmatov's research illustrates the assistance that philology can render the historian, especially the student of the early periods.[56] His persistent analyses of the chronicles resulted in a series of monographs and books, some of which have been lauded by Slavicists the world over. Yet his general deductions met with doubt and criticism. Experts like Alexander Brückner, Reinold Trautmann, or Samuel H. Cross were skeptical of Shakhmatov's methodology. Others criticized his conclusion that the Great Russian, Ukrainian, and White Russian languages, though stemming from a common Old Slavic tongue, developed independently; extreme nationalists among the Great Russians severely took Shakhmatov to task for even admitting the very existence of independent languages.

Schlözer's method was to restore by means of textual criticism and scholarly scrutiny the original text of the *Nestor Chronicle*. This involved a laborious "peeling off" process; that is, by eliminating all detected apocryphal additions and alterations of later writers, he hoped to arrive at the original text. The same method was applied by later students of Russian history, such as Bestuzhev-Ryumin and, notably, Pogodin. Shakhmatov handled the problem by employing historical rather than textual criticism. He began by examining each component of the chronicle as a product of certain historical circumstances. Each examined part was then considered a reflection of the environment in which it must have been recorded. Each detected textual change or new "layer" served as *zeitgebunden* evidence of a period or place. By assiduously dissecting and then reconstructing each part, Shakhmatov set the entire problem in a completely new light. Each textual part, according to Shakhmatov, came to reveal the nature of local history as well as of the time when it had been incorporated by the chronicles.[57]

Philology was only one of the instruments with which Shakhmatov attacked the problem. The primary weapon he employed was a carefully deduced historical narrative. It is particularly for these reasons that Shakhmatov can be rightly considered both as an eminent philologist and a historian. Each of his investigations resulted in a critical essay, based on a particular source, which essentially represented a study of a given period. This process involved minute analyses of political, religious, social, economic, or military conditions of a particular locality. At times the method resulted in startling revelations of the relations between the principalities. Philology thereby became wedded to history and was later employed most effectively by scholars like N. Y. Marr or A. Y. Presnyakov.

Shakhmatov's greatest contribution was in the field of chronology with respect to the numerous chronicles. With considerable ingenuity and scholarly attention he undertook to determine on a linguistic basis the approximate dates of the various sources: the Kievan, Novgorodian, and other chronicles. Thanks to his extraordinary linguistic erudition, Shakhmatov was able to disclose the interdependence of these sources, particularly in the matter of style. In his study of the *Primary Chronicle (Povest' vremennykh lyet)*, published by the Archaeographic Commission in 1916, he accomplished what neither Tatishchev nor Schlözer, nor even Abbot Joseph Dobrovsky—who in 1812 first suggested the method later employed by Shakhmatov—had succeeded in doing, because they lacked sufficient material for comparative study. The task of Shakhmatov was to discover ''the most complete and most accurate, authentic'' *Nestor Chronicle.* By a masterful comparison of the chronicles he established conclusively not only the dates of the various documents but also their origin, place, the nature of the environment in which each document was produced, and the motives of their authors. All this was a genuine revelation to many historians because it threw light on several important moments in the course of Russian history, reclaiming, as it were, the outlook of contemporaries of these periods upon their own time as well as upon the past in general. Of course, many aspects of the chronicles remained obscure; some reconstruction of the past was based on sheer hypotheses, and Shakhmatov himself seemed to have accepted them with serious misgivings. Yet, notwithstanding some of his unfortunate assumptions, Shakhmatov advanced the study of annalistic literature to a point never dreamed of by historians of previous centuries.

Ikonnikov

In the field of historical biography and historiography the name of Vladimir Stepanovich Ikonnikov (1841-1923) is eminent. His research and publications are associated mainly with cultural development of Russia and ideological advancement. Ikonnikov saw political life through the prism of biographical history such as revealed in his work on Russian public leaders of the sixteenth century or in his study of the Mordvinov family.[58] The latter represents also a study of the economic as well as political history of Russia during the early period of the nineteenth century.

Another field of interest of Ikonnikov had been historiography, which also included a good deal of biographical material on such historians as Karamzin, Bestuzhev-Ryumin, Brückner, Boltin, and Schlözer. The result was a separate admirable volume that centered particularly on the "skeptical school."[59] But his chief work undoubtedly remains the extensive study of Russian historiography, an extensive four-volume work that incorporates an extensive portion of annalistic literature, the history of the search of resources throughout Russia, and the process of gathering as well as the publication of the gathered resources.[60]

The two-volume *Study of Russian Historiography* stands not only as a notable achievement in scholarship, but also as proof of remarkable knowledge as well as a rare demonstration of skill to combine quantity of output with high degree of accuracy. Of equal interest is also Ikonnikov's published collection of documents related to the peasant unrest that followed the revolt in December 1825.

Pavlov-Silvansky

In connection with Russian works of broad historical synthesis by earlier writers like Karamzin, Solovyev, Klyuchevsky, or Milyukov, the name of Nikolay Pavlovich Pavlov-Silvansky (1869-1908) must not be overlooked. By his assertion that the institution of feudalism, which had been formerly associated exclusively with Western Europe, had also existed in Russia, he started a lively debate among historians and forced many either to revise or militantly to defend their former views. Today, except for some modifications, the basic contentions of Pavlov-Silvansky have been generally accepted by the majority of students of Russian history.[61]

For many years Pavlov-Silvansky worked with the national archives. His association with university life began rather late and proved of less than a year's duration: his promising academic career abruptly ended when he was barely thirty-nine years old, when the promising scholar contracted cholera. As a student at the University of St. Petersburg he had become keenly interested in Russian feudalism, a subject he studied absorbingly until the very end of his life. A pupil of Sergeyevich, he was deeply impressed by this illustrious teacher and eminent representative of the Juridical School. Later Pavlov-Silvansky came to admire Solovyev's writings even more, in which he discovered a unity of historical forces previously unnoticed. He familiarized himself with the works of Guizot and studied with enthusiasm his views on the development of feudalism. He was fascinated also by Klyuchevsky's theories concerning the origin and development of serfdom. It was under this combined influence of teachers and authors that Pavlov-Silvansky decided to undertake a comparison of medieval institutions in Russia and in the Romano-Germanic countries.

In 1907 Pavlov-Silvansky published his first book, entitled *Feudalism in Early Russia*. The basic problem, as the author saw it, was to prove the absence of any "uniqueness" in the social structure of medieval Russia, which was similar to the order that prevailed in medieval feudal Europe. The book was soon followed by another, *Feudalism in Appanage Russia*, unfortunately published posthumously and in fact not completed by the author. The main thesis pursued the thematic problem a step farther, by way of comparative investigation of feudal and legal institutions between the thirteenth and sixteenth centuries. Pavlov-Silvansky firmly believed that Russian feudalism had developed long before it was formulated by political authority; the latter only sanctioned what had already become a well-established institution.[62] The medieval structure of society, whether in Russia or in the Romano-Germanic countries, was not imposed from without but was brought about by internal conditions, by social and economic strife between the large landowning classes and the peasantry. This in turn led to forcible seizure of land by the former and the suppression and gradual economic enslavement of the latter. As state servants the privileged military class managed to defeat the peasants, and eventually their triumph became a legalized institution within the state. The pattern of historical development as presented by Pavlov-Silvansky can be outlined thus:

> *First period, 1169-1565.* Characterized by communal land ownership, which prevailed within society.
> *Second period, 1565-1760.* Noticeable shift of balance of political and economic power in favor of the rising aristocracy; eclipse of the communal system and defeat of peasant claims to the land.
> *Third period, 1760-1825.* Ascendancy of the state, sanctioning the

claims of the privileged classes. The merging of state and privileged class interests at the expense of the peasantry.

Fourth period, 1825-1861. Emergence of liberationist views followed by gradual emancipation and triumphant assertions of the rights of the masses.

The reign of Peter I was regarded by Pavlov-Silvansky, not as an extraordinary era, but rather as a continuation, only in accelerated form, of social, political, and economic forces that had been in operation prior to the ascendancy of this rebel in purple, and that continued to operate for many decades after his departure from the scene. The distinguishing characteristic of the Petrine era was merely the tempo with which national development kept forging ahead: whereas formerly these changes were creeping, now they were galloping. Attention may be called to the fourth period, which Pavlov-Silvansky traced to the early nineteenth century. The Decembrists, including such of their ideological predecessors as A. Radishchev, marked the dawn of the fourth period, when libertarian ideas from the West entered as the new factor in Russian society. This era, signaled by the Decembrist revolt, initiated an effective opposition by the oppressed masses to the wedded interests of the state and the privileged aristocratic classes. The period carried with it the ideas of the Age of Enlightenment and the slogans of the French Revolution. The year 1825 in Russian history, according to Pavlov-Silvansky, corresponds to the year 1789 in France.

By a parallel study of Western and Russian society, and by tracing identical institutional developments in both, Pavlov-Silvansky arrived at a new historical synthesis. The similarity is particularly noticeable when the legal aspects are analyzed. By his masterful constructive ability and undeniable originality, Pavlov-Silvansky set historians to revising many of their formerly held views of Russia's historical uniqueness. He exploded once and for all the theory that Russian medieval society, with its institution of serfdom, could be described as peculiarly humanitarian, or noted for special virtues, such as Christian socialist qualities not to be found anywhere in the West. Later other writers, notably B. D. Grekov, broadened the thesis pioneered by Pavlov-Silvansky. The Marxian writers enthusiastically accepted the thesis and expanded it to include its economic as well as its political and social implications. Pavlov-Silvansky, Pokrovsky stated, definitely proved that five hundred years ago Russia marched politically in step with Roman-Germanic society, and what was destined to die in Western

Europe was bound to follow the same course in Eastern Europe; the only difference between the two was one of tempo.[63]

Siberian Historiography

Closely related to the borderland provinces is the long-overlooked domain of Siberia.[64] Interest in the vast eastern domain was awakened in the eighteenth century when the "father of Siberian history," Gerhard Friedrich Müller, returned from the Great Northern Expedition after a study of the archives in the east. The fruit of Müller's ten years of exploits in Siberia appeared in 1750 in a work entitled *A Description of the Siberian Kingdom*, followed in 1761 by additional information in his *Compilation of Russian History (Sammlung russischer Geschichte)*.[65] The *Description* presents a dull narrative, poorly synthesized, yet it incorporated a mass of newly discovered materials that served as an aid to many later historians. Soon after the appearance of Müller's work, Johann Fischer published a plagiarized version of Siberian history that did not improve the work either stylistically or architectonically.[66]

For years thereafter, the subject of Siberian history was handled mostly by amateurs like G.I. Spassky, who was by profession a mining engineer. His rendered service, like those of earlier historians, was mostly editorial: he was editor of source material, along with the accounts of travelers and newly discovered Siberian chronicles (the Stroganov, Yesipov, and part of the Cherepanov chronicles). It was not until the middle of the nineteenth century that P. A. Slovtsov, whom the local patriots came to regard as the "Siberian Karamzin," took up the work of Müller in a more able manner. Slovtsov stressed the internal forces of colonization rather than those emanating from the central administrative authority of Moscow.[67]

In spite of certain faults, questionable methodology, and ponderous style, the merit of Slovtsov's work lies in the fact that for the first time the old idea of presenting a strictly chronological narration was abandoned. Even at that the author was very handicapped, for to him Siberia was merely the "Russian backdoor to Asia and America" and therefore only an annex to the empire. This accounts for the considerable space he still devoted to administrative measures by central and local authorities. An additional difficulty, which in the end was bound to defeat Slovtsov's scheme, was the fact that the government was still reluctant to open many of its archives.

Nonetheless Slovtsov succeeded in compiling two volumes of documents, one of which covered the period of 1585-1765. These contain accounts of the conquest of Siberia, the character of the new administration, and of government policy pertaining to the aborigines, trade, commerce, and industry. In attempting to integrate the mass of information, however, Slovtsov demonstrated his inability to dissociate authentic from fictitious material, being apparently unaware that any such confusion existed.

The intensive publication of documents in western Russia by the Archaeographic Commission and the Russian Geographical Society, the latter with branches in Siberia, stimulated further interest in the eastern domain, as did the growing local press and the activities of publicists like N. M. Yadrintsev, G. Yudin, I. Kuznetsov or A. I. Sibiryakov, among others. The new type of student was best represented by Shchapov, of whom more will be said elsewhere. Here it may only be stated that among all his works, his essay on the ethnological development of the Siberian population remains to the present day a significant contribution.

A second writer to whom Siberian historiography is much indebted, a contemporary of Shchapov, is Serafim Serafimovich Shashkov (1841-1882). A pupil of Shchapov at the University of Kazan, Shashkov was the author of a number of monographs, notably on Siberian slavery and on the causes of social unrest in Irkutsk from 1758 to 1760. His writings were published posthumously in two volumes entitled *Historical Studies* (*Istoricheskiye etyudy*) and *Historical Essays* (*Istoricheskiye ocherki*). Shashkov's studies present admirable accounts of the family status among the Siberian aborigines, of the place of the church and clergy in Siberian society, and of the moral decline among the natives; they cast light on the sorrowful exploitation of the aborigines by the administration as well as by individual entrepreneurs who sought quick gains and amassed fortunes. The study brings to mind the remarkable similarity between the American Indian and the Siberian aborigine, whether with respect to economics, politics, or social conflict between and native and invading population.

Two other historians in the general field of Siberian history merit mention. One is N. M. Yadrintsev (1842-1894), who published two studies: *Siberia as a Colony* (*Sibir kak Koloniya*) and *Siberian Aborigines: Their Conditions and Present Status* (*Sibirskiye inorodtsy, ikh byt i sovremennoye polozheniye*). Both studies contain much that retains importance to the very present. The other historian is A. A. Titov, author of a monograph on

Siberia in the Seventeenth Century (*Sibir v XVII veke*), a competent account of the formative period in Siberian history.

For those who search general chronological information, the compilation of data by I. V. Shcheglov will prove most useful.[68] Similar material about administrative measures and various statistical data will be found in the writings of Major General V. K. Andriyevich, based mainly on the complete Code of Laws published by the government during the reign of Nicholas I.[69] A much more important methodological study was made by P. N. Butsinsky (1853-1917), who in a series of monographs stressed further the need for archival investigations, without which he considered the writing of Siberian history completely inadequate.[70] Butsinsky's research in the field of eastern colonization was instrumental in arousing scholarly interest in the field of Siberian historiography. Analyzing more carefully the various means of Siberian colonization, Butsinsky included three main factors: two involved official action, declaratory law and forcible exile; the third, voluntary migration. Though the author failed by far to exhaust the subject, his study had a salutary effect on later research; a considerable portion of his published work was based on archival materials found in the Ministry of Justice and the Ministry of Foreign Affairs. These two important depositories were hardly explored until Butsinsky focused scholarly attention on the wealth they contained. As to Siberian archives, they were barely investigated by Butsinsky, a fact that the author himself regretfully acknowledged.

Other spadework was done by Oksenov, whose most notable contribution was on the relations between Great Novgorod and Yugria or northern Siberia, and between Muscovy and Yugria. Also to be noted is A. A. Adrianov, who compiled most useful data concerning the province of Tomsk, and P. M. Golovachev, who made a special investigation of the population of Siberia in the seventeenth and eighteenth centuries.[71] Even more notable service to Siberian historiography was rendered by N. N. Ogloblin, who compiled a careful catalog of the sources in the Siberian *Prikaz* (department), as well as of many documents pertaining to Siberia in other Russian archives. What Ikonnikov did for Russian historiography, Ogloblin accomplished for Siberia.[72] Equally important are the two works of V. I. Vaghin and S. M. Prutchenko on Sprenaksy's administrative reforms in Siberia, and I. P. Barsukov's two-volume work on the administration of Count Muravyev-Amursky.[73] Finally, there should be noted the single account of the Russian-American Company by P. Tikhmenev and a more recent study of the same organization by S. B. Okun'. The history of the Russian-American Company constitutes part of the drama of eastern expansion that climaxed in Russia's colonial establishments in Alaska and in California.[74]

A general survey of Siberian historiography in the nineteenth century convincingly shows that virgin soil was broken but that little else was done. The first attempt to write a general social and economic history of Siberia was that of Professor N. N. Firsov. It stemmed from the course he offered at the University of Kazan and at the Moscow Archaeological Institute.[75] Though a secondary account, Firsov's work represents an advance in the development of Siberian historiography, a transition from the merely compilatory and monographic to the more general and synthesized method of writing.

Of the more recent historians, whose lives covered the span of two eras, pre- and postrevolutionary, the foremost students in the field are V. I. Ogorodnikov and S. V. Bakhrushin. The two complement each other's writings: Ogorodnikov's study stressed the Siberian aborigines in relation to the incoming tide of Russian settlers and the development of the new administration; Bakhrushin's interest centered chiefly on the general subject of colonization.[76] Both authors endeavored to incorporate writings and present an overall picture of Russian eastward expansion. The increased economic and political importance of Siberia in recent years had led to a steadily rising interest in the past. The long-neglected field is beginning to assume an important place in Russian historiography.

Sergei Vladimirovich Bakhrushin died in 1950, and two years later the Academy of Sciences resolved to honor the memory of the academician by gathering and publishing four volumes which include his most important writings.[77] Our main concern here is the last two volumes, numbers three and four, which deal mainly with Bakhrushin's research in Siberian history, the question of Siberian colonization during the sixteenth and seventeenth centuries, the history of the Krasnoyarsk province during the seventeenth century, and Siberia and Central Asia in the sixteenth and seventeenth centuries. Bakhrushin's interest in Siberian history dated back to 1908. Throughout his lifetime he contributed many essays, reviews, and articles related to the main subject—the eastern domain commonly referred to as Siberia. Thus in 1922 appeared his recognized investigation in the field of

Siberian demography.[78] All told, Bakhrushin wrote during his lifetime about forty studies on Siberia. Most of them dealt with Siberian historiography, including the history of the aborigines, while in 1925 he published his essay *Basic Currents in Siberian History.*[79] Thereafter Bakhrushin never lost his interest in the history of Siberia. And although his attention was often diverted mostly to the sixteenth and seventeenth centuries, the overall effort of his research was much broader and presented a more general picture of the eastern part of the Russian Empire from the earliest times until the end of the nineteenth century. This included such vital subjects as colonization, taxation, trade, travel, and the peasantry during the sixteenth and seventeenth centuries. With the exception of N. N. Ogloblin, Bakhrushin was the man most familiar with the archival wealth that pertained to the past of Siberia.

Bakhrushin's place in Siberian historiography was particularly secured by his thorough research in the field of the so-called Russian Colonization in the East and the role trade had played in the acquisition of the vast eastern area. His life span covered physically and academically the pre- and post-revolutionary periods. At the time of his death, in 1950, he left an impressive legacy—a reevaluation of an enormous amount of archival material as well as a good deal of research—and both enabled him to draw a broader picture of Siberian history. Cumulatively these constituted no small contribution, one that no future student of history will be able to ignore whether in history or in historiography.

Another recent publication that deserves our attention, even though of a date beyond our scope of interest, is the appearance of a five-volume history of Siberia.[80] The general undertaking by the editorial board headed by A. P. Okladnikov constituted a daring enterprise. The vast eastern land, stretching from the Ural Mountains to the Pacific, for some 3,400 miles and 250 miles in width, is more than what some considered as the "bottom of the sack" or the icy prison; instead of a jailhouse Siberia emerges as the treasure house of untold wealth. Economic interest in this sprawling eastern domain was quite natural and understandable, and along with it the interest in its history was bound to rise. Since the 1850s there began to appear many monographic publications, but few general works.[81] The five-volume history of Siberia, despite the characteristic "Soviet line," contains much valuable information in the field of history, geography, economics, and ethnography. The five-volume set offers a wealth of factual information concerning the peasantry, Siberian economy, ethnic difficulties, and climatic conditions.

It is perhaps vital to stress a few peculiarities that are particularly applicable to Siberian historiography. A number of subjects impose themselves in the discussion, as they do in no other phase of Russian historiography (for example, problems such as the character of Siberian colonization). Consequently, the question has been frequently asked whether Siberia was ever a colony in the sense the term is applied elsewhere in the world. Another query is, What was the nature of incorporation of Siberia into the Russian Empire? Other related questions naturally follow, such as the means by which Siberia had been incorporated into the empire and later into the Soviet Union. Furthermore, what was the true nature of the administrative, political, or economic policies prior to 1917 and after? In general terms the history of Siberia is a four-century process of amalgamation of the vast eastern hinterland by the western part of Russia. The subject is as vast as is the territory itself. Interpretations vary widely, and historiography should be of aid to the student of history in familiarizing himself with the important writings and interpretations of this multiphased subject. Historiography should also be of aid in coping with the complexity of historical interpretation, enabling one to arrive at an opinion or interpretation that is based on factual evidence rather than on preconceived views.

The Federalist Idea in History

SHCHAPOV

Russian historical writing was predominantly Great Russian and therefore bore a distinct "Moscow stamp." Only a few men, very few indeed, endeavored to show that not all roads led to Moscow. Those who rebelled against Great Russian particularism or at least demonstrated any awareness of the situation might be grouped into what we may label as the Federalist School. One of the earliest students to stress the federal principle in Russian historical literature was undoubtedly Afanasy Prokofyevich Shchapov (1830-1876), and if he failed to develop this thesis more fully, it was largely because he was silenced by the authorities and had such a short life.[82]

Shchapov was born in a Siberian village, Anga, about 150 miles from Irkutsk. His father was a Russian parish priest, his mother of Buryat origin. His parental background and place of birth made Shchapov a true product of the national and local milieu of his time. While attending the Divinity School of Irkutsk he distinguished himself as a student and was sent to complete his higher education at the Kazan Divinity Academy. Upon graduation he was retained as lecturer in Russian history. Taking advantage of the archives recently transferred from the Solovetsky monastery to Kazan, Shchapov began to examine these sources and soon became interested in church history, especially in the problem of the schism.

Subsequently Shchapov was invited to the University of Kazan, where his academic career began in earnest. Russian history was his chosen field, yet it was Henry T. Buckle whom he esteemed highly and read avidly; Russian historians disappointed him. The reason for this he explained in one of his addresses.

> When I studied Ustryalov and Karamzin, it always seemed strange to me that in their histories one fails to find reference to rural Russia, or to the history of the masses, to the so-called simple, ignorant people. Must the majority remain inaudible, passive, and outside of history? Has not this overwhelming majority the right to enlightenment, to historical development, to life and importance, as have the nobility or the clergy? . . . Yet read the chronicles or the historical records up to the eighteenth century: who built, founded, and populated the land, cleared the Russian soil and forests, drained it of marshes? Who if not the peasants?[83]

In Shchapov's appeal one could discern the earliest and the genuine *vox populi* in Russian historiography, historical materialism, if you wish. With his characteristic wit, G. V. Plekhanov, in describing a debate between Shchapov and Chernyshevsky, referred to it as a verbal duel between a democrat and a social democrat.[84] Like his earlier predecessor, Ivan Pososhkov, Shchapov was the flesh and blood of the peasantry, the ideologist of his class. He approached the study of the past with the typical democratic interest of the peasant, simple, unsophisticated; to Shchapov and to Pososhkov, history was not merely a science, but a weapon for the defense of his class interests.[85]

For his master's dissertation, presented in 1858, Shchapov selected a subject that, for political reasons, students had previously preferred to leave alone—the schism within the Russian church. The new view taken in his thesis was contrary to all former interpretations; the author concluded that the whole matter of the schism was a phenomenon not merely religious in nature, but basically political and social as well. The essence of the schism was not a mere question of ritualism, as is still commonly thought; in the schism Shchapov detected a much deeper meaning—a conflict between the people and policy-making ecclesiastic authorities. It implied popular protest against the church as an agency that collaborated with the state in the enforcement of serfdom and supported the crushing tax system; it condoned administrative abuses and army recruiting. Subtly Shchapov hinted at the close tie between the schism and the subsequent peasant revolts such as the one led by Stenka Razin in 1667-1671. The thesis cast a totally new light on the origins of the schism. To quote the author himself: ''[The schism] proved to be a revolt not only against the church, but against the state, and not only against the reforms of Nikon, but against the changes and reforms.'' The schismatics were more than religious rebels; they represented the general rebellious spirit of the masses against the entire state of affairs in the nation. The merits of his study were acknowledged even by such cool-headed historians as Bestuzhev-Ryumin, who was usually very reserved about committing himself, particularly on such an explosive theme as the one presented by Shchapov.

Shchapov's concept of the Russian state was equally original in interpretation. The leitmotiv in Russian history, Shchapov maintained in his lectures at the University of Kazan, was regionalism, local self-government, and not centralization. He continued to stress this theme in his later writings and throughout his short lifetime. In a series of essays on regionalism during the Time of Troubles, on the village community, and on the institution of the town meeting in Russia, Shchapov saw in them democracy in action and insisted that the solution of Russia's problem was to retain the principle of regional autonomy throughout the far-flung empire. Shchapov differentiated Western European federalism from Russian regionalism: whereas the former was based on ethnographic peculiarities, the latter must be based on historic, economic, and peculiarly local forms of life. Only such a policy can assure successful completion of the continued process of colonization in the nation. Public initiative, and its instinctive reflexes toward national unity without compulsion from above, was an article of faith with Shchapov. This he saw in the village commune, in the locally preserved institution of the town meetings, and in the vanished National Assembly (*Zemsky Sobor*), in which, contrary to Klyuchevsky's interpretation, Shchapov saw genuine native democracy. Because of his unswerving faith in the people rather than in a centralized state, Shchapov attacked the Juridical School with particular vehemence, referring to it as "superstate fanatacism," while the Slavophile interpretation of the past he called the "cobweb-weaving of history."

In another series of essays on geography and history, on the causes of cultural backwardness, and on the role of the state and the people, Shchapov concluded that the state represents a progressive force only as long as it is an instrument of enlightenment, and that thereby it must aid the people to participate in national affairs. Shchapov believed that the theory, as presented by the Juridical School, of the state as an absolute factor in history was not only false, but dangerous, for it would force the masses into a submissive and passive position; such a state would invariably deprive itself of the true creative forces, of national strength and progress. The author logically deduced the necessity for a program of universal education that would enable the people to assume responsibility in the affairs of the state. Only in that case could Russia advance with other nations toward a brighter future. It is not difficult to detect in Shchapov's views the populist philosophy of the 1870s. Shchapov considered the peasantry as the backbone of national life while the intelligentsia was destined to lead the peasantry toward a free social order and economic progress. For this reason Shchapov is considered by some writers as the pioneer populist historian of nineteenth-century Russia.

While at the University of Kazan, Shchapov became involved in a political affair that terminated his academic career. Participating in a session organized by university students to commemorate the victims of the peasant uprising at Bezdna in 1861, he delivered an address that ended with the cry "Long live a democratic constitution!"[86] Shortly afterward he was ordered to appear in St. Petersburg for an investigation, and although the case was hushed up, his relations with the university were severed. While in the capital, Shchapov met some of the leading intellectuals of his generation: Pisarev, Chernyshevsky, Dobrolyubov, and others. They left an indelible impression on him, and vice versa.

Three years later the authorities ordered him to leave the capital and depart for his native city of Irkutsk, where he devoted himself to the study of Siberia. Removed from political events, friends, and libraries, his scholarly pursuits were gravely handicapped; the indigenous intellectual began to wither away. The untimely death of his wife, along with distressing financial difficulties and cultural isolation, thwarted Shchapov's talent and undermined his physical health; he died during the most fruitful period of his life, at the age of forty-six. Despite all that, he managed to leave behind him numerous essays, some constituting highly valued contributions to the study of Russian religious sects, others giving a refreshing view of the theory of regionalism in Russian history, particularly as demonstrated in the administration of Siberia.

While Shchapov, studying Siberia, came to be a firm believer in the principle of regionalism as an answer to local discontent with centralized authority, a number of writers in other parts of the empire, notably in the Ukraine, in the south, drew identical conclusions. The renaissance among the national minorities within Russia aroused a keen popular interest in the past. Among the intellectual groups arose a considerable contingent of Federalists, or "autonomists," who sought political and cultural autonomy as well as opportunities for national development within corresponding regional delimitations. Of these stand out such figures as M. P. Dragomanov (1841-1873), V. B. Antonovich (1834-1908), M. A. Maksimovich (1804-1873), N. I. Kostomarov, of whom more will be said later, and a score of others, most of whom were connected particularly with the University of Kiev. Their extensive writings, editing of documents, and research in folklore, ethnography, archaeology, and history served to agitate regional sentiments and awaken national consciousness among a people traditionally referred to as "Little Russians."

Dragomanov, who combined historical research with Ukrainian national activities, soon disagreed sharply with both university and official authorities. In 1875 he was dismissed from the faculty of the University of Kiev; a year later he emigrated to Geneva, the haven of many political *émigrés*, where he became editor of a Ukrainian publication, *Hromada* (Community). Between 1878 and 1883 he edited five volumes of essays on Ukrainian folklore, history, and ethnography. Dragomanov envisioned a great Slav federation and became a confirmed agrarian socialist. His publication clearly reflected his views though basically he was anti-Marxian, while his nationalistic ideas led him to champion the cause of Ukrainian autonomy within a federal system.[87]

Dragomanov also published a two-volume annotated collection of Ukrainian folksongs with his collaborator, V. B. Antonovich, who remained in Kiev. Here the latter became the editor-in-chief of the Kievan Archaeographic Commission, and under his direction were published nine volumes of collected documents on Ukrainian history, covering the fifteenth to the eighteenth centuries (*Arkhiv yugozapadnoy Rossii*). Antonovich was also the author of a number of works, notably a study of the last period of the Dnieper Cossack communities and a monograph on Lithuania prior to the middle of the fifteenth century. He conducted several archaeological expeditions in southern Russia and was the author of several archaeological maps of the Kiev and Volyn' regions. M. A. Maksimovich, though originally a botanist, later shifted his interest to history. His collection of annotated songs of the south won high praise among men like A. S. Pushkin, P. A. Vyazemsky, and other famed national poets. But above all else these men were strong advocates of federalism as a system that would enable the multinational empire to assure greater harmony within.[88]

KOSTOMAROV

A more colorful and productive member of the Ukrainian Federalist School was Nikolay Ivanovich Kostomarov.[89] Kostomarov was born in the province of Voronezh. His father, a nobleman, was murdered by his own serfs; his mother was of Ukrainian origin, a former serf girl on his father's estate. It is very likely that Kostomarov received from his mother both an interest in southern Russia and sympathy for the oppressed peasant masses. He tells us that his reading of history left him curious and dissatisfied, reminding us of the case of Shchapov. "Why is it," he asked "that all histories talk about eminent statesmen, sometimes about laws and institutions, but disregard the life of the masses? The poor peasant, the tiller of the soil, seems not to exist in history. Why does not history say something about the general life, about the way he thinks and feels, about his happiness and his sorrows?"

Kostomarov came to believe that history did not consist merely of accounts of political life, of diplomacy, wars, and legislative acts. True history must deal with the lives of the peoples who make history, with their aspirations, their vices and virtues, their domestic life, habits, customs, rituals, morals, folk manners. He severely reproached the Slavophiles and criticized historians like Solovyev for giving preeminence to the state at the expense of the people. The purpose of history, Kostomarov argued, was not a matter of chronologically stringing events and facts together like beads: that was perhaps the function of archaeology and ethnography. The historian's mission was the elucidation of the spirit of the people he deals with, embracing all the ramifications and manifold activities of their daily lives.

In his writings Kostomarov sought the causes for the loss of Ukrainian autonomy and the triumph of Muscovite absolutism despite the native Cossack freedom-loving, prairie-dwelling Ukrainian people. Kostomarov endeavored to retrace old democratic institutions among the early Slavs and studied the period of the Novgorod Republic and the causes of it decline. Whatever subject Kostomarov undertook, his object was to see the underlying forces in history rather than the surface of political events. This led him at times to overgeneralization and made him the target of much criticism. His characterization of the Russian and Ukrainian peoples was colorful enough but hardly palatable to many readers, except the romantics who favored Ukrainian separatism.[90]

As a student at the University of Kharkov, Kostomarov studied history, ethnography, and folklore. For his thesis he chose the subject of the Uniate Church in western Russia, but the censor banned it and Kostomarov changed the topic to a study of Russian national poetry in history. In 1846 he joined the faculty of the University of Kiev, though not for long: within less than three years he was arrested as a member of the secret Pan-Slavist Cyril-Methodius Society,[91] imprisoned in the dreaded Peter and Paul Fortress and—though he belonged to the extreme right wing of the group—was banished to Saratov. While in exile, he continued to gather sources on Ukrainian folklore and the peasant revolts led by Stenka Razin and later by Yemelyan Pugachev. It was while exploring this field that Kostomarov also developed an interest in archaeology, participated in several expeditions, and remained an active member of the archaeographic society for the rest of his life.

With the ascendancy of Alexander II, Kostomarov was granted greater freedom, and in 1859 he was allowed to return to the capital, where he joined the faculty of the University of St. Petersburg to lecture in Russian history. Here he interpreted the past of Russia as a centripetal process, emphasizing the part national minorities either had played or were bound to play in the welfare of the empire. From the very dawn of history, Kostomarov maintained, Russian rule was based on the principle of broad federalism.[92] Furthermore, he insisted that the role of the state had been forced too much to the foreground of events at the expense of the masses who had contributed so much to the welfare of the state and in the end had woefully been assigned a backseat in history. The thesis provoked strong displeasure among many of his academic colleagues, frowns among others, and suspicion on the part of official authorities.

In addition to his lectures at the University of St. Petersburg, Kostomarov also consented to take part in the recently formed "Free University." As a middle-of-the-road liberal, Kostomarov came in for conflicts on all sides, particularly with students who regarded him as too conservative and official-dom that thought him too radical. By 1862 he was compelled once again to abandon his university post, this time for good, and he devoted himself entirely to writing and active participation in the archaeological and geographical societies. A prolific writer, he left behind no less than twenty-one volumes of "Historical Monographs" not to mention numerous articles scattered throughout the periodical literature of the country. As a member of the Archaeographic Commission he was responsible for the editing of the nine-volume collection of historical documents on southern and western Russia (*Akty, otnosyashchiyesya k istorii yuzhnoy i zapadnoy Rossii*). Simultaneously he served as editor of a three-volume ethnography published by the Geographical Society. The advancement in the fields of archaeology, ethnography, and archaeography is due to a considerable extent to Kostomarov. These developed sciences proved instrumental in stimulating and advancing the interest in history among other scholars.

Kostomarov's chief works are concerned with the Ukrainian people and their struggle for independence against aristocratic Poland and for autonomy against absolutist Imperial Russia. He published a biography of Ivan Svirhovsky, Ukrainian Ataman of the sixteenth century, and a work on the war led by Bohdan Khmelnitsky and the annexation of southern Ukraine to Russia. Following that he shifted his interest to the history of peasant uprisings in Russia, notably the rebellion under the leadership of Stenka Razin and the mass revolts during the Time of Troubles. Whatever the main subject of study happened to be, the emphasis was always on the ethnographic rather than political or economic aspects. The haste with which he wrote explains in part at least the slipshod generalizations or outright errors one is able to find in his works; the varied activities in which he enthusiastically participated did not help matters either, a fact that rendered him vulnerable to sharp criticism and provided grounds for considering his writings superficial.

A great fault of Kostomarov was perhaps his hero worship and his frequent sweeping interpretations, which on many occasions led him to broad handling of factual material. Characters for whom he felt a personal fondness he painted as legendary knights and relished their part in history with romantic enthusiasm. This fact more than anything else explains the uncritical fecundity of Kostomarov. His vulnerability as a scholar has been readily admitted even by his admirers; yet his voluminous writings stirred deep interest in a field of history that had been formerly deemphasized if not entirely neglected by Great Russian writers, who generally included the Ukraine as a mere annex of Moscow.

There were serious weaknesses and self-contradictions in the historical processes that Kostomarov so laboriously tried to set up against the Juridical School. The exalted role assigned to the masses by Kostomarov somehow dissipates, or leaves one with some misgivings as to either their wisdom or their constructive force in history. Like the Biblical prophet Balaam, Kostomarov begins by cursing the state and ends blessing it. Unwittingly his narrative leads to the deduction that, not the people, but the state did play the primary part in adding meaning and form to national life. Despite the exaltation of the people, after reading Kostomarov one is still left with a constrained sense that the peasant masses emerge as an abstraction whereas the state looms as an imposing reality. Peasants rising in protest prove in the end to have been void of plan or purpose, and thereby defeat themselves and gradually surrender to the very authority against which they initially rebelled. But that was the thesis of the Juridical School, the very opponent that Kostomarov set out at the beginning to disprove!

In his effort to prove his own thesis Kostomarov insisted that contemporary opinion and beliefs were as important as factual documents. What he evidently meant was that the past could be reconstructed without necessarily utilizing available documentary records. The answer of his critics was that the result of such a method must be historical fiction rather than history, a romanticized narrative of the past that must disclaim any pretense to scientific research. And this is precisely what most of Kostomarov's works are; he is the Carlyle of Russian historiography. To be sure, Kostomarov's knowledge of Russian and Ukrainian folklore was impressive, but its application to historical interpretation was often bound to raise eyebrows and expose him to grave criticism.

Aside from a few more enduring contributions to history, most of his writings cite colorful episodes that do not stand up against critical analysis. Hearsay and legendary tales dominate factual evidence; sentimentality and passion overrule rational judgment. The general reader finds most entertaining stories about dashing Cossacks, galloping across the southern steppes, valorous hetmans, and adventurous rebel leaders; to the historian, however, it is fiction, upon which he frowns, and which he puts aside for his bedtime reading.

Though Kostomarov laments the vanished free life of the "Cossack days," he could not but sense that the era had passed into history beyond any hope of restoration as the fiction of "Home on the Range." He seems to have gravely feared that any effort in that direction would resolve itself into a naked nihilism and spell violence, bloodshed, and waste of human lives. A strange circle thus formed itself: fears of possible senseless violence in the present destroyed the idols he built from the past.[93] Yet some of his writings retain value and lasting interest.

The flowing literary style and colorful characterization of historical figures made Klyuchevsky's studies monumental contributions to both history and the Russian language. These qualities were not altered by lack of either accuracy or objective handling of documentary evidence. Kostomarov is noted, too, for his flawless and racy style, yet the conscientious reader seems to sense a degree of theatricality. Actors seem to appear at the footlights of history, cite their lines, and depart; they inspire applause as the curtain is lowered, the lights go out, and the drama comes to an end. "It may not be true, but it is absorbingly exciting," the layman concludes. "It may be absorbingly exciting, but it is hardly in agreement with historical evidence," the historian chimes in.

HRUSHEVSKY

The leading historian among the Ukrainian Federalists is undoubtedly the patriarch scholar Mykhaylo S. Hrushevsky, known better under the Russian name Mikhail Sergeyevich Grushevsky, or the English version as Hrushevsky (1866-1934). He was born in Kholm, formerly Russian Poland, and studied at the University of Kiev under his most admired professor, V. B. Antonovich. Later Hrushevsky taught at the same university though only for a brief period. Because of the cultural discrimination, the ban on the Ukrainian language, and his personal political views, Hrushevsky's difficulties with the administration kept mounting and a final breach became unavoidable. In 1894, on the recommendation of his admired teacher, Antonovich, he accepted a chair at the University of Lvov (Lemberg), then in Austria, where he anticipated a greater degree of cultural freedom and a milder political climate. Within a short time he gained the respect of his academic colleagues and the reverence of his students. His field was southeastern Europe and Ukrainian history, and shortly after his arrival Hrushevsky assumed leadership in the intellectual movement. As president of the Shevchenko Scientific Society, he took charge of its publications.

Hrushevsky was recognized not only as a scholar but also as a statesman, and herein came later the source of his political difficulties. To Hrushevsky history was a tool for implementing his beliefs; yet, it must be noted, he never vulgarized it, but rather managed to remain loyal to true scholarship. Unlike others, he never employed his historical knowledge for popular writing, for propaganda pamphlets, or romantic narration. His whole life was dedicated to a single cause: to erect for his people, in the form of a scholarly history, a monument that could be neither overlooked nor overthrown by academic challenge from his northern opponents. His history of the Ukraine is beyond doubt the standard work in the field and a contribution to which Great Russian historians cannot remain indifferent. The author toiled half of his lifetime over it, as can be judged by the span of time during which the ten volumes appeared, 1898-1937, the last volume being published posthumously. An abridged one-volume history of the Ukrainian people appeared in 1904 in Russian. A few years later his *Illustrated History of the Ukraine* appeared in the Ukrainian language and has since been translated into English and published in the United States. Distracted by turbulent years following 1917, Hrushevsky never completed his great study but ended with the seventeenth century. The Ukraine has been the homeland of war for many centuries; again and again that country served as the battleground of conflicts between the East and the West to the present century. Yet Hrushevsky's ten-volume history represents more than a record of wars: the volumes incorporate valuable accounts of social, economic, and cultural history as well.[94]

Russian historiography has suffered from one serious defect, which might be called Muscovite egocentricity. Many outstanding writers persistently neglected peripheral influence on the general course of Russian national development. Thus, for instance, the Kievan period was most scantily treated, and some still treat it as a casual chapter, a mere episode that only served as a prologue to the rise of the Muscovite state. In most histories the Kievan era seems to vanish after the middle of the thirteenth century as mysteriously as it reappeared in the middle of the seventeenth century. The period that elapses between leaves one with an impression of a vacuum in the history of Eastern Europe. The period that precedes 1240 is often presented as a political dress rehearsal for the national state destined to rise in the North.

With the rise of nationalism in the peripheral regions, such neglect or misinterpretation of historical facts provoked understandable resentment. Ukrainian students of history regarded the deemphasis of the role of the southwestern portion of the nation as nothing less than typical Great Russian distortion. While grumblings against "northern distortion of history" became increasingly audible, it was Hrushevsky who openly revolted and successfully challenged the Great Russian writers. And though Hrushevsky undertook to correct the situation out of some kind of academic revenge, he nevertheless rendered Russian history unintentional service. Furthermore, he inadvertently demonstrated the need to bring the peripheral units together into a unified historical narrative rather than treat them as totally separate and even contrasting entities by themselves.

Hrushevsky's "vengeful" spirit expressed itself in a broadening of historical science; politically, however, it assumed the form of separatism, and here is where the real difficulties enter in full size. Intentional or not, Hrushevsky's thesis came to be widely accepted as advocacy of separatism, that is, a view of the Kievan period as an exclusively Ukrainian chapter in history rather than as part of Great Russian or Muscovite history. Instead of considering Ukrainian, White Russian, Lithuanian, or Great Russian as components of a single national state, the new version came to be interpreted as an account of entirely separate nationalities. A unified narrative might have eliminated Muscovite particularism or chauvinism. Furthermore, fair presentation of the continuous, successive development through the earlier periods that led up to the rise of Moscow is bound to enrich the store of knowledge concerning both Great Russian as well as Ukrainian historiography. This development would have brought into consideration Kievan Russia, Lithuania, and Poland, as well as Moscow; it would not abruptly shift all of history from the "Decline of Kiev" to the "Rise of Moscow," without accounting properly for the economic and political causes that preceded this shift. Kievan Russia could not be allowed suddenly to disappear in the mist of the past, without accounting for the transitional period of peripheral areas. Herein lies the strength of Hrushevsky's thesis or of his school.

Hrushevsky was not a narrow specialist historian; he felt that a knowledge of political events alone could never be sufficient for an understanding of the past—hence his concentration on various aspects of the cultural life of the Ukrainian people. He was keenly interested in literature, philology, economics, sociology, and the natural sciences, and frequently contributed articles in some of these fields. His *History of Ukrainian Literature* vividly attests to the broad cultural knowledge of the author.

Upon his return to Kiev shortly after the revolution, Hrushevsky founded the Scientific Research Center of Ukrainian History. The center brought together leading Ukrainian scholars, who during the 1920s plunged into intensive research and published a number of monographs, mainly on seventeenth-, eighteenth-, and nineteenth-century history. Hrushevsky also set up here the State Publishing House that undertook the publication of studies in various fields, including the Ukraine as well as Galicia. Under his supervision in 1929 six volumes appeared (*Naukovyi Zbirnyk Istorychnoy Sektsii VUAN*), which incorporated a variety of subjects, including judicial developments, census data, military accounts, and various subjects of Ukrainian history. Cumulatively the material covered approximately the seventeenth and eighteenth centuries. Aside from editorial contributions, Hrushevsky labored on a variety of related subjects such as historical science and historiography.

Regrettably, upon his return to Kiev, Hrushevsky plunged into other activities besides the purely academic. He was never the historian to be contented with the ivory tower study and for that reason was soon to be drawn into the whirlpool of politics. Shortly after his return to Kiev he was elected to the presidency of the recently formed Ukrainian National Council (*Rada*). From this moment began a tense struggle between Kiev and Petrograd for recognition and clarification of the status and the degree of autonomy of the Ukraine. The entry of the Soviet government complicated matters further, while the German occupation, followed by civil war and Allied intervention, brought the state of affair to total hopelessness. Hrushevsky left for Vienna, but when he returned a few years later, he was a broken man.

In 1924, at the invitation of the Ukrainian Academy of Science, Hrushevsky was induced to return to Kiev, where he hoped to complete his life work. He was named president of that august institution. However, his hoped-for unmolested scholarship was soon to be shattered: after a short period of relative comfort, he came to realize that the national freedom and cultural autonomy pledged to his people were in reality a myth: the government's constant suspicion of a revival of "Ukrainian chauvinism," which might lead to clamor for national independence, led in turn to repression and interference with his scholarly pursuits.

In 1930 Hrushevsky was arrested and banished to the North, near Moscow. His ceaseless political and literary activities, with all their adversities, hopes, and disillusionments, kept sapping his health, already badly shattered. In 1934 he was allowed to go south to restore his undermined health, but it was too late: he died shortly after his arrival in the Caucasus. Hrushevsky left behind him a rich legacy of historical literature, which, regardless of political feuds, will always have to be taken into account if Russian history is to be seen in its entirety rather than as a series of episodic stages and sporadic developments emerging around the Muscovite state.

Legal Marxists

During the last decades of the nineteenth century the Russian Empire witnessed a noticeable industrial advancement. Railroad construction and extensive foreign investments in industrial enterprises served as harbingers of an encroaching era of industrial revolution with all its familiar attributes: shifts of population, depopulation in certain rural areas, and congestion in others. This caused a disturbance in prices, a fall in market prices in depleted areas, and a rise in the newly formed urban centers. Western capital—lured by prospects of fat returns, abundant resources, cheap labor, and protective government policy—began to flow eastward. The number of factories climbed, the ranks of workers in the cities swelled, Western technology advanced, and markets expanded, while the home-craft industry began to show symptoms of decline. The Russian nation came to face the well-known implications of the transitional period when a backward economy had to yield to an oncoming technological revolution.

Opinions as to how the critical period should be faced were by no means unanimous. While some observers enthusiastically predicted national prosperity and material blessings that would assure mass contentment, thereby hoping to reduce the chances of appeal to mass violence, others felt far less optimistic about the turn of events. There was a strong feeling among some that industrial development was bound to bring with it all the evils of Western society—a restless proletariat and an entrenched bourgeois class clamoring for a more favorable position in government; it held out the prospects of grim periodic crises in the economy of the nation accompanied by unemployment and social disturbances that in the end might imperil the entire social order. Fear of such sorrowful consequences was professed by the agrarian classes, for obvious reasons. There were similar misgivings in the Populist party, whose motivations were not without self-interest. The Populists watched with alarm the economic changes that spelled the end of the "uniqueness" of the national development upon which they based their entire party philosophy. The new order would destroy their revered institution of the village commune, the peasant system of communal landownership to which they were sentimentally attached, and then, they predicted, all the grievious consequences of what had taken place elsewhere would be repeated in Russia.

The interesting feature was the anomaly of the role of government in this industrial development. The government became the owner of an expanded system of railways, mines, and industrial plants; it shared in the benefits that industry came to enjoy. The official attitude, it may be added, was a divided one: while on the one hand it actively supported the industrial revolution, on the other it professed hesitancy as to the potential threat to the existing political and social institutions. If on one hand the imperial government became a partner in or outright owner of numerous industrial establishments and means of transportation, on the other it remained the owner of large estates and by virtue of that fact could not but share the fears of the old privileged landowning class that sulkily looked down on the economic innovations.

It was in the midst of this critical turn of events that we find what might be defined as a Marxist reflection in bourgeois historiography, which in turn led to a school of Marxist interpretation of Russian history. It began with the so-called Legal Marxists who presumably accepted the Marxist economic theory even while refuting its political tenets or implications. They brushed aside the views of orthodox Marxists as well as their doctrines concerning class struggle or the predestined role of the proletariat. The Legal Marxists did accept collectivism and state ownership as a sign of a national evolutionary process in modern society that did not necessarily invite social revolution.

This leads us to the main subject—the essence of Legal Marxism. In Germany a distinguished group of historians, philosophers, sociologists, and economists thought along similar lines, with a slight deviation. Among them were men like Johann K. Rodbertus, Werner Sombart, Georg Simmel, Rudolf Stammler, to mention only a few. In Russia men such as P. B. Struve, M. I. Tugan-Baranovsky, N. A. Berdyayev, and S. N. Bulgakov followed a similar line of thought. They held the view that the universal aim of law was justice, which implied harmonious relationships within a society. Furthermore, they had no intention of challenging capitalism or its implied institutions. Their revolutionary faith was tamed by realities in national life, and for that reason their aims were simpler and more narrow—they hoped that economic and social problems that had arisen with capitalism could be successfully coped with by means of democratic legislation, "legal action," if you please. A properly elected and authorized body of legislators would be able to discover solutions that would enable a society to avoid a catastrophic confrontation within the community with all the consequences of civil strife. A rational government in cooperation with a properly elected body of representatives could find solutions to problems modern society came to face and thereby forestall mass revolution. Such is the basic essence of so-called Legal Marxism. Bearing this in mind, we may now discuss two representatives of this school of thought, P. B. Struve and M. I. Tugan-Baranovsky.

STRUVE

One of the first economic historians to formulate the philosophy of Legal Marxism was Peter Berngardovich Struve (1870-1944). In 1894 he published his *Critical Notes on the Question of the Economic Development of Russia*.[95] The main purpose of the *Notes* was to demolish the contention of the Populists, and the censor saw no harm in this occupation. We can say with a degree of certainty that the appearance of Struve's book on Legal Marxism was the initial step of this new philosophy. It was perfectly "legal" from the official point of view to question the validity of the Populists' contentions concerning the economic role of the village commune; it was equally acceptable to the office of the censor to insist that capitalism in Russia was an established fact or a desirable development as long as there was no reference to labor problems, nor a call for improvement of the workingmen's lot by means of violence or strikes, nor a subtle attack on the institution of private property. In short, Legal Marxism was tolerated and its thematic content admissible in print as long as it was stripped of any revolutionary allusion.

Analyzing the general economic state of affairs, Struve first pointed out the extreme backwardness that prevailed throughout the country and advocated that Russia learn from Western capitalism. This was an immediate challenge to the Populists, who staked their entire philosophy on the "distinct" development of Russian rural economy and social institutions. Pursuing his thesis further, Struve then came to arouse the wrath of the orthodox Marxists when he arrived at the focal point of his theme—that the appearance of capitalism in Russia carried with it a sign of permanent progress. The author departed from the view that capitalism necessarily implied an inevitable social cataclysm, and maintained instead that it held out peaceful means to transform the old order. In a word, it was not by revolution but by evolutionary reforms that an economic system could be secured.

Struve thus rejected the Marxian thesis that hoary capitalism signified a transitory period, at the end of which it was bound to dig its own grave to make for a higher social order to be attained by revolution. According to Struve, capitalist society does not constitute a stepping stone to an advanced society built on bourgeois ruins, but carries with it a stamp of finality. Capitalism, he believed, represents a natural advanced state from which eventually all classes are bound to derive some blessings. He denied the belief of the Marxists that capitalism was bound to disintegrate and to augur nothing but class antagonism within society. Whereas the one endeavored to dissociate political developments from economic evolution, the others professed the two to be absolutely inseparable.

Pointing to the changes that had already taken place in Russia, such as the considerable growth of a commodity economy and the expansion of markets, transportation, and industrial output, Struve concluded that capitalism in Russia was no longer a question of acceptance or denial; capitalism was already the established economy. By virtue of this fact, he declared, the nation could henceforth anticipate not class strife but general welfare; not conflict but peaceful coexistence between the old and the newly established economy. He firmly opposed an interference in its natural development and the notion that the old and new were destined to work at cross-purposes; on the contrary, both were bound to aspire to a common goal—national welfare. Following the same line of thought, Struve later published another study on serfdom in which he endeavored to show that the old agrarian economy coexisted with encroaching capitalism. Occasional conflicts between the two were arbitrated by the state until the old and the new merged into a single economic force that operated for the common good.

The Legal Marxists thus came to believe that the new capitalistic economy could advance despite the presence of a backward rural economy, provided the government extended its protective wings over the economy either by protective tariffs or by actual partnership in a collectivist form. Backward rural conditions would be no impediment to modern technology; on the other hand, technocracy would stimulate the rise of agrarian standards through improved means of transportation and similar developments. The sharper the contrast between the legacy of serfdom and technological advancement, the stronger the Legal Marxists believed would be the country's realization of the need for capitalist expansion. Adjustments, however, should not be enforced from above, since they might result in an artificially imposed superstructure; there must be no interference with the natural course of economic development.

The turbulent events of 1905-1906, however, caused a hasty and serious revision of views among the Legal Marxists. The consternation and panic that the revolution produced in the midst of their camp compelled them to retreat from their position and move sharply to the right. Whereas formerly they looked on the state as the nonpartisan arbitrator instrumental in preventing conflicts of interests, now they ran to the state to secure protection against the rebellious masses. In addition to benevolent economic assistance, they now appealed for more extensive aid against the perilous mass fury displayed in recent years. Strangely, their haunting and desperate search for protection against revolution brought them ideologically much closer to the now-faded Juridical School. The state, Struve now philosophized, could not be considered as either good or evil, but as an indispensable agency singly capable of taming the rebellious elements within the nation, regardless of whether those be eighteenth-century Cossacks or twentieth-century intellectuals. He saw in both nothing but a severed part of the community that seriously threatened the state. Struve was therefore willing to assign the state a primary role and grant it unrestrained freedom for the purpose of suppressing the ever-present spirit of elemental violence or social rebelliousness.

TUGAN-BARANOVSKY

The identical line of thought was followed by Michael I. Tugan-Baranovsky (1865-1919), another Legal Marxist, economist, historian, in his widely known study of the Russian factory during the past century.[96] Basically the thesis of Tugan-Baranovsky did not deviate too far from the one presented by Struve. Peter the Great, according to Tugan-Baranovsky, was the sovereign who introduced capitalism into Russia. There was no conflict between the feudal and capitalist economies; the two functioned side by side harmoniously. Friction stemmed rather from tension at the top, where minor leading groups strove for influence. Whatever other antagonisms were present could be traced largely to the aspirations of labor to shake off its feudal bonds. The state played a decisive part in settling such social or economic maladjustments; it was to capitalism that the state assigned the task of combatting national backwardness and raising the cultural level of the working masses engaged in industry.

Peter I had dealt with the problem when he came to recognize industry as a vital branch of the national economy and relegate power to the middle classes. Capitalism, according to Tugan-Baranovsky, was now destined to pursue the same aims originally perceived by this monarch, securing economic and cultural progress within the state. Therefore, he concluded, Populist fear that capitalism must destroy Russian "uniqueness" or that it was bound to lead to inevitable class warfare had been historically disproved. He firmly believed that continued legislation favoring industrial development was the best assurance of national progress. Furthermore, although the state must render benevolent support or participate wherever necessary, nonetheless it must follow a strict policy of laissez-faire and allow the free play of economic forces for the good of all concerned. As in the case of Struve, under the impact of revolutionary developments Tugan-Baranovsky gradually altered his former views, shifting slowly but surely (and predictably!) into the camp of the extreme right. Legal Marxism passed, as one writer well summarized, "from demonstration of the inevitability and progressiveness of capitalism in Russia to apologetics and glorification; from a bowdlerized Marxism cut to measure for the censor as a matter of reluctant necessity, to a castrated Marxism robbed of its revolutionary vigor; and finally, to open opposition to Marxism.''[97]

Marxist Historians

PLEKHANOV

While discussing Marxist historians a few brief remarks are in order. From our previous description we might have observed that until about the 1880s the heavy weight of compilation in historiography was reflected mainly in homegrown ideologies such as the literary criticism of Belinsky, the nationalistic philosophy of the Slavophiles, or the mild socialist views of Herzen. From the 1860s we note the liberal and radical views of Chernyshevsky followed by rising movement of populism. During the last two decades of the past century, however, we begin to meet a new phenomenon in historiography entering from abroad—the philosophy of Marxism in its full revolutionary armor.

Homespun ideologies seemed to have reached their climax in the spring of 1881, when the assassination of Alexander II clearly demonstrated the futility of the terroristic revolutionary surge. Effective suppression followed but renewed repression during the next decade had convinced many thinkers that something, formerly undetected, called for a total reevaluation of the spirit of protest. It is in this atmosphere, by the end of the 1880s, that we begin to sense the entry of the Marxist application to revolutionary politics as well as to historiography. There was an increased conviction that Marxism might render more meaning to the past and lead to a clearer course toward the future. Among these early writers and thinkers who began to contemplate the application of Marxist dialectics to Russian historical writings was without doubt Georgii Valentinovich Plekhanov (1856-1918).

It was at the turn of the century that Plekhanov began to sense the wisdom of diverting the new generation along the Marxist paths. And although the following prewar years brought a sharp clash between Plekhanov and other socialists who diverted their paths from the one of their teacher, Plekhanov may still be considered as the original formulator, interpreter, and applier of Marxism to Russian historiography. Heresy aside, Plekhanov's writings remain to this day the early classic in Russian Marxist literature, as witness the republication of his writings by the ruling party in the Soviet Union.[98]

Plekhanov was a highly cultured man who had a keen interest in the fields of art, literature, and history. One critic referred to him as a man with "a touch of aristocratic *hauteur*," a quality that made him stand out in the ranks of Marxists. A pioneer with a keenly incisive mind, he boldly undertook to revise and reinterpret Russian history along the new ideas by formerly arcane features leading to a new Marxist interpretation. If Lenin hammered at the situation in Russia with a Machiavellian chillying logic, Plekhanov, his teacher, demonstrated doctrinal rectitude and intellectual superiority. Plekhanov feared and repeatedly expressed suspicion of premature revolutionary action. It was his absolute faith that if Russian democracy was to succeed, it would require enormous restraint and self-control. In revolutionary adventurism Plekhanov could detect only forthcoming social disaster.

Plekhanov came to the revolutionary scene at a time when opponents to autocracy were in search for application of modernization or westernization of native populism, which was undergoing a rapid change as was life itself in the nation. It is here that Plekhanov made his entry, by his endeavor to apply Marxist interpretation to Russian historical writing.

In a series of studies, largely monographic in nature, written while he was a political *émigré* abroad, Plekhanov urged the daring task of undertaking the rewriting of social history of Russia.[99] It was a courageous scheme in view of the numerous adversities and difficulties that seriously kept impeding his progress and which in the end prevented the completion of his projected scheme. Severed from Russian archives, he was compelled to draw information largely from such standard writings as those of Solovyev, Klyuchevsky, Milyukov, and other similar sources. Archival materials being inaccessible to him, his work assumed the nature of reflections upon the subject of social development in Russia. Nonetheless Plekhanov's three-volume history demonstrates an astonishing familiarity with Western philosophy and native events. His wide philosophical knowledge spiced with dialectical materialism ably woven into the pattern of Russian social history makes this work refreshingly original. To this day it represents an interesting attempt at a philosophical interpretation of Russian history, though it falls short of accomplishing the goal at which the author had originally aimed.[100]

ROZHKOV

In the case of Nikolai Aleksandrovich Rozhkov (1868-1927) we meet the "professional" party historian who tried all his life to find himself. He made an honest endeavor to formulate and inject a Marxist interpretation into Russian history, with little success.[101] He graduated from the University of Moscow in 1890 where he had studied and come under the influence of V. O. Klyuchevsky. He defended his master's dissertation on the rural economy of Moscow, a work considered by expert students as a significant contribution to the field of historical literature. Rozhkov was a prolific writer, having produced nearly three hundred books, monographs, and articles. Regrettably most of his writings proved of short-term value and today are hardly known, except to a few students of history. Only his earlier works proved of more durable value, notably his study on the origin of absolutism in Russia or his presentation of economic life of the Muscovite state. Rozhkov was also noted for his remarkably lucid style, one reason for the popularity of his textbooks.

The sad aspect of Rozhkov's life was that he was cast between two revolutions and two parties, the Social Democratic (Mensheviks) and the Communists. He vacillated for many years and only shortly before his death joined the latter, but at heart he remained a man with divided loyalties. This is often revealed in his writings. Many of Rozhkov's mature works, particularly the twelve-volume history of Russia, are not only inferior to his earlier writings, but reveal the painful process of steeping interpretations in Marxism. As one reads the narrative, it is hard to escape the impression of a superimposed Marxist doctrine on a rather mediocre, colorless orthodox narrative. The overall impression one gets is the influence of Spencer's positivism rather than the dialectical materialism of Marx.

Nor is his periodization of Russian history noted for any special originality. The voluminous history cannot be compared with his earlier refreshing and original studies. As one compares Rozhkov's earlier writings with those of a later date, one gets the inescapable impression of a grievous duality in the author. On the one hand Rozhkov displays the best of the liberal traditions of the earlier decades, while on the other he betrays signs of surrender to the later triumphant spirit of the November Revolution. Because he has no firm grip on either tradition, he pathetically falls between the two.

POKROVSKY

One of the early Marxists who came to leave a formidable impact on Russian historiography was undoubtedly Mikhail Nikolayevich Pokrovsky (1868-1932). He pioneered a reinterpretation of the entire course of Russian history at a time when Marxist influence on historical writing was still in an inchoate state. The case of Pokrovsky is entirely different from that of Rozhkov, since his break with Menshevism was much more drastic, but, like Rozhkov, his popularity was to be transitory. The reason is not difficult to discover: whereas Rozhkov remained a lonely figure without any power, Pokrovsky, on the other hand, left behind him an entire school of Soviet historians, a legion of disciples with whom the party later had to deal rather harshly. As a graduate of the University of Moscow in 1891, Pokrovsky had been trained in the best traditions of that institution: he was the pupil of such eminent teachers as V. O. Klyuchevsky and Paul G. Vinogradov, the distinguished scholar in the field of Western feudalism. Klyuchevsky's "economism" and Struve's Legal Marxism were already current topics when Pokrovsky entered his most formative years.

Originally Pokrovsky started in the field of medieval European history. He soon shifted his interest and initiated the thesis, later advanced in more detailed form by Pavlov-Silvansky, of the similarity between Russian and Western feudal institutions and medieval structures of society. While feeling his way, he associated himself with liberal groups who professed Marxist proclivities. The years 1905-1910 represent a soul-searching period for many intellectuals, and Pokrovsky was no exception, shifting from one Marxist grouping to another. It was during this period of vacillations that Pokrovsky commenced his extensive writings.

Among his more noted works may be mentioned first his *Russian History from the Earliest Times* in four volumes, leading up to the nineteenth century, and a two-volume *History of Russian Culture*.[102] The first was supposed to supplement Klyuchevsky's *Course*; the second, Milyukov's *Outlines of Russian Culture*. Both failed to demolish the works at which Pokrovsky aimed his lances; he only formulated a brand of Marxist interpretation that the Marxists themselves later refuted. Contributing to a collective work on the nineteenth-century history of Russia, he later published his own chapters separately under the title of *Diplomacy and Wars of Czarist Russia in the Nineteenth Century*. This represented a novel attempt to demonstrate the relationship between domestic and foreign policies in Russian history.

The fundamental idea that runs throughout the writings of Pokrovsky may be formulated thus: material needs are at the bottom of all human activity and of all history. This simple formula became the keynote, the all-encompassing explanation of every historical phenomenon. Under its domination, history became the record of an inevitable process that left little or no room for the role of leadership or of cultural determinants. Nationalism was eschewed as a bourgeois device, and no trace of national glorification can be found in any of Pokrovsky's writings. This mechanical interpretation of history was laid down in topical form, so that the chronology of events was difficult to follow or made no sense. Even the admiring Lenin was constrained to suggest that a chronological table be appended to Pokrovsky's *Brief History.* Nor can one fail to notice his disregard for national groups within the multilingual Russian Empire, except the fortuitous reference he was compelled to make to the Ukrainian people. The predominant role in history seems to be ascribed to the Great Russian people as surely by Pokrovsky as by the "bourgeois historians" whom he severely took to task.

After Lenin read the *Brief History* of Pokrovsky, he praised the author for displaying originality in his approach to the subject and for making it readable. Yet the praise was extended with some reservation when he suggested:

> To make it a textbook (and this it must become), it must be supplemented with a chronological index. This is, roughly, what I am suggesting: first column, chronology; second column, bourgeois view (briefly); third column, your view, Marxist, indicating the pages in your book. The student must know both your book and the index so that there should be no skimming, so that they should retain the facts, and so that they should learn to compare the old science and the new.

In 1924 Pokrovsky published his *Essays on the Russian Revolutionary Movement of the Nineteenth and Twentieth Centuries.* During the same year Pokrovsky's essays on historiography, entitled *Historical Science and Class Struggle,* also appeared. It consisted largely of the lectures he delivered at the Communist University at Moscow. Aside from the above works one must also refer to the numerous articles he contributed to various papers and magazines, not to mention the virulent debates in which he frequently engaged with his opponents.

To Pokrovsky the revolution was the hour of *a verbis ad verbera*. As a full-fledged member of the Communist party he saw his star ascend with particular speed after November 1917. He began as head of the Moscow Soviet and shortly afterward became Assistant Commissar of Education and head of the historical section. By his order the Institute of History was placed under the Academy of Sciences of the USSR. A Society of Marxist Historians, with chapters in the main towns throughout the Soviet Union, was established in 1925 for the purpose of training a new generation of historians free from the influence of the older generation.

Pokrovsky was also the editor of the various collections of archival materials pertaining to the Pugachev rebellion and to the Decembrist movement, and of the well-known periodical *Krasnyi arkhiv (Red Archive)*, devoted to the publication of documentary sources. He was founder of the militant Marxist Historical Society and of its publication, *Istorik-Marksist*, the aims of which were (1) the maintenance of a united front of all Marxists engaged in historical research, (2) the study of Marxist methodology, (3) the combatting of all anti-Marxist bourgeois distortions in historical writings, (4) the establishment of a Marxist critical literature, (5) assistance to its members in matters of research, and finally, (6) the popularization of the Marxist historical view.[103] During the later years Pokrovsky was also engaged in an elaborate publication of sources concerning Russian foreign policy since 1878.[104]

According to Pokrovsky, Clio was no meek goddess; any historian who dared to digress from the righteous path of Marxist tenets risked invoking the wrath of his authority. As the official judge of historical literature, he saw to it that historians recognized the set Marxist canon or face the consequences. A harsh critic, he spared no one, not even his colleagues, if they happened to be "class enemies" or even their allies. His acrid style made him a dangerous opponent, while his political power often made him a deadly enemy. After the revolution his enemies—some of them eminent figures such as Platonov, Lyubavsky, or Tarlé—suffered from the lash of his tongue, his piercing pen, and, most of all, his lethal political weaponry. Upon him rests a heavy moral responsibility for the utter routing of the old school and for the physical suffering inflicted on its representatives, among them the most eminent members of the historian profession.[105]

Oddly enough, the position of Pokrovsky in the Communist party was that of a relative newcomer and not of a member of the Old Guard; he was not always in harmony with the party line. On this account, from time to time he had been given notice of perilous "deviations," and on as many occasions he would "admit" his ideological errors. Nevertheless Pokrovsky remained until the end of his life in good standing within the ranks of the party, wielding enormous power. In history he saw an effective political weapon, and with unusual vigor he undertook the task of transforming history from an academic "obscure literary form into a real, living, concrete fact." To Pokrovsky, Marxism, was a means, not a dogma; an omnipotent instrument, not an inflexible pattern; and he used the field of history as a battleground on which to meet his political foes. Scarcely any other writer has ever equaled Pokrovsky's skill in subordinating history to politics. "History," he once said, "is politics projected into the past." Whether or not one agrees with Pokrovsky's presentation of historical science, his essential concepts "fitting politics to the past," his erudition as well as talent, cannot be denied. As one writer summarized it, "No future student of Russian history will be able to dispense with his works or to find complete satisfaction in them."

In general terms the periodization of Russian history as developed by Pokrovsky is sound, even if definitions of terms employed are not always lucid or convincing. He divides the past into two main periods: feudal and capitalist. The first he defines as a type of society where a natural economy, a large landholding system, a pyramidal social structure, and a ruling landlord class prevail. While dealing with the Russian feudal period, Pokrovsky followed closely the thesis developed by Pavlov-Silvansky (see above), whom, incidentally, he regarded most highly and lauded publicly in a preface to the latter's work. Pokrovsky refuted the old methodology that started with the shift of population to the northeast, and thereby originated the national state in Russia. Nor did he accept the view that ascribed decisive effects on the state to the Mongolian period. He regarded the development of a natural economy not necessarily as a contributing factor, as formerly believed, since, as he plausibly argued, the Kievan period had already witnessed a similar development. Likely he challenged the method of dividing history according to political institutions; he suggested instead that the past be divided according to the evolution of the material culture, the development of trade, and the appearance of a money economy. This was a depature from former methods of periodization, and many historians subsequently have followed Pokrovsky without either realizing or acknowledging it. Thus far Pokrovsky seemed to have stood on firm ground.

When, however, Pokrovsky undertook to analyze the era of imperialism, his interpretation proved more precarious. He ascribed the origin of imperialism to the introduction of protective policies that led to the formation of national monopolies within the state; these in turn, motivated by schemes of expansion beyond national frontiers, were bound to carry with them the imperialistic policies that led to inevitable conflicts. This was precisely the shape of developments, Pokrovsky maintained, that led Russia to war in the Far East in 1904 and to subsequent conflicts elsewhere.

The interpretation leaves one with a feeling of oversimplification of a much more complex phenomenon. Pokrovsky's entire architectonic system is somewhat flimsily mechanistic and eventually led to violent criticism from the party itself. Though criticizing bourgeois historians, he based his antithesis on the very errors for which he derided his opponents. His economic Marxism did not depart basically from Klyuchevsky's "economism." His effort to demonstrate dialectic unity throughout the entire course of history was overshadowed by his accounts of the socioeconomic formations. By lumping all social developments into a single narrative, he naïvely believed that he would be able to achieve an elucidating synthesis that was bound to explain the underlying forces of history.

Pokrovsky either failed to see or neglected to mention the fact that at various periods the state was closely related to the form of production that he himself considered vital for the understanding of history. Though employing dialectical materialism Pokrovsky failed to prove convincingly the social implications or the relationship between the various forms of production and social changes. Pokrovsky's entire thesis was robbed of its essence and bound to become a lifeless mechanical process, a mere account of an exchange of commodities and a purposeless play of economic factors. The picture was thereby oversimplified: in the absence of commodity exchange, society is defined as feudal; when commodity exchange and trade capital make their entrance, society becomes capitalist. The pattern fits even less when Pokrovsky initiates the subject of class formation and class struggle. These he saw in terms of the international struggle and not as a national phenomenon. Except for the peasant rebellions, which Pokrovsky treated as a local development, he presented the labor movement as an inseparable part of global class struggle. The entire interpretation left many questions unanswered, while a number of answers only multiplied the queries.

In summary, what were Pokrovsky's ideas about history? Primarily that history is an effective branch of politics, or as he phrased it, "history is politics projected into the past.'' Thus Pokrovsky explicitly believed that the frame of reference from which history is written is of far greater importance in determining its validity than the actual research. In his view bourgeois historians were in honest error, for they knew of no other frame of reference than their own. ''Scientific history'' was nothing more or less than a defense of the bourgeois system. Since history, according to Pokrovsky, is fundamentally an account of all human activity, and since the latter is motivated exclusively by material needs, the result was quite obvious: history became a record of an inevitable process with little or no room for the role of leadership or of cultural determinants, as was pointed out previously.

This is important to bear in mind, for Pokrovsky's views led his followers into endless embarrassments after his death and caused violent criticism of his writings. It is well to note also that, though the bourgeois are censured, no antiforeign sentiments appear in Pokrovsky's work. The teaching of history in the schools during Pokrovsky's lifetime serves to throw some light upon the subject. In 1923 the People's Commissar for Education forbade any teaching that might stimulate nationalism or encourage imitation of the past; historical science must not tolerate such bourgeois anachronisms as patriotism and nationalism. Russian political and literary history were virtually discontinued as subjects in the schools.

The rigors of writing history during Pokrovsky's activities were somewhat mitigated during the period of the New Economic Policy (NEP), 1921-1928. In those years Soviet historians went so far as to attend a number of the meetings of the World Conference of Historians. The general course of meetings was uneventful, with the exception of the somewhat tense relations between the Bolshevik and the *émigré* historians. The policy of diffident cooperation with bourgeois historians was, however, short-lived and broke down completely under the strains engendered by the split between Leon Trotsky and Joseph Stalin, the inauguration of the Five-Year Plan (1928), and the Great Depression, which revived hopes for a world revolution.

From 1928 there followed a brief period of four years (Pokrovsky died in 1932), which might be considered as anticlimatic. The tightening of party lines for a renewed struggle was made apparent in several ways. Beginning in 1930, a new drive against ''bourgeois historians'' both at home and abroad was initiated in the pages of the *Istorik-Marksist*, the official organ of Soviet historians. Eugene Tarlé, a nonparty member of the Society of Marxist Historians and a prominent student of the French Revolution, was harshly criticized by Pokrovsky for bourgeois tendencies. Tarlé was banished from the capital and sent east in 1931. His principal errors were the identification of the foreign policy of the USSR with that of czarist Russia and the assigning to Germany of a major share of guilt for World War I. The latter opinion ran directly counter to the Pokrovsky concept of economic pressures as the sole explanatory factor in history.

In March 1931 the Society of Marxist Historians began publication of the journal *Class Warfare* (*Borba klassov*), which was to be devoted to the study of the postwar period, especially in the USSR. Its object was announced as the "militant education of the masses." The appearance of this journal marked the height of Pokrovsky's influence, but his triumph rested on shifting sands. A number of factors caused a radical change. Among these may be mentioned first the increased aspiration for national autonomy, best manifested among the intellectual groups of the Ukraine, Georgia, and Kazakhstan, and the purges of their respective Academies of Sciences.

In due course the pledge of the Communist party to support the various national cultures within the Soviet Union turned into a source of political embarrassment. Especially was this true in the case of the Ukrainians, whose historians, under the leadership of Hrushevsky and others, devoted themselves with intensified fervor to Ukrainian nationalism rather than Marxist tasks. Equally important was the growing disillusionment with the meager results obtained by Soviet historians in the field of education. A survey of schools as early as 1929 had revealed an appalling ignorance of history, a low intellectual level, and the absence of any originality of thought among the pupils.[106]

The lamentable state of affairs in historical writing and in the teaching of history soon resulted in significant changes. In 1921 the party called for a complete overhaul of both study and research in all fields of history. To the quest from above, calling for changes, the Society of Marxist Historians responded with several soul-searching reports denouncing many of their members for "backwardness." At the same time the *Istorik-Marksist*, after being temporarily suspended, reappeared in new form. The change was significant as well as portentous, in that Pokrovsky was editor-in-chief of the suspended journal. Equally significant was the abandonment of the study of foreign history and the concentration on the home front in Soviet parlance. The star of Pokrovsky was rapidly declining, as was his physical health.

The complete *volte-face* in Soviet historiography assumed many different changes during the 1930s. For our immediate concern it should be pointed out that the main victim of the rapidly encroaching changes was Pokrovsky. It was his good fortune to die in 1932, before his work was condemned and demolished. For a number of years it became officially proper to denounce Pokrovsky's work as "schematic sociology" or as "mechanical economism" and questionable history. The sobering fact became clear: the plan of Communist indoctrination by way of history proved impractical and evidently futile. It was officially announced that historians must cease teaching former abstract and formal history textbooks and must abandon the teaching methods practiced to date. Henceforth history must be taught in chronological sequence while students were to be required to memorize important dates and historic events. Equally significant is the fact that the "bourgeois deviationist" and opponent of Pokrovsky, Eugene Tarlé, was allowed to return to the capital from his place of banishment. Momentarily the old-time history textbook and time-tested methods of teaching made their reappearance. Alas, mediocrity also came temporarily to the surface. This situation hardly augured well for scholarship, but it provided at least a breathing spell before the crushing days of Stalinist supremacy. But this is a subject that does not enter into our discussion and one that has already been discussed at sufficient length elsewhere.[107]

For nearly three decades Pokrovsky remained under the shadow of a multitude of heresies while the witch hunt ruled supreme. Pokrovsky was accused of a multitude of crimes: he was accused of schematism, universalism, revisionism, deviationism, pluralism, "selectivism," and other crimes that would not be found even in an authoritative dictionary. Devastating criticism was consistently heaped upon him until the end of the 1950s. It was particularly depressing and somewhat revealing when the witch chorus of opponents was joined by those who only shortly before were his pupils who looked upon Pokrovsky as the guiding light in the field of history. This mass onslaught can be partly explained by the stifling intellectual climate, during which this became a standard practice for sheer survival. It seemed as if students of history had resolved to become propagandists first and historians last.

Following the Twentieth Congress of the Communist party in 1956, there began to emerge signs of a return to sobriety. Level-headed writers cautiously volunteered to suggest a reexamination of Pokrovsky as a Marxist and a student of history.[108] Shortly thereafter, S. M. Dubrovsky in an article in the organ of the historians, *Voprosy istorii*, introduced a reexamination of

Pokrovsky and his role in Soviet historiography, urging a reinterpretation without distortion. It was not, however, until the Twenty-Second Congress that the party passed a resolution that included the following statement: "In [Pokrovsky's] scientific as his political activities there were not a few errors. That is true, of course, and that is to be considered. But it is also well known that he defended Marxism, and contributed much to the development in the field of history." Henceforth, Pokrovsky has been reassigned a more honorable place in the rank of the Marxist historians. Soviet mills grind usually very slowly, and not always finely.

In Retrospect

As one reviews the accomplishments of Russian historiography during the extensive period discussed above, there is a natural temptation not only to summarize the record reviewed, but to indulge in conjecture, based on the assembled data, as to the immediate prospects for the future. One indisputable factor stands out, namely, that for over a century prior to the revolution, Russian historiography demonstrated an amazing advancement in the field of publication of sources as well as in the writing of history. Formed with direct encouragement by the government and by private individuals, special societies commenced publishing activities on a gigantic scale. The most notable of these organizations is the Archaeographic Commission, which managed to publish a staggering amount of source material.

Simultaneously with this feverish activity the art of paleography progressed, as did the study of annalistic literature, which culminated in productive research by such scholars as A. A. Shakhmatov, M. D. Priselkov, A. N. Nasonov, M. N. Tikhomirov, and D. S. Likhachev, to mention only a few. In the field of monographic studies or legal and agrarian history, a number of students proved themselves no less distinguished. Suffice to recall such names as V. I. Sergeyevich, M. I. Semevsky, or M. M. Bogoslovsky. Equally impressive results were obtained in the study of special periods by men like S. F. Platonov, M. K. Lyubavsky, and A. E. Presnyakov. In the realm of Federalist interpretation we have seen such historians as A. P. Shchapov, N. I. Kostomarov, or M. S. Hrushevsky who stand out most promisingly. Finally may be pointed out the works of historical synthesis of general history by such students as V. O.

Klyuchevsky or P. N. Milyukov. These men differed in view, in methods of approach, yet both were stimulating and productive enough to crown all efforts with new research that enriched the field with original and refreshing interpretations.

Yet one must not rest on past achievements or be carried away by positive accomplishments. A more sober evaluation of the records also betrays a lack of monographic treatment of certain periods or certain aspects of Russian history. As one looks closer at the entire field, one notices a degree of uneven development in historical writing in Russia throughout the years we reviewed; there is a glaring one-sided concentration on problems of Russian internal developments and underestimation or reticence concerning, for instance, diplomatic history and foreign relations.

To be certain, a few outstanding monographs in the arid field of diplomatic history have made their appearance such as E. Tarlé's history of the Crimean War, or S. D. Skazkin's account of the Three Emperors' League, or B. A. Romanov's diplomatic history of Russia in the Far East in the early part of this century.[109] Yet the fact remains that when one searches for treatment of broader phases of Russian diplomatic history, one must look to the research done by foreign scholars, such as N. H. Sumner's outstanding volume on the Balkan policy of Russia in the 1870s or W. L. Langer's monograph on the Franco-Russian Alliance.[110] To be sure, these do not by any means fill the gap in Russian diplomatic history, but they mark a considerable advance in the right direction.

There are certain neglected areas in the field of domestic history, most likely because prior to 1917 the majority of Russian historians showed preference for certain fields more than others, and because of censorship, available sources, or "politically undesirable" subjects. Thus the question of institutional history during the first half of the nineteenth century was barely touched, while agrarian history was extensively studied. Equally inadequate is the subject of eastern expansion toward the Pacific and beyond, into Alaska and even as far as California. Russian historical literature compares unfavorably, for instance, with the extent of American historical literature in the field of the westward movement.

Russian history also calls for a more intensive study of imperial administration and imperial policies, particularly in regard to the peripheral people. Here is indeed an almost virgin field. There are too few studies in depth, and the contrast with the wealth of English literature on the history of imperial expansion is most striking. Regional histories and histories of national minorities, although these have begun to appear lately, still have far to go. The same could be said in the field of economic history, particularly industrial development prior to 1917, even though the record is somewhat more favorable.

When we reach the field of historical biography, the situation is equally spotty. There are many eminent historical figures whose biographies would be instrumental in the illumination of history. To cite a few specifically: Nikon and Avvakum among the religious leaders; Catherine II, Alexander I, and Alexander II of the royal members; Gorchakov, the Milyutin brothers, Pobedonostsev, Witte, Stolypin among statesmen; Yermolov, Kaufman, Muraviev-Amursky, or Skobelev among the military figures and empire builders. Recently Professor M. V. Nechkina produced a superb biographical study of V. O. Klyuchevsky that, let us hope, may lead to similar biographies of other distinguished figures of nineteenth- and twentieth-century Russia.

There is also a great need for the study of the decade and a half preceding the revolution, such as that done by Sir Bernard Pares.[111] Other subjects and fields that need further investigation may be added. There is a need for a more adequate study of Russian political parties during the last quarter of the empire, including such parties as the Kadets, the Oktobrists, as well as the Socialists. There is a need for extensive research in the field of religious sectarianism prior to the revolution. A study of the history of the development of modern means of transportation in Russia prior to 1917 would enrich the general field of economic history.

As time goes on, one cannot escape the realization that the legacy of Russian historiography opens wider avenues for research as well as new interpretations. Freshly unearthed sources, steadily growing in number, require analysis and interpretation in light of more recent events. "A new revaluation of old values" is become urgent. For some time the blustering historian came to dominate the footlights, to prove preconceived ideas, inject personal ideologies and beliefs. Sooner or later historiography is bound to reach the crossroads after which mature scholars will be compelled to extricate historical science from its present state and to elevate the field to a deserving level in the social sciences.

In due course it is hoped that the pendulum will swing back to a state where objectivity will be honored and balanced judgment accepted. A number of conditions both internal and external make it imperative to reevaluate the rich past with more light and less agitation. Partisanship still dominates the scene, convictions rule cool judgment. As to the more recent period, it is still too near to permit adequate perspective for an evaluation of its full historic significance. The contemporary observer can assist the future historian in his task of interpreting the complex, confused, multiangled era by assuming the more humble role of *Geschichtssammler*, the famulus of the forthcoming *Geschichtsmaler*. Thus, particularly in the field of more recent history, we are forced reluctantly to assume the role of the scholar of the bygone century if we wish to render a real service to Clio.

Notes

1. Ivashin, "Rukopis' publichnykh lektsii T. N. Granovskogo" [A Manuscript of the Public Lectures of T. N. Granovsky], *Istorichesky zhurnal* (Moscow), Nos. 1-2, 1945.

2. Johann Philipp Gustav Ewers (1781-1830) was a student of Schlözer at Göttingen. In 1803 Ewers came to Russia and established his permanent residence there. His most important contributions are *Vom Ursprunge des russischen Staats* (1808) and *Das älteste Reich der Russen in seiner geschichtlichen Entwickelung* (1826).

3. V. O. Klyuchevsky, *Ocherki i ryechi* [Studies and Addresses] (Moscow, n.d.), pp. 2-3; "Sergey Mikhaylovich Solovyev," *Sochineniya* [Works] (Moscow, 1959), 7: 126-45; M. N. Pokrovsky, *Borba klassov i russkaya istoricheskaya literatura* [Class Struggle and Russian Historical Literature] (Petrograd, 1923), pp. 59-60.

4. S. M. Solovyev, *Ob otnosheniyakh Novgoroda k velikim knyazyam* [Relations Between Novgorod and the Grand Princes] (Moscow, 1845); *Istoriya otnosheny mezhdu russkimi knyazyami Ryurikova doma* [A History of the Relations Among the Russian Princes of the Rurik Dynasty] (Moscow, 1847); *Sobraniye sochineny* [Collected Works] (St. Petersburg, n.d.) (This includes Solovyev's monographic studies such as the essays on Russian historiography, the history of the fall of Poland, the Near Eastern Question, and others); *Geschichte des Falles von Polen*, trans. Spörer (Gotha, 1865); *Imperator Aleksandr I. Politika-Diplomatiya* [Politics and Diplomacy in the Reign of Alexander I] (St. Petersburg, 1877); *Istoriya Rossii s drevneyshikh vremyon* [History of Russia from Earliest Times], 29 vols. (St. Petersburg, 1897); another edition, 29 vols. in 15 books (Moscow, 1959-1966). See also K. Bestuzhev-Ryumin, *Biografii kharakteristiki* [Biographical Essays] (St. Petersburg, 1882), pp. 255-72; N. L. Rubinstein, *Russkaya istoriografiya* [Russian Historiography] (Moscow, 1941), pp. 312-42.

5. *Russky biografichesky slovar*, (St. Petersburg, 1896-1918) 19: 85, 86.

6. Y. F. Shmurlo, "S. M. Solovyev," *Entsiklopedichesky slovar* (Brockhaus-Efron) 30: 798-803.

7. Klyuchevsky, *Ocherki i ryechi*, p. 39.

8. A. S. Presnyakov, "S. M. Solovyev v ego vliyanii na razvitiye russkoy istoriografii [S. M. Solovyev, His Influence on the Development of Russian Historiography]," *Voprosy istorigrafii i istochnikovedeniya istorii SSSR. Sbornik statey* (Moscow, 1963), pp. 76-86.

9. A. I. Herzen, *Byloye i dumy* [Past and Thoughts] (Moscow, 1932), 3: 531-33.

10. K. D. Kavelin, *Sobraniye sochineny* [Collected Works], 4 vols. (Moscow, 1897-1900); "Zapiska Kavelina o nigilizme" [Memorandum Concerning Nihilism], *Istorichesky arkhiv*, No. 5, 1950.

11. *Russky biografichesky slovar*, 8: 364-65.

12. A. N. Pypin, *Istoriya russkoy etnografii* [A History of Russian Ethnography] (St. Petersburg, 1890-1892), 2: 19 ff.

13. V. I. Sergeyevich, *Drevnosti russkogo prava* [Early Russian Law] (St. Petersburg, 1911).

14. B. N. Chicherin, *Oblastniye uchrezhdeniya Rossii v XVIII v.* [Regional Institutions of Russia in the Eighteenth Century] (Moscow, 1856); *Opyty po istorii russkogo prava* [Studies of Russian Law] (Moscow, 1858); *O narodnom predstavitelestve* [Popular Representation] (Moscow, 1866; 2nd ed., 1899); *Russky dilettantizm i obshchinnoye zemlevladeniye* [Russian Dilettantism and Communal Landownership] (Moscow, 1878); *Sobstvennost i gosudarstvo* [Private Property and the State], 2 parts (Moscow, 1882-1883); *Polozhitelnaya nauka, filosofiya i yedinstvo nauki* [Positive Science, Philosophy, and the Unity of Science] (Moscow, 1892); *Nauka i religiya* [Science and Religion] (Moscow, 1879; 2nd ed., 1901); *Philosophische Forschungen* (Heidelberg, 1899); *Vospominaniya* [Reminiscences], 4 parts Moscow, 1929-1934). Rubinstein, *Russkaya istoriografiya*, pp. 301-12, 445-47, 462-63 (see above, note 4).

15. A. D. Gradovsky, *Sobraniye sochineny* [Collected Works], 9 vols. (St. Petersburg, 1899-1904).

16. The reader's attention is invited to an excellent critical appraisal of the Juridical School by P. N. Milyukov, entitled "Yuridicheskaya shkola v russkoy istoriografii: Solovyev, Kavelin, Chicherin, Sergeyevich," in *Russkaya maysl'* 6 (1886): 80-92.

17. K. N. Bestuzhev-Ryumin, *Biografii i kharakteristiki* [Biographical Essays] (St. Petersburg, 1882); *Russkaya istoriya* [Russian History], 2 vols. (1872-1875); *Geschichte Russlands*, trans. T. Schiemann (Mitau, 1877); *O tom, kak roslo Moskovskoye knyazhestvo i sdelalos russkim tsarstvom* [How the

Muscovy Principality Grew and Became the Russian State] (St. Petersburg, 1866).

See also Y. F. Shmurlo, *Ocherk zhizni i nauchnoy deyatelnosti Konstantina Nikolayevicha Bestuzheva-Ryumina* [A Study of the Life and Scholarly Activites of K. N. Bestuzhev-Ryumin] (Yuriev, 1899); S. F. Platonov, *Stati po russkoy istorii* [Articles on Russian History], 2nd ed. (St. Petersburg, 1912); Rubinstein, *Russkaya istoriografiya*, pp. 411-14 (see above, note 4).

18. *Russky istorichesky zhurnal* 8 (1922): 225-28.

19. M. V. Nechkina, *Vasily Osipovich Klyuchevsky. Istoriya zhizni i tvorchestve* [V. O. Klyuchevsky: A History of His Life and Creative Works] (Moscow, 1974), p. 59.

20. M. V. Nechkina, "Istoriya issledovaniya V. O. Klyuchevskogo" [A History of the Study of V. O. Klyuchevsky], *Istoricheskie zapiski* 84 (1969): 216.

21. V. O. Klyuchevsky, *Opyty i issledovaniya* [Essays and Studies] (Moscow, 1915), pp. 1 ff.

22. *V. O. Klyuchevsky. Kharakteristiki i vospominaniya* [V. O. Klyuchevsky: Essay and Recollections] (Moscow, 1912), pp. 13-14.

23. Published in *Ocherki i ryechi*, pp. 57-89, 117-39, 279-311 (see above, note 3).

24. V. A. Maklakov, *Iz vospominaniy* [Reminiscences] (New York, 1954), p. 191.

25. *Russky istorichesky zhurnal* 8 (1922): 184-85.

26. V. O. Klyuchevsky, *Kurs russkoy istorii* (Moscow, 1923), 3: 82-83. English translation, 3: 64-65.

27. F. I. Chaliapin, *Pages from My Life* (New York, 1927), pp. 194-95.

28. *Russky istorichesky zhurnal* 8 (1922): 204 ff. See also two excellent essays on this subject in *V. O. Klyuchevsky. Kharakteristiki i vospominaniya*, pp. 45-58, 59-93.

29. Klyuchevsky, *Opyty i issledovaniya*, pp. 212-310.

30. See *Sbornik statey, posvyashchennykh S. F. Platonovu* [Collection of Essays Dedicated to S. F. Platonov] (St. Petersburg, 1912), p. 299. Note also Klyuchevsky, *Opyty i issledovaniya*, pp. 417 ff.

31. Klyuchevsky, *A Course in Russian History*, Vol. 4, Chapters 3-6, 10. See also Klyuchevsky's interpretation of the reign of Catherine II in *Ocherki i ryechi*, pp. 312-85.

32. For the most recent and super study of V. O. Klyuchevsky, see Nechkina, *Vasily Osipovich Klyuchevsky* (cited in note 19, above). Equally interestingly written and presented with a great deal of admiration is the essay by G. Fedotov in *Sovremenniye zapiski* (Paris) 50 (1932): 340-62. Also, M. Karpovich, "Klyuchevsky and Recent Trends in Russian Historiography," *Slavonic and East European Review* 21 (1943): 31-39.

33. *V. O. Klyuchevsky. Kharakteristiki i vospominaniya*, pp. 20-22.
34. V. O. Klyuchevsky, *Sochineniya* [Works] (Moscow, 1959), Vol. 6. The following works of Klyuchevsky may be regarded as the important contributions as well as the basic ones. *Sochineniya* [Works], 8 vols. (Moscow, 1956-1959); *Drevnerusskiye zhitiya svyatykh, kak istorichesky istochnik* [Lives of Early Russian Saints as a Source of History] Moscow, 1871); *Pis'ma V. O. Klyuchevsky k P. P. Gvozdevu (1861-1870)* [Letters of V. O. Klyuchevsky to P. P. Gvozdev] (Moscow, 1870); *Kurs russkoy istorii* [A Course in Russian History], 5 vols. (Moscow, 1904-1921); trans. J. Hogarth, 5 vols. (London, 1911-1931); *Istoriya soslovy v Rossii* [A History of Social Classes in Russia] (Moscow, 1913; Petrograd, 1918); *Boyarskaya duma drevney Rusi* [The Boyar Council in Early Russia] (Moscow, 1883); *Ocherki i ryechi* [Studies and Addresses] (Moscow, n.d.); *Opyty i issledovaniya* [Essays and Studies] (Moscow, 1915); *Otzyvy i otvety* [Reviews and Replies] (Moscow, 1914); *Skazaniya inostrantsev o Moskovskom gosudarstve* [Accounts of Foreigners Concerning the Muscovite State] (Petrograd, 1918). Studies and essays concerning Klyuchevsky: M. V. Nechkina, *Vasily Osipovich Klyuchevsky. Istoriya zhizni i tvorchestva* [V. O. Klyuchevsky: A History of His Life and Creative Works] (Moscow, 1974); S. I. Tkhorzhevsky, "V. O. Klyuchevsky, kak sotsiolog i politichesky myslitel" [V. O. Klyuchevsky as Sociologist and Political Thinker], *Dyela i Dni* (Petrograd) 2 (1921): 152-79; A. E. Presnyakov, "V. O. Klyuchevsky (1911-1921)," *Russky istorichesky zhurnal* (Petrograd) 8 (1922): 203-24; M. N. Pokrovsky, *Istoricheskaya nauka i borba klassov* [Historical Science and the Class Struggle] (Moscow, 1933), see pp. 167-205; A. A. Golubtsov, "Teoreticheskiye vzglyady V. O. Klyuchevskogo" [Theoretical Views of V. O. Klyuchevsky], *Russky istorichesky zhurnal* (Petrograd) 8 (1922): 178-202; N. L. Rubinstein, *Russkaya istoriografiya* [Russian Historiography] (Moscow, 1941), pp. 441-69; *V. O. Klyuchevsky. Kharakteristiki i vospominaniya* [Characterizations and Reminiscences] (Moscow, 1912); "V. O. Klyuchevsky, kak istorik istoricheskoy nauki" [V. O. Klyuchevsky as Historian of Historical Science], *Istoriya i istoriki* (Moscow: 1964); V. I. Astakhov, *V. O. Klyuchevsky—vydayushchiysya predstavitel' burzhuaznoy istoriografii*, Part II (Kharkov, 1962); A. A. Zimin, "Formirovaniye istoricheskikh vzglyadov V. O. Klyuchevskogo v 60-ye gg. XIX veka" [Formation of the Historical Views of V. O. Klyuchevsky During the 1860s], *Istoricheskie zapiski*, Book 69, pp. 178-97; *Ocherki istorii istoricheskoy nauki v SSSR* [Studies of the History of Historical Science in the USSR], 2: 146-70, 564-68, 593-95.
35. S. F. Platonov, *Ocherki po istorii smuty v Moskovskom gosudarstve XVI-XVII v.v.* [A Study of the Time of Troubles in the Muscovite State in the

Sixteenth and Seventeenth Centuries] (St. Petersburg, 1899); *Lektsii po russkoy istorii* [Lectures on Russian History] (St. Petersburg, 1915); *Boris Godunov* (Petrograd, 1921); *Ivan Groznyi* [Ivan the Terrible] (Berlin, 1924); *Histoire de la Russie des origines à 1918* (Paris, 1929); *La Russie moscovite* (Paris, 1932).

36. For a complete list of Lappo-Danilevsky's works, see *Russky istorichesky zhurnal* 6 (1920): 29-41. His most important works are the following: *Organizatsiya pryamogo oblozheniya v Moskovskom gosudarstve so vremyen smuty do epokhi preobrazovany* [The Administration of Direct Taxation in the Muscovite State from the Time of Troubles to the Period of Reforms] (St. Petersburg, 1890), and see a critical review of this work by P. N. Milyukov entitled *Sporniye voprosy finansovoy istorii Moskovskogo gosudarstva* [Debatable Questions Concerning the Financial History of the Muscovite State] (St. Petersburg, 1892); *Skifskiye drevnosti* [Scythian Antiquities] (St. Petersburg, 1887); *Russkiye promyshlenniye kompanii v pervoy polovine XVIII stoletiya* [Russian Industrial and Trading Companies in the First Half of the Eighteenth Century] (St. Petersburg, 1899); *Ocherk istorii obrazovaniya glavneyshikh razryadov krestyanskogo naseleniya v Rossii* [A Study of the Formation of the Main Categories Within the Peasant Population of Russia] (St. Petersburg, 1905); *Metodologiya istorii* [The Methodology of History] (St. Petersburg, 1913); "The Development of Science and Learning in Russia," in J. D. Duff, ed., *Russian Realities and Problems* (Cambridge, 1917).

37. *Russky istorichesky zhurnal* 6 (1920): 97 ff.

38. M. K. Lyubavsky, *Oblastnoye deleniye i mestnoye upravleniye litovsko-russkogo gosudarstva* [Provincial Division and Local Administration of the Lithuanian-Russian State] (Moscow, 1892); *Litovsko-russky seym* [The Lithuanian-Russian Diet] (Moscow, 1901); *Ocherk istorii Litovsko-russkogo gosudarstva do Lyublinskoy unii vklyuchitelno* [A Study of the Lithunian-Russian State Including the Union of Lublin] (Moscow, 1910); *Obrazovaniye osnovnoy gosudarstvennoy territorii velikorusskoy narodnosti* [The Territorial Basis of the Great Russian State] (Leningrad, 1929).

39. A. Y. Presnyakov, *Obrazovaniye velikorusskogo gosudarstva. Ocherki po istorii XIII-XV vekov* [The Formation of the Great Russian State. Studies in the History of the Thirteenth through the Fifteenth Centuries] (Petrograd, 1918); *Knyazhoye pravo v drevney Rusi* [Prince Law in Early Russia] (St. Petersburg, 1909); *Aleksandr I* (Petrograd, 1924); *Apogey samoderzhaviya: Nikolay I* [The Apogee of Autocracy. Nicholas I] (Leningrad, 1925); *14 Dekabrya 1825 goda* [December 14, 1825] (Leningrad, 1926).

40. *Istorik-Marksist*, 13: 269.

41. *Bolshaya sovetskaya entsyklopediya*, 34: 440.

42. Here are some of the most important studies of Milyukov. P. N. Milyukov, *Gosudarstvennoye khozyaystvo v Rossii v pervoy chetverti XVIII stoletiya i reforma Petra Velikogo* [State Economy in Russia During the First Quarter of the Eighteenth Century and the Reforms of Peter the Great] (St. Petersburg, 1922; 2nd ed., 1903); *Sporniye voprosy finansovoy istorii Moskovskogo gosudarstva* [Debatable Questions Concerning the Financial History of the Muscovite State] (St. Petersburg, 1892); *Glavniye techeniya russkoy istoricheskoy mysli* [Main Currents in Russian Historical Thought] (Moscow, 1898); *Ocherki po istorii russkoy kultury* [Studies in the History of Russian Culture], 3 vols. (St. Petersburg, 1896-1903); rev. ed., 3 vols. in 4 (Paris, 1933-1937); *Russia and its Crisis* (Chicago, 1905); *Iz istorii russkoy intelligentsii* [Essays on the Russian Intelligentsia] (St. Petersburg, 1902); *Le mouvement intellectuel russe*, trans. J. W. Bienstock (Paris, 1918); *Histoire de Russie* (in collaboration with C. Seignobos and L. Eisenmann), 3 vols. (Paris, 1932-1933); *Zhivoy Pushkin* [The Living Pushkin] (Paris, 1937).

43. Milyukov, *Ocherki po istorii russkoy kultury*, 1: 235-38.

44. Milyukov, *Ocherki po istorii russkoy kultury*, 2: 394-96.

45. See, for example, P. Paradizov, *Ocherki po istoriografii dekabristov* [Studies of Decembrist Historiography] (Moscow, 1929), pp. 161 ff.

46. Biographical data concerning V. I. Semevsky may be found in the periodical *Golos minuvshego*, Vols. 9-10, 1917.

47. E. N. Vodovozova, *Na zare zhizni* [At the Dawn of Life] (Moscow, 1934), 2: 339 ff.

48. See V. I. Semevsky's "Address" delivered before the examination board, defending his master thesis, cited in *Russkaya starina* 34 (1882): 577-78.

49. V. I. Semevsky, *Krestyane v tsarstvovaniye Imperatritsy Yekateriny II* [Peasants in the Reign of Catherine II], 2 vols. (St. Petersburg, 1903); *Kresyansky vopros v Rossii v XVIII i pervoy polovine XIX veka* [The Peasant Question in Russia in the Eighteenth and First Half of the Nineteenth Century], 2 vols. (St. Petersburg, 1888); *Rabochiye na sibirskikh zolotykh promyslakh* [Laborers in the Sibierian Goldmining Industry], 2 vols. (St. Petersburg, 1898); *Politicheskiye i obshchestvenniye idei dekabristov* [Political and Social Ideas of the Decembrists] (St. Petersburg, 1909); *M. V. Butashevich-Petrashevsky i Petrashevtsy* [M. V. Butashevich-Petrashevsky and his Circle] (Moscow, 1922).

50. Additional references concerning V. I. Semevsky are as follows: Rubinstein, *Russkaya istoriografiya*, pp. 405-409; (cited above, note 4); *Ocherki istorii istoricheskoy nauki v SSSR*, [Studies on the History of Historical Science in the USSR], 2: 207-18; *Istoriografiya istorii SSSR s drevneyshikh vremyen do Velikoy Oktyabrskoy Sotsialisticheskoy Revolyutsii* [A Historiography of the History of the USSR from Earliest Times to the Great October Socialist

Revolution] (Moscow, 1961); A. L. Shapiro, *Russkaya istoriografiya v period imperializma* [Russian Historiography During the Period of Imperialism] (Leningrad, 1962), pp. 135-51.

51. *Russkaya starina*, 34: 578-84.

52. *Golos minuvshego* 9-10 (1917): 38.

53. S. Svatikov, "Opalnaya professura 80-kh godov" [Dishonored Professor of the Eighties], *Golos minuvshego*, Vol. 2, 1917.

54. G. L. von Maurer, *Einleitung zur Geschichte der Mark-, Hof-, Dorf-, und Stadtverfassung* (n.p., 1854). Also his *Geschichte der Fronthöfe, der Banerhöfe under der Hofverfassung in Deutschland*, 4 vols. (n.p., 1863).

55. V. I. Semevsky, *Rabochiye na sibirskikh zolotykh promyslakh*, 1: iii-iv ff.

56. *Russky istorichesky zhurnal* 7 (1921): 114-20.

57. About Shakhmatov, see the following. Volume 25 (1922) of the *Izvestiya otdeleniya russkogo yazyka i slovesnosti Rossiyskoy Akademii Nauk* includes several superb essays on Shakhmatov. See also V. V. Vinogradov, *A. A. Shakhamatov* (Petrograd, 1922); S. P. Obnorsky, ed., *A. A. Shakhmatov, 1864-1920. Sbornik statey i materialov* (Moscow-Leningrad, 1947); D. S. Likhachev, "Shakhmatov kak issledovatel russkogo letopisaniya," in the preceding collection of essays; *A. S. Shakhmatov, 1864-1920. Biografiya* (Leningrad, 1930).

Among the most notable works of A. A. Shakhmatov may be cited the following: *Rozyskaniya o drevneyshikh letopisnykh svodakh* [Investigations Concerning the Earliest Chronicles] (St. Petersburg, 1903); *O yazyke novgorodskikh gramot* [The Language of the Novgorodian Charters] (St. Petersburg, 1885); *Issledovaniye o Dvinskikh gramotakh* [A Study of the Dvinsk Charters] (St. Petersburg, 1903); *Neskolko zametok o yazyke Pskovskikh pamyatnikov* [A Few Notes Concerning the Language of the Pskov Records] (St. Petersburg, 1909); *Ocherk drevneyshogo perioda istorii russkogo literaturnogo yazyka* [A Study of the Russian Literary Language of the Earliest Period] (St. Petersburg, 1915); *Vvedeniye v kurs istorii russkogo yazyka* [An Introduction to the History of the Russian Language] (Petrograd, 1916); *Drevneyshiye sud'by russkogo plemeni* [Concerning the History of the Earliest Russian Tribe (Petrograd, 1919).

58. V. S. Ikonnikov, *Russkiye obshchestvenniye deyateli XVI veka* [Russian Public Workers of the Sixteenth Century] (Kiev, 1866); *Graf N. S. Mordvinov [Count N. S. Mordvinov]* (St. Petersburg, 1873).

59. V. S. Ikonnikov, *Skepticheskaya shkola v russkoy istoriografii i eё protivniki* [The Skeptical School in Russian Historiography and its Opponents] (Kiev, 1871).

60. V. S. Ikonnikov, *Opyt russkoy istoriografii* [A Study of Russian Historiography], 2 vols. in 4 (Kiev, 1891-1908); *Maksim Grek*, two parts

(Kiev, 1865); "Krestyanskoye dvizheniye v Kiyevskoy gubernii v 1826-27 gg. v svyazi s sobytiyami togo vremeni" [The Peasant Movement in the Kiev Province During 1826-1827 in Connection with the Events of the Time], in *Sbornik statey, posvyashchennykh V. I. Lamanskomu* (St. Petersburg, 1908), Part 2, pp. 657-742.

61. See G. V. Vernadsky, "Feudalism in Russia," *Speculum* 14 (1939): 300-23.

62. See N. Kareyev, *V kakom smysle mozhno govorit o sushchestvovanii feodalizma v Rossii* [In What Sense can We Talk About Feudalism in Russia] (St. Petersburg, 1910).

63. N. P. Pavlov-Silvansky, *Feodalizm v drevney Rusi* [Feudalism in Early Russia] (St. Petersburg, 1907); *Feodalizm v udelnoy Rusi* [Feudalism in Appanage Russia] (St. Petersburg, 1910); *Gosudarevy sluzhilyye lyudi: proiskhozhdeniye russkogo dvoryanstva* [The Sovereign's Servant-Men: The Origins of the Russian Nobility] (St. Petersburg, 1898); *Dekabrist Pestel pered verkhovnym ugolovnym sudom* [The Decembrist Pestel Before the Supreme Criminal Court] (Rostov, 1907); *Proekty reform v zapiskakh sovremennikov Petra Velikogo* [Reform Projects in Memoranda of Contemporaries of Peter the Great] (St. Petersburg, 1897); *Ocherk po istorii XVIII-XIX vv. Sochineniya* [A Study of the History of the Eighteenth and Nineteenth Centuries] (St. Petersburg, 1909), vol. II. Cf. B. D. Grekov, *Feodalniye otnosheniya v Kievskom gosudarstve* [Feudal Relations in the Kievan State], (Moscow, 1935).

64. V. G. Mirzoyev, *Istoriografiya Sibiri. Pervaya polovina XIX veka* [Historiography of Siberia], (Moscow, 1960). V. G. Mirzoyev, *Istoriografiya Sibiri. Domarksistsky period* [A Historiography of Siberia. Premarxist Period] (Moscow, 1970). A discussion of Siberian historiography may be found in A. N. Pypin, *Istoriya russkoy etnografii* [A History of Russian Ethnography], Vol. 4, Part 2; also in V. I. Ogorodnikov, *Ocherk istorii Sibiri* [A Study of the History of Siberia] (Irkutsk, 1920), pp. 1-92. See also V. I. Mezhov, *Sibirskaya bibliografiya* [Siberian Bibliography] (St. Petersburg 1891-92). 3 vols.

65. See G. F. Pekarsky, *Istoriya Akademii Nauk* [A History of the Academy of Sciences], (St. Petersburg, 1870-1873) 2 vols. 1: 366-68, 427.

66. G. F. Müller, *Opisaniye sibirskogo tsarstva* [A Description of the Siberian Kingdom] (St. Petersburg, 1750; 2nd ed., 1787); *Sammlung russischer Geschichte*, 9 vols. (St. Petersburg, 1732-1764); vol. 10 (Dorpat, 1816); Johann Eberhard Fischer (1697-1771), *Sibirische Geschichte von der Entdekkung bis auf die Eroberung dieses Lands durch die russischen Waffen* . . . , 2 vols. (St. Petersburg, 1768); a new edition of Müller's history was published by the Soviet Academy—*Istoriya Sibiri*, 2 vols. (Moscow, 1937-1941). Other works related to the subject discussed are: G. V. Lantzeff,

Siberia in the Eighteenth Century: A Study of Colonial Administration,
(Berkeley, Cal., 1943); M. G. Levin and L. P. Potapov, eds., *The Peoples of
Siberia* (Chicago, 1964); V. I. Ogorodnikov, *Ocherk Sibiri do nachala XIX
stoletiya* [A Study of Siberia to the Beginning of the Nineteenth Century]
(Irkutsk, 1920); *Narody Sibiri* [People of Siberia] (Moscow, 1956); S. V.
Ivanov, *Ornament narodov Sibiri kak istorichesky istochnik* [Ornaments of
the Peoples of Siberia as a Source of History] (Moscow, 1963).

67. P. A. Slovtsov, *Istoricheskoye obozreniye Sibiri* [A Historical Survey of
Siberia], 2 vols. (St. Petersburg, 1838-1844). The latest publication is *Istoriya
Sibiri s drevneyshikh vremyen do nashikh dney* [A History of Siberia from
Earliest Times to the Present] 5 vols. (Moscow, 1968-1969).

68. I. V. Shcheglov, *Khronologichesky perechen vazhneyshikh dannykh iz istorii
Sibiri (1032-1882)* [A Chronological List of Most Important Data in the
History of Siberia, 1032-1882] (Irkutsk, 1883).

69. V. K. Andriyevich, *Istoriya Sibiri* [A History of Siberia], 5 vols. in 2 (St.
Petersburg, 1889).

70. P. N. Butsinsky, *Zaseleniye Sibiri i byt pervykh eya naselnikov* [The
Settlement of Siberia and Life of the First Settlers] (Kharkov, 1869); *K istorii
Sibiri: Surgut, Narym i Ketsk do 1645 goda* [Notes on the History of Siberia:
Surgut, Narym, and Ketsk to 1645] (Kharkov, 1893); *Mangazeya i Man-
gazeysky uyezd (1601-1645)* [Mangazeya and Mangazeysk District, 1601-
1645] (Kharkov, 1893).

71. P. M. Golovachev, *Rossiya na Dalnem Vostoke* [Russia in the Far East] (St.
Petersburg, 1904); N. M. Yadrintsev, *Sibir kak koloniya* [Siberia as a Colony]
(St. Petersburg, 1892).

72. N. N. Ogloblin, *Obozreniye stolbtsov i knig sibirskogo prikaza 1592-1768
g.g.* [A Survey of the Rolls and Books of the Siberian Department 1592-
1768], 4 vols. (Moscow, 1859-1900).

73. V. I. Vaghin, *Istoricheskiye svedeniya o deyatelnosti gr. M. M. Speranskogo
v Sibiri s 1819 to 1822 g.* [Historical Data on the Activities of Count M. M.
Speransky in Siberia from 1819 to 1822], 2 vols. (St. Petersburg, 1872); S. M.
Prutchenko, *Sibirskiye okrainy* [Siberian Borderlands], 2 vols. (St.
Petersburg, 1899); I. P. Barsukov, *Graf N. N. Muravyev-Amursky* [Count N.
N. Muravyev-Amursky], 2 vols. (Moscow, 1891).

74. P. Tikhmenev, *Istoricheskoye obozreniye obrazovaniya Rossiysko-
amerikanskoy kompanii i deystv eya do nastoyashchego vremeni* [A Historical Survey of the Formation of the Russian-American Company and its
Activities to the Present], 2 vols. (St. Petersburg, 1861-1863); S. B. Okun',
The Russian-American Company, trans. Carl Ginsburg (Cambridge, Mass.,
1951).

75. N. N. Firsov, *Chteniya po istorii Sibiri* [Readings in the History of Siberia], 2

vols. (Moscow, 1920-1921); *Polozheniye inorodtsev severo-vostochnoy Rossii v Moskovskom gosudarstve* [Position of the Natives of Northeastern Russia in the Muscovite State] (Kazan, 1866).

76. V. I. Ogorodnikov, *Ocherk istorii Sibiri do nachala XIX stoletiya. Vvedeniye. Istoriya do russkoy Sibiri* [An Outline of Siberian History to the Nineteenth Century: Introduction. History to the Russian Conquest] (Irkutsk, 1920); *Zavoevaniye russkimi Sibiri* [The Russian Conquest of Siberia] (Vladivostok, 1924); S. V. Bakhrushin, *Kazaki na Amure* [Amur Cossacks] (Leningrad, 1925); *Ocherki po istorii Sibiri XVI i XVII v.v.* [Studies of Siberian History of the Sixteenth and Seventeenth Centuries] (Moscow, 1927); *Pokruta na sobolinnykh promyslakh semnadtsatogo vyeka* [Contracts in the Sable Trade in the Seventeenth Century] (n.p., n.d.); "Sibirskiye sluzhiliye Tatary v XVII vyeke" [Siberian Tartar Vassals in the Seventeenth Century], *Istoricheskiye zapiski* (Moscow) 1 (1937): 55-80.

77. S. V. Bakhrushin, *Nauchnye trudy* [Scholarly Works], 4 vols. (Moscow, 1952-1954).

78. See *Sbornik statey po russkoy istorii, posvyashchennyi S. F. Platonovu* (Petrograd, 1922), pp. 269-85.

79. *Severnaya Aziya*, Nos. 1-2, 1925.

80. *Istoriya Sibiri s drevneyshikh vremyen do nashikh dney* [A History of Siberia from Earliest Times to the Present], 5 vols. (Leningrad, 1968-1969).

81. Here are a few of the monographs that may be cited at random: *Ocherki goroda Tomska* [Essays on the City of Tomsk] (Tomsk, 1954); N. N. Protopopov, *Novosibirskaya oblast. Ekonomiko-geografichsekaya kharakteristika* [The Novosibirsk Province: An Economic-Geographic Description] (Novosibirsk, 1955); *Narody Sibiri* [Peoples of Siberia] (Moscow-Leningrad, 1956); V. D. Sokolov, *Kuznetsky ugolniyi basseyn* [Kuznetsk Coal Basin] (Moscow, 1957); A. A. Stepanov, *Khabarosky Kray* [Khabarovsk Province] (Khabarovsk, 1957); A. B. Margolin, *Problemy narodnogo khozyaistva Dalnego Vostoka* [Economic Problems of the Far East] (Moscow, 1963); I. I. Komogortsev, *Sibir industrialnaya* [Industrialized Siberia] (Novosibirsk, 1968).

82. P. A. Shchapov, *Zemstvo i raskol* [Zemstvo and the Schism] (St. Petersburg, 1862); *Sochineniya* [Works], 3 vols. (St. Petersburg, 1906-1908); *Sochineniya. Dopolnitelniyi tom k izdaniyu 1906-1908 gg.* [Works. Supplementary volume to the edition of 1906-1908], prepared by A. N. Turunov (Irkutsk, 1937); *Neizdanniye sochineniya* [Unpublished Works] (Kazan, 1928). Works concerning Shchapov: N. Y. Aristov, *A. P. Shchapov* (St. Petersburg, 1883); P. Kabanov, *Obshchestvenno-politicheskiye i istoricheskiye vzglyady A. P. Shchapova* [Socio-Political and Historical

Views of A. P. Shchapov] (Moscow, 1954); *A. P. Shchapov v Irkutske. Neizdanniye materialy* [A. P. Shchapov in Irkutsk: Unpublished Materials] (Irkutsk, 1938).

83. *Istorik-Marksist* 3 (1927): 9-10.

84. G. V. Plekhanov, *Sochineniya* [Works] (Moscow, 1923), 3: 19.

85. *Zhurnal Ministerstva Narodnogo Prosveshcheniya* 9-10 (1875): 72.

86. *Krasnyi arkhiv*, 4: 407-10; *Russky biografichesky slovar*, 24: 5.

87. D. Zaslavsky, *M. P. Dragomanov. K istorii ukrainskogo natsionalizma* [M. P. Dragomanov: History of Ukrainian Nationalism] (Moscow, 1934); M. Pavlyk, *Mykhaylo Petrovich Drahomanov, 1841-1895* (Lvov, 1896); *Mykhaylo Drahomanov. A Symposium and Selected Writings. A Special Issue of the Annals of the Ukrainian Academy of Art and Sciences in the United States* (New York, 1952), Vol. II, No. 1 (3); D. Doroshenko, "M. Drahomanov and the Ukrainian National Movement," *Slavonic Review* (London), April 1938.

88. See P. Ponomarev, "M. A. Maksimovich," *Zhurnal Ministerstva Narodnogo Prosveshcheniya*, No. 10, 1871. Also D. K. Ostryanin, *Svitoglyad M. Maksimovicha* [The World View of M. Maksimovich] (Kiev, 1960).

89. N. I. Kostomarov, *Istoricheskiye monografii i issledovaniya* [Historical Monographs and Studies], 21 vols. (St. Petersburg, 1903-1906); *Russkaya istoriya v zhizneopisaniyakh eya glavneyshikh deyateley* [A History of Russia in Biographies of Her Leading Statesmen], 2 vols. (St. Petersburg, 1903-1907); *Posledniye gody Rechi-Pospolitoy* [The Closing Years of the Polish Commonwealth] (St. Petersburg, 1870); *Bunt Stenki Razina* [The Rebellion of Stenka Razin] (St. Petersburg, 1859).

On Kostomarov: G. Karpov, *Kostomarov, kak istorik Malorossii* [Kostomarov as a Historian of the Ukraine] (Moscow, 1871); A. N. Pypin, *Istoriya russkoy etnografii*, 3: 151-87; V. I. Semevsky, "N. I. Kostomarov," *Russkaya starina* 49, No. 1 (1886): 181-212; Rubinstein, *Russkaya istoriografiya*, pp. 421-40 (cited above, note 4); N. I. Kostomarov, *Avtobiografiya* [Autobiography], ed. V. Kotelnikov (Moscow, 1922).

90. Semevsky, "N. I. Kostomarov"; I. Zhitetsky, "Professorskaya deyatelnost N. I. Kostomarova" [Professorial activities of N. I. Kostomarov] *Golos minuvshego*, No. 5, 1917; L. K. Polukhin, *Formirovannya istoricheskikh poglyadiv N. I. Kostomarova* [The Development of Historical Views of N. I. Kostomarov] (Kiev, 1959).

91. See P. A. Zaionchkovsky, "Kirillo-Mefodiyevskoye obshchestvo," *Trudy istoriko-arkhivnogo obshchestvennogo instituta*, Vol. 3, 1947; N. I. Kostomarov, "Avtobiografiya," *Russkaya mysl'*, Nos. 5-6, 1885.

92. N. I. Kostomarov, *Mysli o federativnom nachalye drevney Rusi* [Thoughts on the Origin of Federalism in Early Russia] (St. Petersburg, 1872).

93. N. I. Kostomarov, *Istoricheskye monografii i issledovaniya* [Historical Monographs and Studies] (St. Petersburg, 1903), Book 1, 412.

94. M. S. Hrushevsky, *Istoriya Ukrainy-Rusi* [History of Ukraine-Rus'], 10 vols. (Lvov-Kiev, 1898-1937); *Istoriya ukrainskoy literatury* [A History of Ukrainian Literature], 3 vols. (Lvov-Kiev, 1923); *Zherela do istorii Ukrainy-Rusi* [Sources Pertaining to the History of Ukranian Russia] (Kiev-Lvov, Vols. 1-8 and 12, 1895-1913; 22, 1913; 26, 1924); *Istoriya Kiyevskoy zemli* [History of Kievan Russia] (Kiev, 1891); *A History of the Ukraine*, ed. O. J. Frederiksen (New Haven, 1941); *Ocherk istorii ukrainskogo naroda* [A Study of the History of the Ukrainian People] (St. Petersburg, 1904); *Abrégé de l'Histoire de Ukraine* (Paris, 1920); *Geschichte des ukrainischen (ruthenischen) Volkes* (Leipzig, 1906); D. Doroshenko, *A Survey of Ukrainian Historiography* (New York, 1957).

95. P. B. Struve, *Kriticheskiye zametki k voprosu ob ekonomicheskom razvitii Rossii* [Critical Notes on the Question of the Economic Development of Russia] (St. Petersburg, 1894); *Krepostnoye khozyaistvo: issledovaniya po ekonomicheskoy istorii Rossii v XVIII i XIX v.v.* [Serfdom: A Study of the Economic History of Russia in the Eighteenth and Nineteenth Centuries] (Moscow, 1913).

96. M. I. Tugan-Baranovsky, *Russkaya fabrika v proshlom i nastoyashchem. Istoricheskoye razvitiye fabriki v XIX v.* [The Russian Factory in the Past and Present: Historical Development of the Russian Factory in the Nineteenth Century], 7th ed. (Moscow, 1938).

97. Bertram D. Wolfe, *Three Who Made a Revolution*, (New York, 1948) p. 122.

98. G. V. Plekhanov, *Sochineniya* [Works], 24 vols. (Leningrad, 1923-1927). Also *Literaturnoye naslediye G. V. Plekhanova* [The Literary Heritage of G. V. Plekhanov], Sbornik 1-8 (Moscow, 1934-1940).

99. G. V. Plekhanov, *Istoriya obshchestvennoy mysli* [A History of Russian Social Thought], 3 vols. (Moscow, 1925). In his *Collected Works*, Vols. 20-22 (Moscow, 1923-1927). See also the illuminating study by S. H. Baron, *Plekhanov, the Father of Russian Marxism* (Stanford, Cal., 1963).

100. S. M. Levin, "G. V. Plekhanov kak istorik revolyutsionno-narodnicheskogo dvizheniya 70-kh godov" [G. V. Plekhanov as Historian of the Revolutionary-Populist Movement in the 1970s], in *Voprosy Istoriografii i Istochnikovedeniya Istorii SSSR* (Moscow, 1963).

101. N. A. Rozhkov, *Selskoye khozyaistvo moskovskoy Rusi v XVI veke* [Rural Economy in Muscovite Russia in the Sixteenth Century] (Moscow, 1899); *Gorod i derevnya v russkoy istorii* [Town and Country in Russian History] (Moscow, 1904); *Proiskhozhdeniye samoderzhaviya v Rossii* [The Origin of

Absolutism in Russia] (Moscow, 1906); *Russkaya istoriya* [Russian History], 12 vols. (Moscow, 1919-1926). On Rozhkov, see "Istoricheskiye vzglyady N. A. Rozhkova" [Historical Views of N. A. Rozhkov], *Istorik-Marksist*, vol. 13, 1929; O. Volobuyev, "N. A. Rozhkov—metodist istorik" [A. A. Rozhkov—Methodologist-Historian], *Ucheniye zapiski Moskovskogo Oblastnogo Pedagogicheskogo Instituta*, No. 121, 1965.

102. M. N. Pokrovsky, *Russkaya istoriya s drevneyshikh vremyen* [Russian History from the Earliest Times], 4 vols. (Moscow, 1913-1914); later ed. (Moscow, 1932-1933); *History of Russia*, trans. J. D. Clarkson (New York, 1931); *Diplomatiya i voyny tsarskoy Rossii v XIX stoletii* [Diplomacy and Wars of Czarist Russia in the Nineteenth Century] (Moscow, 1923); *Ocherki russkogo revolyutsionnogo dvizheniya XIX-XX v.v.* [Essays on the Russian Revolutionary Movement of the Nineteenth and Twentieth Centuries] (Moscow, 1924); *Ocherk istorii russkoy kultury* [A Study of the History of Russian Culture], 2 vols. (Petrograd, 1923); *Istoricheskaya nauka i borba klassov* [Historical Science and Class Struggle] (Moscow, 1953); for a complete list of Pokrovsky's publications see *Istorik-Marksist* 1-2 (1932): 216-48; *Frantsiya do i vo vremya voiny* [France to and During the War] (Leningrad, 1924).

On Pokrovsky: Rubinstein, *Russkaya istoriografiya*, pp. 575-99 (cited above, note 4); Rubinstein, "Pokrovsky—istorik Rossii" [Pokrovsky—Historian of Russia], *Pod znamenem marksizma*, No. 11, 1924; *Ocherki istorii istoricheskoy nauki v SSSR* [Studies of the History of Historical Science in the USSR], 3: 218-35; 4: 180-201, and passim; E. A. Lutsky, "Razvitiye istoricheskoy kontseptsii M. N. Pokrovskogo" [The Development of the Historical Concepts of M. N. Pokrovsky], *Istoriya i istoriki. Istoriografiya istorii SSSR. Sbornik statey* (Moscow, 1965), pp. 334-71.

103. *Istorik-Marksist* 1 (1926): 320.

104. *Mezhdunarodniye otnosheniya v epokhu imperializma, 1878-1917* [International Relations During the Era of Imperialism, 1878-1917] (Moscow, 1931-); to date the project remains incomplete.

105. See the list of imprisoned and exiled scholars in the *Slavonic Review*, April 1933, pp. 711-13. On the early controversies within the ranks of the Society of Marxist Historians and the sad lot that befell some of the men, see R. Stuart Tompkins, "Communist Historical Thought," *Slavonic Review*, January 1935, pp. 298 ff. On the persecution and continuous nagging of eminent scholars by the rank and file members of society, see G. Zaidel and M. Tsvibak, *Klassoviy vrag na istoricheskom fronte. Tarlé i Platonov i ikh shkoly* [The Class Enemy on the Historical Front: Tarlé and Platonov and Their Schools] (Moscow-Leningrad, 1931).

106. L. Mamet, "Istoriya i obshchestvenno-politicheskoye vospitaniye" [A

History of Socio-Political Education], *Istorik-Marksist* 14 (1929): 159 ff.

107. See Antole G. Mazour, *The Writing of History in the Soviet Union* (Stanford, Cal., 1971).

108. M. E. Naidenov, ''Velikaya Oktyabrskaya sotsialisticheskaya revolyutiys v sovetskoy istoriografii'' [The Great October Socialist Revolution in Soviet Historiography], *Voprosy istorii* 10 (1957): 171; V. G. Ruslyakova, ''Borba s falsifikatsiyey i vulgarizatsiey istorii Velikoy Oktyabrskoy sostialisticheskoy revolyutsii (1917-1937)'' [The Struggle with Falsification and Vulgarization of the History of the Great October Socialist Revolution], in *Sbornik statey po Istorii Rabochego Klassa i Sovetskoy Istoriograffii* (Moscow, 1958), pp. 249-50; V. F. Inkin and A. G. Chernykh, ''O pervom etape razvitiya sovetskoy istoricheskoy nauki'' [The First Stage in the Development of Soviet Historical Science], *Istoriya SSSR* 1 (1961): 81-96. See also the article on Pokrovsky by A. S. Roslova in *Istoriografiya istorii SSSR s drevneyshikh vremyen do Velikoy Oktyabrskoy Sotsialisticheskoy Revolyutsii* (Moscow, 1961), Chapter 29.

109. E. V. Tarlé, *Krymskaya voyna* [The Crimean War], 2 vols (Moscow, 1950); S. S. Skazkin, *Konets avstro-russko-germanskogo soyuza* [The End of the Austro-Russo-German Alliance], (Moscow, 1928), Vol. 1, B. A. Romanov, *Rossiya v Mandzhurii. Ocherki po istorii vneshney politiki samoderzhaviya v epokhu imperializma* [Russia in Manchuria: A Study of Russian Foreign Policy During the Age of Imperialism] (Leningrad, 1928). B. A. Romanov, *Ocherki diplomaticheskoy istorii russko-yaponskoy voyny, 1895-1907 gg.* [A Study of Diplomatic History of the Russo-Japanese War, 1895-1907] (Moscow, 1947).

110. B. H. Sumner, *Russian in the Balkans, 1870-1880* (Oxford, 1937); W. L. Langer, *The Franco-Russian Alliance, 1890-1894* (Cambridge, Mass., 1929).

111. Sir Bernard Pares, *The Fall of the Russian Monarchy* (New York, 1939).

Bibliography

Books

Astakhov, V. I. *Kurs lektsii po russkoy istoriografii, epokha promyshlennogo kapitalizma* [A Course of Lectures on Russian Historiography, the Epoch of Industrial Capitalism]. Kharkov, 1962.

———. *Kurs lektsii po russkoy istoriografii do serediny XIX veka* [A Course of Lectures on Russian Historiography to the Middle of the Nineteenth Century]. Kharkov, 1959.

———. *Kurs lektsii po russkoy istoriograffi do kontsa XIX veka* [A Course of Lectures on Russian Historiography to the End of the Nineteenth Century]. Kharkov, 1965.

Bestuzhev-Ryumin, K. N. *Biografii, kharakteristiki* [Biographical Essays]. St. Petersburg, 1882.

Bezkrovnyi, L. G. *Ocherki po istochnikovedeniyu voennoy istorii* [Studies of Sources on Military History]. Moscow, 1957.

———. *Ocherki voennoy istoriografii Rossii* [Studies in Military Historiography of Russia]. Moscow, 1962.

Bibliografiya russkoy istorii [A Bibliography of Russian History]. Moscow, 1957.

Black, Cyril E., ed. *Rewriting Russian History; Soviet Interpretations of Russia's Past.* New York, 1956.

Butterfield, Herbert. *Man on His Past: The Study of the History of Historical Scholarship.* Cambridge, England, 1955

Cherepnin, L. V. *Russkaya istoziografiya do XIX veka* [Russian Historiography of the Nineteenth Century]. Moscow, 1957.

Chumachenko, E. G. *V. O. Klyuchevsky—istochnikoved* [V. O. Klyuchevsky—Source Expert]. Moscow, 1970.

Dmitrieva, R. P., comp. *Bibliografiya russkogo letopisaniya* [A Bibliography of Russian Chronicle Writing]. Moscow, 1962.

Doroshenko, D. *Oglyad ukrainskoy istoriografii* [A Survey of Ukrainian Historiography]. Prague, 1923.

———. *A Survey of Ukrainian Historiography: A Special Issue of the Annals of the*

Ukrainian Academy of Arts and Sciences in the United States. New York, 1957.

Dovnar-Zapolsky, D. *Iz istorii obshchestvennykh techeny v Rossii* [A History of Social Movements in Russia]. Kiev, 1905. (See pp. 232-67.)

Entsyklopedichesky slovar [Russian Encyclopedia], 41 vols. St. Petersburg, 1890-1904.

Gapanovich, I. *Russian Historiography Outside of Russia.* Peking, 1935.

Hecker, Julius. *Russian Sociology.* New York, 1934.

Histoire et historiens depuis cinquante ans: méthodes, organisation et résultats du travail historique de 1876 à 1926. Paris, 1927. (See Vol. 1, pp. 341-70.)

Hösch, Edgar. *Evgenj Viktorovich Tarlé (1875-1955) und seine Stellung in der sowjetischen Geschichtswissenschaft.* Wiesbaden, 1964.

Ikonnikov, V. S. *Opyt russkoy istoriografii* [A Study of Russian Historiography], 2 vols. in 4. Kiev, 1891-1908.

Illeritsky, V. E., and Kudryavtsev, I. A., eds. *Istoriografiya istorii USSR* [A Historiography of the USSR]. Moscow, 1961.

Istoricheskaya nauka i nekotoryye problemy sovremennosti [Historical Science and some Contemporary Problems]. Moscow, 1961.

Istoricheskaya nauka v Sibiri za 50 lyet [Historical Science in Siberia for the Last Fifty Years]. Novosibirsk, 1972.

Istoriya i istoriki [History and Historians]. Moscow, 1965-

Istoriya istoricheskoy nauki v SSSR [A History of the Historical Science in the USSR], 4 vols. Moscow, 1955-1966.

Kireyeva, P. A. *V. O. Klyuchevsky kak istorik russkoy istoricheskoy nauki* [Klyuchevsky as the Historian of Russian Historical Science]. Moscow, 1966.

Klyuchevsky, V. O. [In Memoriam] *Kharakteristiki i vospominaniya* [Essays and Recollections]. Moscow, 1912.

———. *Ocherki i ryechi* [Studies and Addresses]. Moscow, n.d.

———. *Pisma, Dnevniki, Aforizmy i Mysli ob Istorii* [Letters, Diaries, Aphorisms, and Thoughts about History]. Moscow, 1968.

———. *Sochineniya* [Works], 8 vols. 1956-1959.

Koyalovich, M. I. *Istoriya russkogo samosoznaniya* [History of Russian Self-Realization]. St. Petersburg, 1893.

Krandiyevsky, S. I., *Ocherki po istoriografii ekonomicheskoy istorii XVII-XIX v. v.* [Studies of Historiography of Economic History of the Seventeenth to the Nineteenth Centuries]. Kharkov, 1964.

Kritika noveyshey burzhuaznoy istoriografii. Sbornik statey. [A Collection of Critical Essays of the Latest Bourgeois Historiography]. Leningrad, 1967.

Lomonosov, Schlözer, Pallas. Deutsch-Russische Wissenschaftsbeziehungen in 18 Jahrhudert. Berlin, 1962.

Milyukov, P. N. *Glavniye techeniya russkoy istoricheskoy mysli* [Main Currents of Russian Historical Thought]. Moscow, 1898.

————. *Le mouvement intellectuel russe*. Paris, 1918.

Mirzoyev,V. G. *Istoriografiya Sibiri. Pervaya polovina XIX veka.* [Historiography of Siberia, First Half of the Nineteenth Century]. Kemerovsk, 1965.

————. *Istoriografiya Sibiri* [Historiography of Siberia]. Moscow, 1970.

Nechkina, M. V. *Vasily Osipovich Klyuchevsky. Istoriya zhizni i tvorchestva* [V. O. Klyuchevsky: A History of His Life and Creative Works]. Moscow, 1974.

Peshtich, V. I. *Russkaya istoriografiya XVIII veka* [Russian Historiography of the Eighteenth Century]. Leningrad, 1961.

Petrovich, Michael Boro. *The Emergence of Russian Panslavism, 1857-1870.* New York, 1956.

Picheta, V. I. *Vvedeniye v Russkuyu Istoriyu* [An Introduction to Russian History]. The Hague, Russian Reprint Series 48, 1967.

Platonov, F. S. *Lektsii po russkoy istorii* [Lectures on Russian History]. St. Petersburg, 1915. (See introductory chapter.)

Pokrovsky, M. N. *Borba klassov i russkaya istoricheskaya literatura* [Class Struggle in Russian Historical Literature]. Petrograd, 1923.

————. *Russkaya istoricheskaya literatura v klassovom osveshchenii* [Class interpretation in Russian Historical Literature], 2 vols. Moscow, 1927-1930.

Priselkov, M. D. *Istoriya russkogo letopisaniya* [A History of Russian Annalistic Literature]. Leningrad, 1940.

Protiv istoricheskoy kontseptsii M. N. Pokrovskogo [Against the Historical Concepts of M. N. Pokrovsky]. Moscow, 1939. A collection of essays.

Pypin, A. N. *Istoriya russkoy etnografii* [A History of Russian Ethnography], 4 vols. St. Petersburg, 1890-1892.

Rubinstein, N. L. *Russkaya istoriografiya* [Russian Historiography]. Moscow, 1941.

Shakhmatov, A. A. *Povest vremennykh lyet* [A Narrative of Bygone Years]. Petrograd, 1916.

————. *Rozyskaniya drevneyshikh russkikh letopisnykh svodakh* [Investigations of the Earliest Russian Chronicle Codes]. St. Petersburg, 1908.

Shakhnazarov, I. D. *Russkoye revolyutsionnoye prosveshcheniye b borbe s burzhuazno-dvoryanskoy istoriografiey* [Russian Revolutionary Education in its Conflict with Bourgeois-Gentry Historiography]. Leningrad, 1934. (See also *Problemy marksizma* 5 [1933]: 48-73.)

Shapiro, A. L. *Russkaya istoriografiya v period imperializma* [Russian Historiography During the Period of Imperialism]. Leningrad, 1962.

Sokolov, O. D., *M. N. Pokrovsky i sovetskaya nauka* [M. N. Pokrovsky and Soviet Science]. Moscow, 1970.

Tarnovsky, K. N. *Sovetskaya istoriografiya rossiiskogo imperializma* [Soviet Historiography of Russian Imperialism]. Moscow, 1964.

Tikhomirov, M. N. *Istochnikovedeniye istorii* [Historical Resources], 2 vols. Moscow, 1940.

————. *Istochnikovedeniye istorii SSSR s drevneyshego vremeni do kontsa XVIII veka* [Historical Resources of the USSR from the Earliest Times to the End of the Eighteenth Century]. Moscow, 1964.

————. Ed. *Ocherki istorii istoricheskoy nauki v SSSR* [Studies of the History of Historical Science in the USSR], 5 vols. Moscow, 1955-1965.

Zharikov, D. A. *I. N. Boltin, kak istorik* [I. N. Boltin as a Historian]. Samarkand, 1941.

Articles

"Arkhiv Semevskogo" [The Archive of Semevsky]. *Literaturnoye nasledstvo*, 7-8: 418-30.

Azadovsky, D. "Zadachi Sibirskoy bibliografii" [Problems of Siberia Historiography]. *Sibirskiye zapiski*, Vol. 6, 1919.

Bakhrushin, S. B. "Müller kak istorik Sibiri" [Müller as the Historian of Siberia]. See Müller's latest edition of *Istoriya Sibiri* [History of Siberia], published in 1937 by the Academy of Sciences, pp. 5-55.

Bidlo, Jaroslav, "Remarques à la défense de ma conception de l'histoire de l'orient Européen et de l'histoire des peuples slaves." *Bulletin d'Information des Sciences Historiques en Europe Orientale*, Vol. 6, fasc. 3-4. Varsovie, 1934. See also N. Derzhavin. "Iz itogov VII mezhdunarodnogo kongressa istoricheskikh nauk v Varshave" [Observations on the 7th Congress of Historical Sciences in Warsaw]. *Trudy instituta slavyanovedeniya Akademii Nauk SSSR* (1934): 475-82.

Epstein, F. "Die marxistische Geschichtswissenschaft in der Sovjetunion seit 1927." *Jahrbücher für Kultur und Geschichte der Slaven*, Vol. 6, No. 1, 1930.

Fedotov, G. "Rossiya Klyuchevskogo" [Klyuchevsky's Russia]. *Sovremenniye zapiski* 50 (1932): 340-62.

Florovsky, A. "La littérature historique russe-émigration." *Bulletin d'Information des Sciences Historiques en Europe Orientale* (Varsovie), 1: 82-121; 3: 25-79.

————. "Russkaya istoricheskaya nauka v emigratsii" [Russian Historical Science in Emigration]. *Trudy V-go S'yezda russkikh akademicheskikh organizatsy zagranitsey* (Belgrade), Vol. 1, 1931.

————. "The Works of Russian Emigrés in History (1921-1927)." *Slavonic Review* 7 (1928): 216-18.

Gautier, G. "Histoire de Russie: publications des années 1917-1927." *Revue Historique* 157 (1928): 93-123.

Golubtsov, S. A. "Teoreticheskye vzglyady V. O. Klyuchevskogo" [Theoretical views of Klyuchevsky]. *Russky istorichesky zhurnal* 8 (1922): 178-202.

Gorin, P. "M. N. Pokrovsky—Bolshevik-istorik" [M. N. Pokrovsky—Bolshevik-historian]. *Vestnik Kommunisticheskoy Akademii* 4 (1933): 42-48.

Gurko-Kryazhin, B. "M. N. Pokrovsky i izucheniye istorii Vostoka" [M. N. Pokrovsky and the Study of History of the Orient]. *Noviy vostok* 25 (1929): 29-46.

Hrushevsky (Grushevsky), M. S. "Ob ukrainskoy istoriografii XVIII vyeka. Neskol'ko soobrazheny" [A Few Reflections on Ukrainian Historiography of the Eighteenth Century]. *Izvestiya Akademii Nauk, O.O.N.* 8 (1934): 215-23.

Jonas, Hans. "Die Entwicklung der Geschichtsforschung in der Sovjet-Union seit dem Ausgang des Weltkrieges." *Zeitschrift für osteuropäische Geschichte* 5 (1931): 66-83, 386-96.

Karpovich, Michael. "Klyuchevsky and Recent Trends in Russian Historiography." *The Slavonic and East European Review* 21 (1943): 31-39.

Khodorov, A. E. "M. N. Pokrovsky i izucheniye Dalnego Vostoka" [M. N. Pokrovsky and the Study of the Far East]. *Noviy vostok* 25 (1929): 1-28.

Kiesewetter (Kizeveter), A. "Histoire de Russia: travaux des savant russes émigrés 1918-1928)." *Revue Historique* 163 (1930): 160-83.

Korablev, V. N. "Akademik A. N. Pypin i slavyansky vopros" [Academician A. N. Pypin and the Slav Question]. *Vestnik akademii nauk SSSR*, 8-9 (1933): 67-78.

Lappo-Danilevsky, A. S. "The Development of Science and Learning in Russia." In J. D. Duff, ed., *Russian Realities and Problems*. Cambridge, 1917. pp. 153-229.

Leppmann, W. "Die russische Geschichtswissenschaft in der Emigration." *Zeitschrift für osteuropäische Geschichte* 5 (1931): 215-29.

Lukin, N. M. "Akademik M. N. Pokrovsky" [Academician M. N. Pokrovsky]. *Izvestiya Akademii Nauk SSSR, O.O.N.*, Ser. VII, 9 (1932): 773-82.

Maklakov, B. "Klyuchevsky." *Slavonic Review* 13 (1935): 320-29.

Mazour, Anatole G. "Modern Russian Historiography." *Journal of Modern History* 9 (1937): 169-202.

Mazour, Anatole G., and Bateman, Herman E. "Recent Conflicts in Soviet Historiography." *Journal of Modern History*, March 1951, pp. 56-68.

Milyukov, P. N. "Eurasianism and Europeanism in Russian History." *Festschrift zum 80. Geburtstage* (Supplement to *Der russische Gedanke*, Bonn) 1 (1930): 225-36.

———. "Velichiye i padeniye M. N. Pokrovskogo" [The Greatness and Fall of M. N. Pokrovsky]. *Sovremenniye zapiski* (Paris) 65 (1937): 368-87.

"Neskolko dokumentov iz tsarskikh arkhivov o M. N. Pokrovskom" [Several documents from czarist archives concerning M. N. Pokrovsky]. *Krasnyi arkhiv* 3 (1932): 5-53.

Nevsky, V. M. "M. N. Pokrovsky—istorik oktyabrya" [M. N. Pokrovsky—Historian of the October Revolution]. *Istoriya proletariata SSSR* 12 (1932): 3-20.

Pfitzner, J. "Die Geschichte Osteuropas und die Geschichte des Slawentums als Forschungsprobleme." *Historische Zeitschrift* 150 (1934): 21-85.

Piksanov, N. K. "Akademik A. N. Pypin" [Academician A. N. Pypin]. *Vyestnik Akademii Nauk SSSR* 4 (1933): 39-44.

Piontkovsky, S. "Velikoderzhvniye tendentsii v istoriografii Rossii" [Autocratic Tendencies in Russian Historiography]. *Istorik-Marksist* 17 (1930): 21-26.

―――. "Velikorusskaya burzhuaznaya istoriografiya poslednego desyatiletiya" [Great-Russian Bourgeois Historiography of the Last Decade]. *Istorik-Marksist* 18-19 (1930): 157-76.

Pokrovsky, M. N. " 'Noviye' techeniya v russkoy istoricheskoy literature" ["New" Currents in Russian Historical Literature]. *Istorik-Marksist* 7 (1928): 1-17.

Powell, A. "The Nationalist Trend in Soviet Historiography." *Soviet Studies*, April 1951, pp. 372-77.

Presnyakov, A. Y. "V. O. Klyuchevsky." *Russky istorichesky zhurnal* 8 (1922): 203-24.

Rubinstein, N. "M. N. Pokrovsky—istorik vneshney politiki" [M. N. Pokrovsky—Historian of Foreign Policy]. *Istorik-Marksist* 9 (1928): 58-78.

―――. "Osnovniye problemy postroyeniya russkoy bibliografii" [Basic Problems of Russian Bibliography]. *Voprosy istorii* 2 (1948): 89-94.

Schlesinger, Rudolf. "Recent Discussions on the Periodization of History." *Soviet Studies*, October 1952, pp. 152-69.

―――. "Recent Soviet Historiography." *Soviet Studies*, April 1950, pp. 293-312; July 1950, pp. 3-21; October 1950, pp. 138-62; January 1951, pp. 265-88.

Shcheglov, A. "Metodologicheskiye istoki oshibok M. N. Pokrovskogo" [Methodological Sources of the Errors of M. N. Pokrovsky]. *Pod znamenem marksizma* 5 (1936): 55-69.

Skubitsky, T. "Klassovaya borba v ukrainskoy istoricheskoy literature" [Class Struggle in Ukrainian Historical Literature]. *Istorik-Marksist* 17 (1930): 27-40.

Struve, P. "Ivan Aksakov." *Slavonic Review* 2 (1924): 514-18.

Sukhotin, L. M. "Kratky ocherk russkoy istoriografii" [A Brief Outline of Russian Historiography]. *Sbornik arkheologicheskogo obshchestva* (Belgrade), 1927, pp. 61-76.

Szporluk, Roman. "Pokrovsky and Russian History." *Survey* (London) 58 (October 1954): 107-18.

Tikhomirov, M. "Russkaya istoriografiya XVIII veka" [Russian Historiography of the Eighteenth Century]. *Voprosy istorii* 2 (1948): 94-100.

Tompkins, Stuart R. "Trends in Communist Historical Thought." *Slavonic Review* 13 (1935): 294-319.

"Uebersicht der historischen Literatur Russlands für die Jahre 1860-1865." *Historische Zeitschrift* 16: 126-74.

Yugov, M. "Polozheniye i zadachi istoricheskogo fronta v Belorussii" [The Situation and Problems Concerning the Historical Front in White Russia]. *Istorik-Marksist* 17: 41-50.

Index

ABOUT THE AUTHOR

Anatole G. Mazour spent his early years in Czarist Russia. Born and educated in Kiev, Dr. Mazour fought in World War I and the Russian Civil War. After living briefly in Europe as a Russian emigré, he came to the United States. Dr. Mazour received his Ph.D. from the University of California at Berkeley and began his teaching career there. Among Dr. Mazour's recent books are *Men and Nations, The Rise and Fall of the Romanovs,* and *The Writing of History in the U.S.S.R.*